POCKET GUI

DINOSAURS

POCKET GUIDE TO
DINOSAURS

Maria Costantino

Published by SILVERDALE BOOKS
An imprint of Bookmart Ltd
Registered number 2372865
Trading as Bookmart Ltd
Blaby Road
Wigston
Leicester LE18 4SE

© 2007 D&S Books Ltd

D&S Books Ltd
Kerswell
Parkham Ash, Bideford
Devon, England
EX39 5PR

e-mail us at:- enquiries@d-sbooks.co.uk

This edition printed 2007

ISBN 13: 9-781-84509-466-9

DS0167. Dinosaurs

Creative director: Sarah King
Designer: Debbie Fisher and Co
Project editor: Clare Haworth-Maden

Material from this book previously appeared in The Dinosaur Handbook.

Fonts: Avenir and Gill Sans

Printed in Thailand

1 3 5 7 9 10 8 6 4 2

CONTENTS

WHAT IS A DINOSAUR?

In 1841, the British anatomist Richard – later Sir Richard – Owen (1804-92) addressed the annual meeting of the British Association for the Advancement of Science in Plymouth, England. Owen's presentation at the meeting was a review of all of the fossil reptiles that had been found in the British Isles to that date.

With his training in anatomy, Owen was able to recognise from the remains of three fossil reptiles – *Megalosaurus, Iguanodon* and *Hylaeosaurus* – that these were completely different to any other fossilised or living creature. Owen described how these three fossil reptiles were all extremely large – about the size of a full-grown elephant – that they all lived on land and that they all had distinctive, 'pillar-like' legs that were 'tucked in' underneath the body. Owen noticed that this position of the legs was totally different to the 'splayed' leg position – where the upper leg joins the body at the sides – that is typical of other reptiles, and he named these strange reptiles 'dinosaurs', which is derived from the Greek words *deinos* and *saurus*, which mean 'terrible reptiles'.

To be precise, dinosaurs were members of a particular group of reptiles: they were all creatures that had four limbs (although some did walk 'upright' on their two hind legs) and they lived on land. While a few may have waded into shallow, swampy water, dinosaurs were not 'designed' to be efficient swimmers, and they didn't live in the sea. The gigantic sea reptiles mentioned later in this book – such as plesiosaurs, mosasaurs and ichthyosaurs – were not, in fact, dinosaurs at all. In the same way, dinosaurs did not fly. The 'flying reptiles' of the 'age of the dinosaurs', like the pterosaurs, were also not dinosaurs.

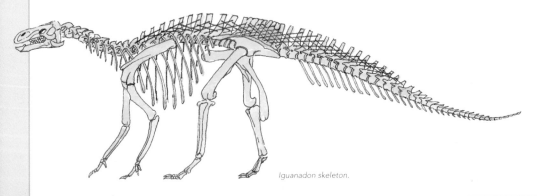

Iguanadon skeleton.

Dinosaurs belonged to the group of reptiles known as archosaurs, which means 'ruling reptiles'. The archosaur group includes some now extinct creatures, such as the theocodonts, as well as some very well-known extant (or still living) creatures, such as crocodiles, and some very familiar living descendants: birds!

Not a dinosaur, but a flying reptile.

Not a dinosaur, but a marine reptile.

The crocodile is an extant member of the dinosaurs.

Birds are living descendants of dinosaurs.

FOSSILS

Everything we know about dinosaurs is based on their fossilised remains. The most common fossils are the naturally preserved remains of once living organisms that have become entombed in sediments – layers of sand, silt, mud and rock. Gradually, the original material from which the organism was composed is replaced by minerals. In other fossils, the original organism or object was destroyed by the acidic

T. rex teeth: the hard remains, such as of teeth, bones and claws, are among the most common finds.

effects of ground water, and minerals later formed a replica of the object or organism. These fossils are therefore composed of new, replacement minerals that are harder and heavier versions of the original material. Not only can fossils often be very different in colour to the object that originally formed them, because of pressure inside the rocks in which they are found, fossils can also be distorted in shape. It is also important to remember that over millions of years, the shifting of the continental plates means that the sediments containing fossil remains may have moved far away from their original resting place.

BODY FOSSILS

The remains of plants and animals, such as shells and teeth, bones and leaves, are among the best-known fossil remains. These are called body fossils. The soft parts of organisms – such as flesh, skin and internal organs – are usually lost before the fossilisation process begins, having been broken down by bacteria or even eaten by scavengers. Consequently, the fossil remains of soft-bodied animals like jellyfish are extremely rare. Sometimes, though, a very rapid burial in soft sediment, combined with the presence of certain types of bacteria, mean that the soft parts of bodies are retained and fossilised. In these exceptional circumstances, palaeontologists have the opportunity to study not only the fossilised remains of hard body parts like bones and teeth, but the skin and internal organs, too.

TRACE FOSSILS

Traces – the things left behind by organisms, such as egg shells, footprints, marks made by claws, nests and even droppings – can also become fossilised. These are called trace fossils. Trace fossils are the most numerous type of fossil, but because these traces are not always found next to the organism that made them, they are very difficult to identify precisely. Fossils can also be preserved in materials, such as amber, tar, peat and ice. Dinosaur fossils, however, are all found in rock, but of the millions of dinosaurs that must have died, only a mere handful became fossilised.

THE DISCOVERY OF DINOSAURS

More than 2,400 years ago, ancient Greek scholars were collecting and describing fossil seashells, but it was only during the past 300 years or so that the mystery of what fossils were, and how they were formed, was unravelled. By the late 18th century, most educated people recognised that fossil seashells were parts of animals that lived beneath the seas, but they had a problem working out how these fossils came to be embedded in rocks on land – high up the side of cliffs at the shore line and even in mountains way inland from the sea. The reason most often given was taken from the Bible: these animals had been stranded by the great flood that had been sent by God as a punishment for humankind's misbehaviour. For the most part, early fossil discoveries were regarded as dead members of species that still existed. This fitted in the religious concept known as the plenum, which said that God had created and populated the Earth with every conceivable type of living thing. With this in mind, it was beyond belief that he would have allowed any of his creations to become extinct.

It was only around 200 years ago that scientists began to posit a new theory to explain the appearance of these fossils: that the rocks beneath our feet had once been mud or sand on the sea floor. These sediments had been subjected to great pressure – literally squashed – and had hardened into rock, and the movement in the earth had raised the rock above the level of the sea, along with the fossils embedded in it. In some instances, wind, rain, sun, frost and running water wore away at the rock, leaving the fossil exposed.

In 1770, deep in a chalk mine near Maastricht, in The Netherlands, the important discovery of the jaws of a huge fossil animal was made. The discovery provoked a great deal of interest – and controversy. Baron Georges Cuvier (1769–1832), the father of modern palaeontology and comparative anatomy, described the jaws and recognised them as belonging to a gigantic marine lizard which he called *Mosasaurus*, meaning 'Meuse reptile', after the river that flows through the region. To Cuvier, the jaws were clearly an example of his long-held belief that there had, in fact, been extinctions of animals in earlier times. Cuvier paved the way for the scientific acceptance of extinction, so that by the beginning of the 19th century, many people began to accept that many of the fossils that they were finding represented creatures that were not like any that were alive.

Ammonites are the fossilised remains of cephalopod molluscs.

A new theory to explain the appearance of fossils was formed only 200 years ago.

AMATEURS AND ENTHUSIASTS

By 1800, there were a number of very keen fossil hunters who began collecting specimens. Not all were scientists, though: one of the first and greatest discoveries was, in fact, made by an 11-year-old girl called Mary Anning (1799–1847). In 1811, Mary discovered a complete Jurassic-age ichthyosaur fossil skeleton in the sea cliffs at Lyme Regis, in Dorset, on England's southern coast. She became the first person to make a living from fossil hunting! Mary went on to discover the first plesiosaur in 1821, and the first pterodactyl in 1828. Most of her finds she sold to collectors and institutions: Mary's fossilised ichthyosaur skeleton can be seen today in London's Natural History Museum, for instance. While the rocks of Lyme Regis that Mary was searching did come from the age of the dinosaur, the discoveries of dinosaurs themselves came from further east in England.

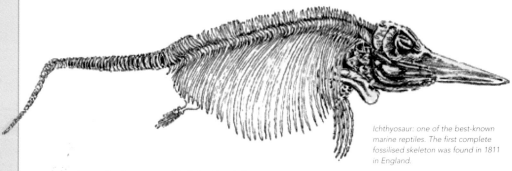

Ichthyosaur: one of the best-known marine reptiles. The first complete fossilised skeleton was found in 1811 in England.

THE *IGUANODON* AT THE SIDE OF THE ROAD

In 1822, Gideon Algernon Mantell, a family doctor from Lewes, in Sussex, and an enthusiastic amateur geologist and fossil hunter, set off with his wife, Mary Ann, in their horse and carriage to visit a patient. While Dr Mantell ministered to his patient, Mrs Mantell took a short stroll to stretch her legs. Walking along the country road, she noticed a pile of stones and gravel used for filling in ruts and potholes. Among the rubble, Mrs Mantell noticed some teeth. After informing her husband, Dr Mantell traced the stones and gravel back to the quarries in the Tilgate Forest near Cuckfield, where he soon discovered more remains.

At first, Dr Mantell had trouble identifying the teeth, and so they were shown to the eminent anatomists of the time – Georges Cuvier in Paris and William Buckland in Oxford – but these two were, in fact, sceptical about Dr Mantell's information about the age of the rocks in the quarries and disregarded his 'dental finds'. Dr Mantell, however, firmly believed that the teeth were from secondary, or Mesozoic, rocks, and were reptilian.

Teeth discovered by a Sussex roadside in 1822 once belonged to the giant Iguanodon.

With further comparisons, he finally revealed that the teeth that he (and his wife) had discovered were very similar to those of the South American lizard, the iguana. In 1825, Mantell published his findings: the teeth, he claimed, belonged to a giant, 12m- (40ft-) long herbivorous fossil lizard that he called *Iguanodon* ('iguana-tooth'), an extinct relative of the living iguana. After so much research, even Baron Cuvier was forced to admit that he had made a mistake, and Mantell's article published Cuvier's apology.

MEGALOSAURUS

A year earlier, in 1824, William Buckland (1784–1856) had also described the partial remains of a large reptile, but this time a carnivorous one. The remains had been found in Stonesfield, in north Oxfordshire, and were named by Buckland *Megalosaurus* ('big reptile'). The remains are still on view today at the University Museum, Oxford. Both *Megalosaurus* and *Iguanodon* seemed to belong to the *Mosasaurus* category of fossil reptiles, except that both were land, rather than marine, dwellers. Despite the fact that they were major discoveries, the true significance of these fossil remains – along with the partial fossil skeleton of the 'armoured reptile', named *Hylaeosaurus,* that was also described by Dr Mantell in 1833 – remained unrecognised until Sir Richard Owen revealed that these three fossil reptiles were truly unlike any living lizards with which they had been compared. Owen recognised the *Iguanodon*, *Megalosaurus* and *Hylaeosaurus* as a separate suborder: the *Dinosauria*.

Owen's conception of dinosaurs as 'elephantine reptiles' gained a great deal of prominence in the mid-1850s, particularly after he asked the sculptor Waterhouse Hawkins to make a complete 'zoo' of life-sized concrete models, which were placed in the gardens surrounding the reconstructed Crystal Palace at Sydenham, in south-east London. Hugely popular at the time, these models can still be seen in the park today, and are worth visiting by any dinosaur hunter (although we now know that they are inaccurate: the *Iguanodon* sported a horn on its nose!)

Megalosaurus was a carnivorous dinosaur.

NEW DISCOVERIES, NEW INSIGHTS

Throughout the 19th century, it seemed that everyone, everywhere, had caught 'dinosaur fever'! More and more remains were being unearthed in Britain and in Europe, but it was in America that the most exciting finds were to be made. In fact, Americans had been finding fossil dinosaur bones and footprints long before anyone else – they just didn't realise it! In 1800, Pliny Moody found huge fossil footprints in the Connecticut Valley: the bird-like shape of the prints led many to believe that they were the very footprints of the raven sent by Noah from the Ark to find dry land. In fact, what Moody had discovered were the tracks left by a dinosaur in the Triassic age as the creature had crossed mud flats.

The Megalosaurus jaw housed sharp teeth designed for a meat-eating diet.

The year 1855 marked the real beginning of American dinosaur discoveries. Ferdinand Hayden (1829–87) was a young geologist conducting surveys of the western territories for the US government, who collected fossils and recorded the geological composition of the land in which they were found. In 1855, Hayden was surveying the Upper Missouri, and while in Montana, found some scattered teeth that seemed to resemble those of the *Iguanodon* and *Megalosaurus* found in Britain. In 1858, these teeth were examined by Joseph Leidy (1823–91), professor of anatomy at the University of Pennsylvania, who identified some of the teeth as belonging to a herbivorous dinosaur that he called *Trachodon* ('Rugged-tooth') – today we know this dinosaur as the duckbilled *Anatosaurus* – and others belonging to a ferocious *Megalosaurus*, which he named *Deinodon horridus*, which translates as 'The most horrible of the terror-teeth'.

In the same year, 1858, Leidy also examined a partial skeleton found in Haddonfield, New Jersey. This creature, named *Hadrosaurus*, once again had teeth like *Iguanodon*, but also had its fore and hind legs preserved intact. Leidy discovered that unlike Owen's vision of a large, elephantine creature, his *Hadrosaurus* had a posture that was more like a kangaroo.

Leidy's discovery would take us closer to a greater and more accurate understanding of this type of dinosaur than anyone's so far, and once again the sculptor Waterhouse Hawkins was called upon to build models of the dinosaurs Leidy described.

Discovered by Joseph Leidy in 1858, the Hadrosaurus skeleton shows its 'kangaroo'-type posture.

Leidy's views on dinosaurs, rather than Owen's, were finally confirmed in the 1880s, following the discovery by coal miners, in 1878, in the village of Bernissart, in south-west Belgium, of no fewer than 40 complete and partial *Iguanodon* skeletons. The scientific description of the remains was recorded by Louis Dollo (1857–91), and for the first time, Owen's *Iguanodon* – which he knew only from its teeth – could be accurately reconstructed.

MARSH AND COPE: RIVALS IN THE RACE FOR KNOWLEDGE

In 1877, just before the the significant finds in Bernissart were uncovered, even richer deposits were discovered in Colorado, USA, by two schoolmasters working independently of each other. One of the teachers, Arthur Lakes, discovered bones at Morrison, Colorado, which he sent for examination to Orthniel Charles Marsh (1831–99), a professor at Yale College, later Yale University. One of the great pioneers of dinosaur studies, Marsh built up one of the most extensive fossil collections in the world, and later persuaded his uncle, George Peabody, to establish the Peabody Museum of Natural History at Yale. Marsh's own teams had already made a number of important discoveries: in 1871, they had found the first American pterodactyl fossils, as well as the remains of the earliest horses in North America.

Marsh's great rival in the quest for knowledge of dinosaurs was Edward Drinkwater Cope (1840–97). The son of a Quaker family, Cope would discover more than 1,000 species of extinct vertebrates (animals with backbones) in the USA, and would publish more than 1,200 books and papers adding to our knowledge of evolutionary history. In 1877, schoolmaster O W Lucas had been exploring rocks near Canyon City, Colorado, where he found the fossils that he sent to Cope for analysis.

The discoveries by the two schoolmasters fuelled the rivalry between Cope and Marsh that had begun in 1870, when Cope had shown Marsh the skeleton of *Elasmosaurus*, a plesiosaur found in Kansas.

Pterodactyl: a reptile of the air. Many species of wing-finger reptiles have now been discovered.

Marsh quickly pointed out a dramatic error in Cope's study: the head of the animal had been placed on the wrong end. Cope would never forgive Marsh for pointing this out, and the bitter battle between the two was on! Soon teams hired by Cope and Marsh extended their excavations beyond Colorado to Wyoming at Como Bluff, to Montana, to the Connecticut Valley and into New Mexico.

The teams spied on each other, and the rivalry even encouraged acts of vandalism: smashing each other's fossils with hammers, and even damaging the food, water and tents at each other's camps. Despite the intense competition, between 1877 and the late 1890s, Cope and Marsh between them described about 130 new species of dinosaurs, with many of the fossil remains finding their way into museums in America, in particular, the Peabody Museum at Yale University, the Smithsonian Institution in Washington, DC, and the American Museum of Natural History in New York.

BONE CABIN AND THE DINOSAUR NATIONAL MONUMENT

Following Cope's and Marsh's deaths, a much more co-ordinated – and less violent – exploration of regions of North America was instituted by the American Museum of Natural History. In 1898, a small cabin, built as a shelter by a shepherd, was discovered in Wyoming. Called 'Bone Cabin', the shelter had been made out of some of the hundreds of dinosaur bones that were to be found scattered across the area.

But by far the richest finds of dinosaur skeletons that the world has ever known were discovered near Vernal, in the Uinta mountains of Utah, in 1909, by Earl Douglass (1862–1931). Working for the Carnegie Museum in Pittsburgh, Utah, between 1909 and 1923, Douglass discovered 355,600kg (350 tons) of fossilised dinosaur remains in the Carnegie Quarry, including those of *Allosaurus*, *Diplodocus*, *Aptosaurus*, *Camarasaurus* and *Stegosaurus*. So vast were the finds that, in 1915, by presidential decree, the site was named Dinosaur National Monument. Today, a working museum stands on the site, surrounded by fossil-bearing rocks, with fossils still in place and visible. In honour of his work, the quarry itself was renamed the Douglass Quarry.

One of the richest finds of dinosaur bones was made in 1909 in Utah, by Earl Douglass.

WORLDWIDE FINDS

While the end of the 19th century marked the end of the great pioneering age of dinosaur discoveries, there were still plenty of dinosaur remains to be discovered across the world.

Compsognathaurus, a carvivorous dinosaur whose name means 'pretty jaw', was only the size of a modern chicken.

In Europe, in spite of a long tradition of dinosaur discovery and excavation, finds in the 20th century were to be greatly outshone by huge discoveries elsewhere in the world. Nevertheless, in the sandstone region of Solnholfen, in Germany, amazing fossils of great detail revealed the tiny *Compsognathaurus* and the first-known bird, *Archaeopteryx*, while in the south of France, in Aix-en-Provence, some of the largest fossil dinosaur eggs, measuring 30cm (12in) long – about five times larger than a hen's egg – were found and were believed to have been laid by the herbivorous *Hypselosaurus*.

In Canada, in 1884, Joseph Tyrell uncovered the fossil remains of *Albertosaurus* in the Red Deer River area of Alberta. Tyrell was followed to the region by Barnham Brown, known affectionately as 'Mr Bones', of the American Museum of Natural History, in 1910. Brown would find the first *Tyrannosaurus rex* fossils, and would describe and name *Ankylosaurus* and *Corythosaurus*.

In 1912, the Sternberg family, led by father Charles H (1850–1943), made many spectacular discoveries in the Red Deer River region, and developed the technique of 'jacketing' fossil bones in a protective cast. Son Charles M (1885–1981) was famous for his skills in 'reading' the ground for dinosaur remains, while George F (1883–1959) found an impression of dinosaur skin that belonged to *Anatosaurus,* and then discovered the hadrosaur (meaning 'duck-billed') *Edmontosaurus* in 1909.

T. rex, one of the most famous of all dinosaurs.

Levi (1894–1976) developed the jacketing method further and devised a latex casting technique that was used to duplicate fossils.

So important was the Red Deer River region in Alberta, Canada, that the area was designated the Dinosaur Provincial Park and is now a United Nations' World Heritage Site, a status enjoyed by important historical monuments like the Pyramids of ancient Egypt.

At the other end of the Americas, in South America, a great number of finds were made in the 20th century, in particular in Argentina by Jose Bonaparte and Fernando Novas, who, in 1985, found fossils of *Carnatosaurus*. While Bonaparte and Novas were professional palaeontologists, discoveries were also being made by amateurs: the first *Herrerasaurus* bones were found by an Argentinean farmer called Victorino Herrera in the 1960s. These fragments were the only ones known until 1985, when scientists working in the Valley of the Moon, a desert region in the foothills of the Andes, found a near complete specimen. Some of the biggest of all dinosaurs –

Carnatosaurus, the 'Meat-eating bull', was found in Argentina in 1985.

including the carnivorous and appropriately named *Gigantosaurus* – and the huge, herbivorous *Argentinosaurus*, were found in Argentina, while other important fossil finds have been made in recent years in Colombia, Chile, Brazil, Uruguay and Peru.

AFRICA

The first major discoveries of dinosaur fossils in Africa were made as recently as 1908. These came from Tendaguru, in present-day Tanzania, in east Africa, and were excavated by the German palaeontologists Edwin Hennig and Werner Janensch, from the Berlin Museum of Natural History. Between 1908 and 1912, the pair excavated more than 254,000kg (250 tons) of fossil bones and rock, which were then carried by native bearers for over 65km (40 miles) to the nearest port for shipment to Germany. Hennig and Janensch found some remarkable dinosaurs, including the giant, giraffe-like *Brachiosaurus*, a smaller dinosaur that they called *Dicraeosaurus* and the stegosaur-like armoured dinosaur, *Kentrosaurus*.

Later finds on the vast continent included those from Morocco and Egypt in the north (*Cetiosaurus* and the huge, sail-backed *Spinosaurus*), from Niger, in central Africa (*Camarasaurus*, a 20,320kg (20 ton) plant-eater), and from Zimbabwe, in southern Africa (*Barosaurus*, and the 6m- (20ft-) long *Vulcanodon*).

ASIA AND AUSTRALIA

Discoveries of dinosaurs in Asia and Australia date back to the early part of the 20th century, but the most significant discoveries in these regions have been made far more recently. Some of the most exciting finds have come from Australia – of dinosaurs found nowhere else in the world. One of the major sites is 'Dinosaur Cove', in the Otway–Strzelecki mountain range, on the coast near Melbourne, Victoria, where the remains

Velociraptor, the 'fast thief' of the Cretaceous period, had some 80 extremely sharp teeth and a sickle-shaped claw on each foot for slashing.

of *Leaellynasaurus* were found. In Queensland, the remains of the large, herbivorous *Muttaburrasaurus* (named after Muttaburra, the site of the remains) were found, while near Winton, the tracks of around 130 dinosaurs passing by are preserved in more than 3,000 trace fossil footprints.

In India, the remains of a huge, plant-eating dinosaur, *Titanosaurus*, were uncovered near Umrer, in central India. *Titanosaurus* lived some 70 million years ago, was a staggering 12m (40ft) long and is estimated to have weighed somewhere around 10,160kg (nearly 10 tons). Other major finds include *Dravidosaurus*, found near Tirunchirapalli, in southern India. This is a dinosaur of the stegosaur group that lived much later than other stegosaurs, in the Late Cretaceous period, about 70 million years ago.

In Asia, most of the dinosaur fossils that have been found so far were discovered in the Gobi Desert, in Mongolia, Central Asia, and in present-day China. The first expeditions to the Gobi Desert took place in 1922, and were led by Roy Chapman Andrews (1884–1960), Henry Fairfield Osborn and Walter Granger, of the American Museum of Natural History. The initial aim of this expedition was to find evidence regarding the origin of humankind, but the most significant finds that the team made were, in fact, dinosaurs. Between 1992 and 1925, four expeditions to the region collected a number of specimens, all of which were brand-new to science: *Pinacosaurus*, *Saurornithoides*, *Oviraptor* and *Velociraptor*. Most significant was the discovery not only of *Protoceratops*, but of its nests and eggs – the first of any dinosaur eggs to be discovered.

Brachiosaurus, or 'arm lizard', grew up to 16m (50ft) high. Its thigh bones alone were over 1.8m (6ft) long.

Dinosaur fossils had been found for centuries in China, but were identified as belonging to the magic creatures of Chinese folklore: dragons! Systematic and scientific study of dinosaur fossils began in the 1930s, and was led by Professor Yang Zhong-jian (known to his colleagues in the West as C C Young), who in 1941, found the remains of *Lufangosaurus* in China's southern province of Yunnan.

Following the establishment of the People's Republic of China in 1949, and the country's political and cultural isolation, all dinosaur research in China was concentrated on the Institute of Vertebrate Palaeontology in Beijing, which has co-ordinated much of the work since then. In the 1950s, Chinese scientists discovered *Tsintaosaurus* and *Mamenchisaurus*. These were followed in subsequent decades by the important discoveries of *Shantungosaurus*, *Psittacosaurus*, *Tuojiangosaurus* and *Avimimus*. Today, China is an area of 'dinosaur fever'! Its important finds, including 'feathered dinosaurs' like *Sinosauropteryx*, have astounded scientists across the world, and are causing many to alter long-held ideas. A few of the existing dinosaur finds in China have also captured the world's imagination, but have turned out to be clever fakes.

THE SEARCH CONTINUES

While the vast majority of dinosaurs are known from only a few fossil parts, occasionally remains are found of a dinosaur body that has dried out very rapidly, so that quite a number of its parts are preserved as mummified fossils. One of the best-known, part-mummified dinosaur fossils is 'Sue', the biggest, and most complete, preserved specimen of a female *Tyrannosaurus* ever found. Sue was found in 1990, in South Dakota, USA, and was named after her finder, fossil hunter Susan Hendrickson, of the Black Hills Institute of Geological Research. Not only was Sue a very important specimen in scientific terms, she was extremely valuable: in 1997, Sue was sold for more than $8.3 million to the Field Museum in Chicago.

Almost all of the continents, excluding Antarctica, have yielded, and continue to yield, dinosaur remains, and even Antarctica is likely to have some. The obvious problem here is that the rocks that most likely contain them are covered by thick ice sheets. This icy continent has not always been inhospitable, though: the remains of an early Triassic-period, mammal-like reptile called *Lystrosauris* were found here, and scientists are hopeful that one day dinosaur remains will also be discovered.

With its horny 'beak' and small frill at the back of its head, Psittacosaurus was a light, long-tailed herbivore.

NAMING DINOSAURS

Chances are, there are many more dinosaurs waiting to be unearthed, but for any dinosaur, enough fossils need to be found for a panel of scientists to be sure that it is a distinct type so that they can estimate its size and give it a scientific name.

Each dinosaur has a scientific name that is usually made up of Latin or Greek words. Each of the dinosaur names in this book is written in italics. This is in order to distinguish individual dinosaurs from their 'groups'. Some of the dinosaur 'groups' are themselves named after the first-discovered or major dinosaur of their kind, like the tyrannosaurs and stegosaurs.

Still hard at work: the search for dinosaur remains continues.

For example, *Velociraptor* (which means 'speedy predator') and *Deionychus* (which means 'terrible claw') are both members of the group of dinosaurs known as dromaeosaurs. They are called dromaeosaurs (which means 'running reptiles') after the major, or first, specimen of this type of dinosaur to be found, *Dromaeosaurus*. All of the dinosaurs in the dromaeosaur group shared similar characteristics: they were medium-sized, meat-eating dinosaurs, with a large, curved claw on each foot.

Euoplocephalus (which means 'well-armoured head') belongs to the group of dinosaurs called ankylosaurs (meaning 'fused reptiles'). These dinosaurs all had a protective armour of outer body plates and a large lump of bone at the end of their tails, which they used as a hammer or swing, rather like a club.

Dromaeosaurus was a small, fast-moving dinosaur whose remains were first discovered in 1914, in Canada.

As you can see, many dinosaur names end in -*saurus*, which some people say means 'reptile', while others say it means 'lizard', even though dinosaurs were not lizards. Some of the Latin and Greek names can be real tongue-twisters, but most refer to a unique feature: the dinosaur *Opsisthocoelicaudia* (pronounced 'owe-pis-thowe-see-lee-cord-ee-ah'!) means 'posterior tail cavity' and refers to the unique formation of this dinosaur's joints between the vertebrae in its tail.

Some of the more modern dinosaur finds are also named after the place where the remains were found or the people who found them. *Minmi* takes its name from Minmi Crossing in Queensland, Australia, while *Riojasaurus* was found in Rioja, Argentina.

The duck-billed *Lambeosaurus* was named in honour of the great Canadian fossil expert Lawrence Lambe (1853–1919). *Baryonyx*, which means 'heavy claw', a name that it got from the massive claw on its thumb, is properly known as *Baryonyx walkeri*, in honour of Bill Walker, an amateur fossil hunter and quarryman who, in 1982, found a 'massive claw' in a claypit in Surrey, England. *Leaellynasaura*, found in Australia, was named in honour of Lea Ellyn, the daughter of one of the dinosaur's discoverers.

Who knows, maybe one day, you, too, will
find – and name – a dinosaur!

CHAPTER 1

WHEN DINOSAURS RULED THE EARTH

THE CHANGING EARTH

Geologists and palaeontologists divide the past into several different periods called eras, which are then further subdivided into periods, each of which lasted for millions of years. Some periods are subdivided further into smaller units called epochs. The milestones of the main geological eras or epochs are the orogenetic (mountain-forming) periods. During these periods, the distribution of the land and seas was changed. This in turn affected the environment that supported life: life either adapted to its environment or it became extinct. Consequently, new and more advanced forms of life originated at the same time as those that were incapable of transforming and evolving died out.

According to many scientists, the history of the Earth begins only at the time when the solid crust of the Earth was formed; this occurred during the Archaean or Archeozoic era, around 2,100 million years ago. This era is divided into two periods: the first is called the Anhydric (waterless) period, and the second, later period is called the Primeval Oceanic period, during which air temperatures dropped and made the water vapour condense and form the first primeval oceans in the hollows of the solidifying crust of the Earth. This was a period of great volcanic activity, when immense lava flows solidified both on the surface of the Earth and below it, and were transformed into rocks that weathered and crumbled and were carried away by the first rivers to be deposited at the bottom of the oceans to form the first sediments.

LIFE BEGINS

Of this very early period in the Earth's history – the Precambrian era – we know very little. What is apparent, though, is that the history of the Earth, and life on it, stretches back over millions of years. The trail that leads to dinosaurs begins really in the Palaeozoic era, the first era in which a variety of complex living things were produced. In the first 200 millions years or so of the Palaeozoic era – through the Cambrian, Ordovician and Silurian periods – almost all life on Earth remained beneath the seas. By the Cambrian period, seaweed and many of the groups of invertebrates (back boneless) animals had appeared. There were soft-bodied jellyfish and worms, but there were also trilobites and brachiopods, which produced lime to make hard shells to protect their bodies.

In the seas of the Ordovician period, corals, molluscs and the ancient relatives of octopus and squid colonised the waters, while the ancestors of the modern starfish were beginning to give rise to small, fish-like animals – the first animals to make bones. The ability to grown internal bones was gigantic step forward: the skeleton protects the inner organs of an animal in the same way as the outer shell of a crab.

But unlike a crab, an animal with an internal skeleton does not have to shed its protective armour when its inner body grows too big for its 'case' – its bones grow in size with it. Having an internal skeleton also allows for a greater degree of mobility. The advent of internal skeletons would help animals move out of the sea and on to land.

TABLE OF GEOLOGICAL TIMES

ERA	PERIOD	How many million years ago (approx)
ARCHAEAN	1st: Anhydric (waterless period)	at least 2,500
	2nd: Primeval Oceanic period (origins of life)	
PROTEROZOIC	1st: Huronian }	1,200
(Eozoic)	2nd: Algonkian }	
Development of Invertebrates		
PALAEOZOIC	Lower Cambrian	600
Age of Invertebrates	Ordovician	500
Fishes & Amphibia	Silurian	440
	Devonian	395
	Upper Carboniferous	345
	Permian	280
MESOZOIC	Triassic	225
Age of Reptiles	Jurassic	193
	Cretaceous	136
TERTIARY	Paleogene Paleocene }	
(Cenozoic/Kainozoic)	Eocene }	
Age of Mammals	Oligocene }	65
	Neogene Miocene }	
	Pliocene }	
QUATERNARY	Pleistocene }	
(Anthropozoic)	Holocene (present age) }	1.8
Age of Man		

PLANT LIFE

The move to land by vertebrates occurred during the Devonian period, about 395 to 345 million years ago. But before anything animal could colonise the land, there had to be plants, since all animals depend on plants for food at first or second hand: herbivorous (plant-eating animals) feed on plants and carnivorous animals (meat-eating animals) feed on herbivores. The soft seaweed – which was rootless – could not have survived either the dry air or the effects of gravity, but by 400 million years ago, a relative of the seaweed had evolved a stiffened stem, along with fine, hair-like roots and an internal tube system that allowed it to suck up water and nutrients.

Because these early plants were still evolving, they clung to the edges of land alongside rivers, lakes and seas, and it would be here that the aquatic animals would also first come ashore. The first creatures to come ashore were the ancestors of millipedes, centipedes, wood lice and scorpions and other arthropod (jointed-leg) creatures.

The Carboniferous period saw very favourable living conditions, and the well-watered basins at the feet of mountains were the perfect environment for luxurious plant growth. These plants formed forests covering much of what is now eastern Europe and North America; the hot, wet forests of the Carboniferous period, lying just above sea level, may have resembled the dense, lush forest that can be seen in the tropical regions of the Earth today. The plants, though, were very different. Under tree-like plants, such as the giant club mosses *Lipidodenron* and *Calamitina,* which grew to heights of over 30m (100ft), grew a rich undergrowth of mosses and ferns. Some of these ferns wound themselves around the trunks of taller plants, others grew tree-like themselves, and up to 14m (45ft) high. The tallest trees of the Carboniferous forest were the *Cordaites*: richly branched, with long, ribbon-like leaves and a smooth trunk, these could reach heights of 44m (145 ft). The remains of these plants became the basis of present-day coal deposits.

The first winged insects flew through the Carboniferous forests, and fossil remains show that a few of these insects – such as dragonflies and cockroaches – would have looked very similar to present-day species, only much larger. Scorpions grew to more than 60cm (24in) long, while the *Arthopleura*, a flat-bodied millipede, was a mighty 2m (6ft 6in) long. The primitive dragonfly *Meganeura,* with its wingspan of around 60cm (24inches), was over three times the size of the dragonfly *Tetracanthagyna plagiata* from Borneo, the largest dragonfly species still living today. Because insects are generally small and delicate, fossil remains are rare because their bodies most likely rotted away before they could be trapped in sediment, or amber, and fossilised. With little fossil evidence, scientists are still trying to work out how insects actually evolved.

LOBE-FINNED AMPHIBIANS

Most of the waterside-dwelling insects would have provided food for the first vertebrates that ventured ashore. These vertebrates were rhipidistians, a group of now extinct, lobe-finned amphibians that evolved some 360 million years ago from fish. Because they had evolved from fish, the rhipidistians still had fish-like features, but with long, fleshy, muscular, lobed fins that looked a little bit like legs with which they pulled themselves out of the water and on to the land. Unlike modern fishes, rhipidistians had lungs, but they were still fishes and were not designed to spend long periods out of the water.

By the late Devonian period, the lobed fins of some rhipidistians had evolved into legs with five-toed feet, and these rhipidistians were now at home on land, as well as in the water. *Ichthyostega*, an early amphibian from the Devonian period, had some fish-like features – a tail fin and small scales – combined with a distinctly amphibian body. It also had fewer skull bones, making its head lighter to carry, and legs that were now suited to walking. For the first time on Earth, there were creatures with a skeleton whose basic design foreshadowed that of the dinosaurs.

REPTILES

The amphibians only managed to gain a toehold on the moist edges of land, and the first truly land-based vertebrates to venture further into the dry, inland areas were reptiles. They were uniquely suited to this adventure, thanks to their body design and their breeding habits. Where amphibians have moist, soft skins that soon dry up if overexposed to warm, dry air, reptiles have a tough, waterproof, outer covering of thick, dry scales that trap moisture inside the body.

Reptiles' bones, too, underwent changes, especially in the hips and feet, which allowed them to run, unlike the restricted wriggling motion of, for example, a salamander. Bursts of activity – such as a sprint after some tasty morsel of prey – were fuelled by more effective respiratory and circulatory systems than amphibians had. But it was possibly the reptiles' breeding habits that freed them the most from the dependence on water.

A reptile fossil.

Most male amphibians scatter their sperm haphazardly over eggs laid in water by the females, but male reptiles fertilise the female's eggs while they are still inside her body. Amphibians' eggs, encased in their jelly-like blobs, would dry up if they were laid on land, but reptiles' eggs, whether leathery or hard-shelled, carry protective linings that keep the contents moist, even when they are deposited in hot, desert sands. When, in the Permian period that ended the Palaeozoic era, the swampy forests were replaced by drier, desert-like conditions, the reptiles, unlike many amphibians, were therefore ideally suited to the new landscape and climate and were colonising new regions.

By the Permian period, several early reptile groups had evolved. First, there were the small, low cotylosaurs, named because of their cup-shaped vertebrae. Cotylosaurs called captorhinomorphs had sharp teeth and hunted insects and amphibians in the forests and swamps. Second, there were the much larger, man-sized reptiles called diadectomorphs, or 'broad-toothed forms', which had blunter teeth better designed to grind up plant material. So by Permian times, there were herbivores (plant-eaters) and carnivores (meat-eaters) among the vertebrates.

Scientists believe that from the primitive cotylosaur reptiles, other kinds of species, including mammals, evolved. One reptile offshoot was a group known as pelycosaurs. These were the size of a rhinoceros and roamed largely across what are now the south-western states of the USA. Pelycosaurs had a 'skin web', or 'sail', that grew between spiny growths from its backbone. It is believed that these cold-blooded creatures used the 'sail' as a body-temperature control system: by angling the 'sail' to the sun, the pelycosaur could speed up – or slow down – the rate at which its body heated up or cooled down. This ability to control body temperature is something that crocodiles also display today.

SYNAPSIDS

As the Permian period continued, mammal-like reptiles were to evolve from these pelycosaurs. These included the slow-moving, but immensely powerful, plant-eating dicynodonts, or 'two dog teeth', whose fore limbs were splayed out sideways, but whose back legs were erect, like those of mammals. The dicynodonts were synapsids, which means 'with arch' and comes from the name given to a large hole low in the skull, behind each eye. The muscles that operated the jaw passed through these holes and gave the synapsids very large gapes and an immensely powerful bite. The synapsids formed a separate group from the true reptiles that gave rise to the dinosaurs.

THE AGE OF DINOSAURS

The 'age of the dinosaur' corresponds to the time period that geologists call the Mesozoic era, from about 248–65 million years ago. The Mesozoic – which literally means 'middle life' – is divided into three shorter time spans: the Triassic, Jurassic and Cretaceous periods. Throughout these periods, different dinosaurs lived and died, and each species may have lived for only 2 or 3 million years.

During the Triassic period (about 248 to 208 million years ago), dinosaurs began to evolve. The Jurassic period (about 208 to 144 million years ago) was the time of the largest, and smallest, of the dinosaurs, while during the Cretaceous period (about 144 to 65 million years ago), the dinosaurs varied most.

PANGAEA: THE SUPERCONTINENT

There are good reasons for the early evolution and spread of the dinosaurs: when the lower Permian period ended and the magnificent Carboniferous forests disappeared from the surface of the Earth, the upper Permian period began, and striking changes took place in the plants and creatures. Most of the land was warm, which suited the reptiles, and the continents, as we now know them, were gathered together in one great land mass, forming a single supercontinent called Pangaea. Consequently, the animals that were evolving in one place during the Triassic period were able to travel across the land mass: a curious, pig-like dicynodont called *Lystrosaurus* was to be found in Australia, Antarctica, China, India and in South Africa. Almost everywhere on this supercontinent, the climate was tropical or subtropical, with many areas of desert.

Throughout the Mesozoic era, the super-continent Pangaea that straddled the Equator, and that was evident in the Triassic period, was also to undergo slow, almost invisible, changes due to the process called continent drift. This is the name given to Alfred Wegener's theory of 1915, whereby the great sheets of the Earth's crust – known as tectonic plates – very slowly (only a few centimetres each year) moved apart to form the continents as we know them today.

A Sauroposeidon.

LAURASIA AND GONDWANA

By the Jurassic period, Pangaea was gradually splitting into two huge land masses or continents: in the north was Laurasia, which was made up of a number of large land masses and smaller islands, while in the south was the continent of Gondwana. The 'modern' southern continents – South America, India, Antarctica, Africa and Australia – had begun to pull away from what are now Europe and North America with the formation of a narrow seaway to the east called Tethys and the very small beginnings of the Atlantic Ocean to the west. By the middle of the Jurassic period, another sea, the Turgai Sea, would begin to separate Europe from Asia. Despite the movement of the continents, there appears to have been some contact remaining between these areas because palaeontologists have found that various Jurassic-period dinosaurs, such as diplodocids, brachiosaurids and iguanadontids, were very similar in both North America and Africa during this time.

The largest and the smallest of all of the dinosaurs lived during the Jurassic period in the warm, wet forests, thick with ferns and horsetails by river banks, or in the drier, inland areas that supported gingkoes, conifers and cycads – palm-like plants, with large, leafy crowns from which sprouted pine-like cones. Many of the creatures that had lived during the Triassic period had all but died out and had been replaced by others: dinosaurs now replaced the mammal-like reptiles, such as the dicynodonts, while the big, aquatic reptiles like ichthyosaurs and plesiosaurs roamed the seas. By the end of the Jurassic period, the air was filled with flying animals and early birds, which had evolved from reptiles.

THE FORMATION OF MODERN CONTINENTS

By the early Cretaceous period, Laurasia and Gondwana were themselves splitting further into the continents that exist today, and were drifting into to their now familiar positions on the globe. Africa and South America had drifted apart, and India was moving across the Indian Ocean, while in the north, the continents, while not physically separated to the same degree, were subdivided by inland seas that covered parts of Laurasia. Consequently, western North America and eastern Asia were still in contact with each other across the Bering Straits, and Europe and eastern North America were also still in contact with each other. The distribution of dinosaur remains reflects these contacts, with some species found only in Asia and western North America and others found only in Europe and eastern North America.

With the movement of the continents came climate changes. Overall, the Earth's climate became cooler. The more temperate climate favoured the spread of flowering plants, the seeds of which grow inside a protective case, more familiarly known as a fruit. The new plants that appeared during this period included very familiar 'modern' plants and trees, such as oaks, aspens and magnolias. Alongside these new plant species, in the northern continents, biped and quadruped – two- and four-legged – dinosaurs evolved, and many fed on the plant life. In turn, these herbivores were themselves the prey of carnivorous dinosaurs. Mammals were also around, but they remained small and furtive. In the air, the giant, skin-winged gliding animals, the largest ever airborne creatures, flew through the air alongside a widening variety of birds, some of which were not too different from some alive today. But by the end of the Cretaceous period, the dinosaurs, along with many other ancient life forms, had disappeared from the Earth. About 65 million years ago, the last dinosaurs lay dead. What killed them on land, in the sea and in the air remains one of the great unsolved mysteries of prehistoric life on Earth.

CHAPTER 2

DINOSAUR ANATOMY

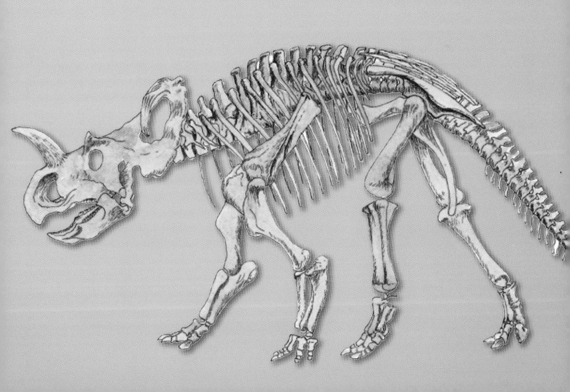

THE THECODONTIANS

Dinosaurs belonged to a very large group of diapsid (or 'two-arched') reptiles, which include the now extinct dinosaurs and flying reptiles, or pterosaurs, as well as some living animals, such as snakes, crocodiles and lizards. The diapsid-reptile group also included a not-so-well-known group called the thecodontians.

A Giganotosaurus.

Palaeontologists believe that the thecodontians paved the way for the dinosaurs because in the structure of their hips and hind legs, the thecodontians were able to change the angle that their back legs made between their bodies and the ground when they walked. The femur, or upper leg bone, of thecodontians was curved, and their hip joints were socketed in a way that allowed them either to hold their legs out at the sides of their bodies – like a lizard does – or to hold their legs partly underneath their bodies, which allowed them to lift their bodies clear of the ground when they walked. This was a much more efficient way of walking, and it also allowed the thecodontians to have much larger body weights that were carried on legs, rather than having a huge belly resting on the ground. This altering of the range of leg positions would make it possible for dinosaurs to achieve immense body sizes.

The increased weight now carried on the thecodontians' legs would in turn affect the structure of the ankle bones: small animals, like lizards, with their legs at the sides of their bodies, do not require really strong or stable ankle bones; instead, they need ankles with a great deal of flexibility. Theocodontians, and later the dinosaurs, with their much larger size and more varied gaits, required much greater strength and stability. So instead of rows of small bones that slide past each other (as lizards have), the theocodontians developed the much stronger ball-and-socket type of ankle joint. The new leg position of the dinosaurs was, in many ways, the key to their success: their upright posture meant that they did not have to expend huge amounts of energy just keeping their bodies off the ground. Instead, they were able to develop much more active lifestyles.

During the Mesozoic era around 248 to 65 million years ago, dinosaurs formed the single (but most diverse) group of reptiles that completely dominated life on land. The very first dinosaurs were probably biped carnivores (two-legged meat-eaters) that were not much larger than a medium sized dog. Soon, however, dinosaurs were to evolve into a huge variety of shapes and sizes, from as small as a farmyard hen to as large as a whale. No individual dinosaur species lived for more than a few million years, but there were always new ones evolving to take the place of the ones that had died out.

BIRD-HIPPED AND LIZARD-HIPPED DINOSAURS

The dinosaurs that eventually evolved from the theocodontians at the end of the Triassic era are divided into two groups: saurischians, or 'lizard-hipped' dinosaurs, and ornithischians, or 'bird-hipped' dinosaurs. All dinosaurs had four limbs: unlike some other reptile-like snakes, dinosaurs did not lose their limbs as they evolved during the Mesozoic era.

SAURISCHIAN DINOSAURS: KEY FEATURES

The saurischian (lizard-hipped) dinosaurs included the sauropodomorph ('lizard-foot form') dinosaurs, which were usually quadruped (walking on all four legs) herbivores (plant-eaters) of often enormous size, and all of the therapods ('beast feet'), which were bipedal (two-legged), carnivorous (meat-eating) dinosaurs of varying sizes. The saurischian dinosaurs were characterised by having a pelvis in which the three bones – the ilium, ischium and pubis – as in most other reptiles, radiate outwards from one another in different directions from the hip joint or socket. In most of the saurischian dinosaurs, the pubic bones pointed forwards, as in lizards, but in some other saurischians, the pubic bones pointed backwards. Unlike other reptiles, though, the saurischians had an opening in the hip socket called the acetabulum. Above this was an outwardly projecting lip, or ridge, against which the femur was pressed: this ridge allowed the joint to rotate, but stopped the ball-shaped head of the femur from slipping out of the hip socket. The saurischian dinosaurs had knee joints and ankle joints that were simple hinges, rather than the more complex ball-and-socket joints of the theocodontians.

ORNITHISCHIAN DINOSAURS: KEY FEATURES

The ornithischian dinosaurs shared the same leg structure as the saurischian dinosaurs, but their pelvis was different. The ornithischian dinosaurs had a downwards- and backwards-pointing pubis bone that lay parallel to the ischium, as it does in living birds, hence the name 'ornithischian'. But in spite of their appellation, it was the therapod saurischian dinosaurs (and not the ornithischians) that would give rise to birds.

Along with a different hip structure, the ornithischian dinosaurs were distinguished by bony rods on either side of their spine along their backs, and by a strange, 'U'-shaped, horn-covered bone called the predentary at the front tip of their lower jaws. In most ornithischians, the predentary bone formed the lower half of a toothless, horn-covered beak designed for grasping and cropping leafy vegetation. Further back inside the jaw were cheek teeth designed for cutting up and chewing leaves and stalks.

An example of lizard-like hips.

The ornithischian dinosaurs were all herbivores, but they can be further subdivided into three main groups: thyreophorans, which were armoured and plated quadrupeds; marginocephalians, which had heads with bony frills or horns; and, ornithopods, the bipedal herbivores.

WARM- OR COLD-BLOODED?

Although palaeontologists know a great deal about the anatomy, life cycle, breeding habits and diets of dinosaurs, so far it has not been established whether they were cold- or warm-blooded. Reptiles are exothermic (cold-blooded) creatures, which means that they rely on the temperature outside their bodies, such as the heat from the sun if they live in their natural habitats, or from heating bulbs if they are kept in vivaria. Lizards spend a great deal of their time basking in the heat of the sun in order to raise their body temperature to a level where it can work properly. To avoid overheating, lizards cool off in the shade. But if it is too cold – for instance, at night or in winter – reptiles become inactive. Endothermic (warm-blooded) animals, such as mammals, produce their body heat from the food that they eat, and have hair or fur to keep them warm and sweat glands to help them to cool down.

What is puzzling to scientists is that although dinosaurs were reptiles, much of their behaviour was more like that of warm-blooded mammals. Being warm-blooded would have allowed dinosaurs to stay warm and active during the day and night and in colder weather conditions. This would have allowed them to hunt for prey for greater lengths of time. If dinosaurs were endothermic, they would have needed to eat at least 10 times more food than if they were exothermic, in order to burn off calories to keep them warm and give them the energy that allowed them to run faster.

Two further arguments for dinosaurs being endothermic have been offered, firstly, by the evidence that many lived in herds and raised families of young. This type of very complex lifestyle is common to many birds and mammals, but is rare in reptiles (although Nile crocodiles do display a great deal of parental care in that they respond to their offsprings' calls and break open their nests to release their young, then carry them protectively in their jaws to special crocodile nurseries, where the babies grow and develop while being carefully watched over by the adults).

Secondly, there is dinosaur posture. Most dinosaurs stood upright on straight legs: this posture is common to endothermic creatures, but not to other, cold-blooded reptiles.

A Brachiosaurus.

Furthermore, dinosaurs had bones that were more like mammals' than reptiles': mammal bones contain far more blood vessels than reptile bones. The huge, sauropodomorph dinosaurs like the *Brachiosaurus*, with its very long neck, needed a strong heart and very high blood pressure so that blood could be pumped to its brain — its head was probably about 13m (43ft) from the ground, But lower down its body, at the level of its lungs, such a high blood pressure would have been fatal. Endothermic animals have a 'twin-pressure' system, in so far as they have a fully divided heart: it is divided into a 'lung-circulation' and a 'body-and-head' circuit, which makes for an efficient circulatory system because there is no mixing of oxygenated and deoxygenated blood in the heart. In reptiles, which have only a semidivided heart, there is mixing of deoxygenated and oxygenated blood in the heart that is regulated by a pressure-sensitive valve. In order that massive bleeding due to high pressure bursting the thin blood vessels in *Brachiosaurus'* lungs did not occur, *Brachiosaurus* must have had a divided heart that kept the blood pressure in the lung circuit lower than in the body-and-head circuit. Therefore, since dinosaurs had divided hearts, they may well also have been endothermic (warm-blooded).

SEXUAL DIMORPHISM & CHARACTERISTIC FEATURES

In dinosaurs – and in many other animals – any difference between the sexes, either in size or in specific features, is known as sexual dimorphism. This can present problems to palaeontologists attempting to study fossilised remains: are the differences between male and females of the same species to be expected? Since it is the female of the species that bears the young, differences in pelvic anatomy have helped to distinguished male and female dinosaurs. Sometimes, though, it is difficult to tell whether differences are really just variations in the normal range for the species – think how many different shapes and sizes there are of dogs, or even of human beings – or could it be that the differences found in two sets of fossilised remains mean that, in fact, the two are completely different species? These problems are made more difficult because no complete fossilised dinosaur – with allof its bones and all of its soft parts, like skin, eyes, muscles and organs, has ever been found. Most dinosaurs are reconstructed from the fossils of their hard parts, and chief among these are their teeth, bones, horns and claws. But the vast majority of dinosaurs are, in fact, known from only a very few fossil parts.

Because there are no living dinosaurs to study, scientists have to make educated guesses based on comparisons with living forms. Consequently, many think that like many living reptiles, female dinosaurs were larger than the males, an idea that is further supported by evidence of 'Sue', the biggest, and most complete, preserved *Tyrannosaurus rex,* which was found in South Dakota, USA, in 1990. (With this in mind, perhaps the king of the dinosaurs should be renamed *Tyrannosaurus regina*!)

A further marker of sex in some dinosaurs, in particular, the hadrosaurs (duck-billed dinosaurs), were the head crests of the lambeosaurines. As a result of investigations by Dr Peter Dodson, of the University of Pennsylvania, we now know that some examples of *Lambeosaurus* that had been earlier identified as different species were, in fact, simply male, females and juveniles of a small number of species. Some had short, rounded main crests, with small, spike-like spurs pointing upwards and backwards, others had a large, angular main crest, with a large spur pointing upwards and backwards.

A lambeosaurine.

CRESTS, HORNS, SPIKES AND FRILLS

Dr Dodson's work showed that the crests on some hadrosaurs were related to growth stages in life, and were probably used as indicators of sex. It is most likely that the crests, frills, horns and spikes that adorned the heads of many other dinosaurs served the same purpose. Such devices would have helped dinosaurs to distinguish one another – for purposes of courtship and mating, as well as in territorial disputes – and perhaps the dinosaur with the largest and most attractive head adornment was marked out as the leader of the pack.

The internal anatomy of the crests of some hadrosaurs has given rise to a number of theories about other possible functions. One theory suggests that the elongated, tubular crest of *Parasaurolophus* was a snorkel that allowed the dinosaur to breathe while it was feeding under water. A variation suggests that the crests were self-contained air-storage compartments, like the air tanks of scuba divers. This is unlikely, given the amount of air that could be contained in the crest, especially in relation to the size of dinosaur. A third theory suggests that the cranial crests were the site of salt glands. Since many living reptiles have these glands in their nasal or ocular cavities to regulate the salt levels in their bodies – the perpetual tears in turtles' eyes when on land are produced by these salt glands – it seems reasonable to suggest that large, herbivorous dinosaurs, such as hadrosaurs, might have had them, too. The problem, however, with this idea is that if the crests were used to house salt glands, why were there so many different shapes and sizes of crests, and what system for regulating salt was available to those hadrosaurs that didn't have crests, or to those that had solid crests?

Parasaurolophus.

Another theory suggests that the crests on lambeosaurines functioned as foliage detectors – a sort of antenna device – to stop their heads from getting knocked about by branches as they ran through thickly wooded areas. By far the most widely accepted theory, though, is that the crests were used for making sounds. Air blown through the head-crest passages could have made the entire crest vibrate. The huge variety of shapes and sizes of crests must have made it possible for a range of sounds to be emitted, from very low-pitched and deeply resonating rumbles to more high-pitched, trumpeting blasts. Such sounds may have been part of mating rituals, as well as being used to intimidate rivals and frighten away predators. It is possible that in common with other herd animals, such calls and noises were made to call the herd together to form a massed defence.

HORNS AND FRILLS

Like head crests, dinosaurs' horns got bigger as the animals matured and grew in size. The horns and frills of the ceratopsian (which means 'horn-face') dinosaurs were the defensive armour required by herbivores to keep them safe from attack by predatory, carnivorous dinosaurs, especially as ceratopsians had no teeth in the front of their hooked, beak-like mouths. The ancestor of all of the ceratopsians, these horn-faced dinosaurs, was *Psitticosaurus* ('parrot reptile') which lived in China and Mongolia in the early Cretaceous period. What distinguished *Psitticosaurus* – and gave it its name – was its deep skull, which ended in a parrot-like beak. But the first truly horn-faced dinosaur, which scientists named *Protoceratops*, had a crest that formed a large shield covering the neck and shoulders and may have helped to guard the neck and the vital nerves and blood supplies running through the neck to the brain. As the ceratopsians evolved, each line had its own frill-and-horn design. One of these lines included *Chasmausaurus,* which had a long, swept-back, bony frill, a small nasal horn and two larger horns that jutted from its brows. *Pentaceratops* ('five-horned face') was a much bigger beast, with larger horns and an additional pair of horn-like, bony projections on the cheeks. Later still would come *Torosaurus,* with its huge brow horns and a frill that extended beyond the shoulders. A second line comprised the short-frilled ceratopsians, of which the most famous is *Triceratops* ('three-horned face'), which was also the last, and the largest, of all ceratopsians. While its nasal horn was short, a pair of horns nearly 1m (3ft) long projected from its brows.

Psitticosaurus.

Meanwhile, the pachycephalosaurs, or 'thick-headed reptiles', which were hornless beasts, may have defended themselves by charging their enemies head first as they were equipped with a very thick, domed bone on the top of their heads – a bit like a crash helmet. It's also likely that at mating times, males fought each other in head-butting contests.

NECKS

Because *Triceratops* had an extension at the rear of its skull made of solid bone that could have weighed as much as 50kg (110lb), ceratopsian dinosaurs had short, stout necks that needed to be very strong to support the huge weight of their skulls and horns. Meanwhile, the herbivorous dinosaur *Barosaurus* required a longer, and much more flexible, neck to enable it to crop leaves from low-lying vegetation while standing still, as well as enabling it to reach up to tender shoots and leaves in the tall trees. The long, flexible neck of *Barosaurus* was composed of 15 vertebrae, which had deep hollows inside them. These hollows made the vertebrae lighter in weight, while keeping the bones strong. The tough ligaments that supported the neck ran along a series of notches in the top of each vertebra.

BEAKS AND TEETH

Some of the most common fossil remains of dinosaurs are of their teeth. These are most common because, like us, it seems that dinosaurs lost teeth, either in fights or perhaps even through dental problems. But like reptiles, dinosaurs grew new teeth to replace old, broken or worn ones. Consequently, individual teeth were replaced at different times. They are also among the most common dinosaur finds because teeth are made of the hardest bodily substance and are therefore more likely to turn up as finds. Consequently, many dinosaurs have been named after their dental deposits.

Dinosaur teeth varied greatly in shape. Sharp, dagger- and knife-like teeth were suited to ripping flesh. There were also peg-shaped, comb- and rake-like teeth; rows of rasp- or file-like teeth; and teeth designed for flattening and crushing. The shape, number and arrangement, or layout, of dinosaurs' teeth have

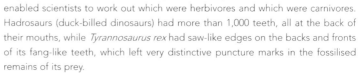

enabled scientists to work out which were herbivores and which were carnivores. Hadrosaurs (duck-billed dinosaurs) had more than 1,000 teeth, all at the back of their mouths, while *Tyrannosaurus rex* had saw-like edges on the backs and fronts of its fang-like teeth, which left very distinctive puncture marks in the fossilised remains of its prey.

A typical, herbivorous dinosaur had a toothless beak and 'cheek teeth', which were used for grinding up leaves and were all of one type. *Hypsilophon*, meaning 'high-ridged tooth', was named because it had grooved, high-ridged cheek teeth that made it an effective chewer of tough vegetation. Because its jaws were hinged at the level of the teeth, as its upper jaw moved out, the lower jaw moved in, and consequently the upper and lower teeth constantly sharpened each other.

Spinosaurus' teeth.

Heterodontosaurus, which means 'different-tooth reptile', had three distinct types of teeth: sharp upper incisors, which bit against a tough, horny, toothless beak in the lower jaw; ridged, high-crown cheek teeth to chew plant food to a pulp; and long, curved, canine teeth on the upper and lower jaws to the front of the cheek teeth, which were used as weapons. Dinosaur teeth came in a huge range of sizes. Some of the largest teeth, 18cm (7in) long, belonged to *Daspletosaurus*, a *Tyrannosaurus-like* carnivore.

Heterodontosaurus.

CLAWS

Like reptiles today, dinosaurs had claws or similar hard structures at the ends of their digits (fingers and toes), which were probably made of keratin, the same hard substance that formed their horns and from which our own fingernails and toenails are made. Because different dinosaurs varied greatly in size, so, too, did their claws' shapes and sizes. Many dinosaurs had five-clawed digits on their feet, but others, like the *Tyrannosaurus*, had only three clawed toes on each foot. The huge carnivores, like *Diplodocus*, had claws on elephant-like feet that resembled hooves, while many of the carnivorous dinosaurs that ran on their two back legs had claws on their fingers that were long and sharp, ideally suited to slashing and ripping flesh.

Some of the largest claws belonged to *Deinocheirus,* a gigantic, ostrich-like dinosaur that lived during the late Cretaceous period in Mongolia. Only parts of its fossilised hands and arms have been found, but its massive finger claws were more than 25cm (over 8in) long. The fossil found in southern England by Bill Walker in 1982 that gave *Baryonyx* ('heavy claw') its truly justified name had a long thumb claw a massive 35cm (over 13in) long.

Coelophysis claws.

TAILS

All dinosaurs had tails, although some may have lost theirs in accidents or attacks. Like the dinosaurs themselves, tails varied in both size and function: *Diplodocus* had 73 caudal vertebrae (bones relating to the tail and lower back), while *Camarasaurus* had 53. *Seismosaurus* ('earthshaking reptile'), found in New Mexico, was one of the longest dinosaurs of all, measuring around 34m (110ft) and weighing around 30,480kg (30 tons). Long tails like these were needed to counterbalance the weight of the neck. It is possible also that some dinosaurs, like *Saltasaurus*, with its muscular tail, would have used the strength in their tails to help to prop them up if they reared their bodies up, on to their back legs.

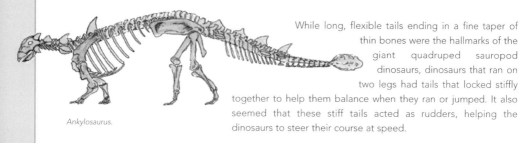

While long, flexible tails ending in a fine taper of thin bones were the hallmarks of the giant quadruped sauropod dinosaurs, dinosaurs that ran on two legs had tails that locked stiffly together to help them balance when they ran or jumped. It also seemed that these stiff tails acted as rudders, helping the dinosaurs to steer their course at speed.

Ankylosaurus.

It is possible that *Diplodocus* may also have used its tail as a whip to defend itself against attackers. Meanwhile, other dinosaurs' tails were more obviously designed as part of their armoury. The smaller, yet heavier, ankylosaurids (fused lizards), which were also slow-moving and could not rely on speed as their defence, used their tails as weapons. At the tips of their tails, four bony lumps – two large and two small – were fused together and to the tail-tip vertebrae to form a club that was further stiffened by tendons. The powerful muscles in the tail allowed the ankylosaurids to swing their club-ended tails from side to side to deliver mighty blows to their attackers. In other dinosaurs, the danger was not so much under the skin (or scales) of the tail, but on it: sticking out from the end of *Stegosaurus'* tail were at least two pairs of long, sharp, bony spikes covered in horn. Standing broadside to an attacker, by swinging its spiked tail, *Stegosaurus* would have been able to deliver a deeply penetrating wound to the flanks of a dinosaur predator, or to a rival for a female's affection.

SKIN AND ARMOUR-PLATING

A representation of how dinosaur skin might have looked.

Like reptiles – lizards, snakes, turtles and crocodiles – dinosaurs had scaly skin. Because skin is soft tissue, in most cases, when a dinosaur died, this would have rotted away, or have been eaten by another dinosaur, very quickly. In a rare find, a 65-million-year-old fossil of *Edmontosaurus* shows that the dinosaur's dead body dried and shrivelled up instead of rotting away, so that the skin impression was preserved wrapped around the skeleton. This find showed that *Edmontosaurus* was covered in thousands of small scales like little pebbles, with larger lumps (called 'tubercules') spaced among them. In other instances, dinosaur skin has been preserved in clay or silt as imprints showing the pattern of scales or nodules on the skin.

As in crocodiles, dinosaur scales were deeply embedded in a thick, tough and leathery hide rather than lying on top of its skin and overlapping, as in snakes. The scaly skin would have offered some protection against the claws and teeth of other dinosaurs, and would have also proved effective against smaller pests, such as mosquitoes.

Some dinosaurs had more protective armour. *Saltosaurus* had two types: while closely packed, pea-sized lumps toughed its skin, on its flanks, it had 50 or so hand-sized, bony 'scutes' (literally, 'shields') or plates. But undoubtedly the most armour-plated skins belonged to the ankylosaurs and nodosaurs, which were protected by bony plates and spikes: *Stegosaurus* ('roof-reptile') could be as big as a bus and had huge oesteoderms, or bony plates, along its back, while *Gastonia* (named after its finder, Robert Gaston) was as big as a family car and had huge spines sticking out sideways from its shoulders and tail, while two rows of long spines ran down its back. In between the larger spines were smaller spines, while a bony shield protected its hips.

While a great deal of knowledge has been gained about the structure of dinosaur skin and scales, we still cannot tell what colour dinosaurs were, since their remains are fossilised and are therefore stone coloured. Some scientists suggest that they may have been similar in colour to crocodiles, which would have given them useful camouflage. Without evidence to suggest otherwise, it may be that dinosaurs were as brightly and beautifully coloured as many living lizards and snakes. It is also quite possible that dinosaurs acquired colours as they matured, or perhaps during mating seasons. Microscopic examinations of dinosaur skin and scales have shown that there were patterns of ridges on the surface. It seems that some dinosaur scales reflected light, like mirrors or sequins. This means that they would have taken on some of the colour of their immediate surroundings as the reflected light was bounced off their scales.

Dinosaur skin was probably similar in appearance and texture to crocodile skin.

BRAINS AND THE SENSES

In general, there is a link between the size of an animal's brain compared to the size of its body and to the level of its intelligence. The human brain accounts for 1/50th of the weight of the human body, but *Brachiosaurus'* brain was a tiny 1/100,000th of the weight of its whole body. Nevertheless, this tiny, walnut-sized brain, located about 13m (43ft) in the air (over twice as high as a giraffe's) was quite sufficient to 'work' this giant plant-eater. The brightest dinosaur – if we use the brain-size/body-weight and intelligence correlation – may well have been the small carnivore *Troodon,* whose brain was about 1/00th of the weight of its body. This means that we humans are only twice as clever as *Troodon*!

Like other soft tissues, the brains of dinosaurs have not been preserved. What we have instead are fossilised skulls that have preserved the brain cavity, which indicate its approximate size and shape, and in some cases, lumps of rock that have formed casts inside the skull cavities, taking on the size and shape of the brain. It was once thought that the tiny brain of *Stegosaurus* was far too small to control such a large animal, and that it had a second, larger brain at the base of its tail. This second brain is now thought to be a nerve junction, a point where a bundle of nerves join. These nerves controlled the hind legs and tail movement and stored glycogen, food-derived energy for powering the muscles.

It is apparent from fossilised skulls and skull casts that some dinosaurs had large bulges called optic lobes in their brains, suggesting that their sense of sight was well developed. While we don't know if dinosaurs could see in colour, the size and position of their eyes would have affected the image that their brains received: small-eyed dinosaurs probably only had good daytime vision, while larger-eyed dinosaurs, like *Troodon*, could probably see quite well in darker circumstances. Frontally placed eyes are more common in carnivorous animals, and allow them to see in detail and judge distances. Eyes placed on the sides of the face or head are more common in herbivorous animals, giving them all-round vision, vital as they need to keep an eye open for hungry carnivores!

In either case, well developed senses, such as sight, smell and hearing, were vital to the dinosaurs' existence. These senses were needed for hunting – tracking prey by scent and sound – and for defence, as many dinosaurs lived in family groups or herds and protected their young by being alert for predators.

Troodon.

CHAPTER 3
DINOSAUR LIFESTYLES

From the beginning of the Mesozoic era, around 200 million years ago, to its end, about 65 million years ago, dinosaurs ruled the Earth. In the space of around 140 million years, some of the most awesome – and terrifying – animals evolved. There were carnivorous predators, some standing more than 6m (20ft) tall, and herbivorous giants measuring up to 26m (85ft) long. Yet no matter how great or large, by the end of the Cretaceous period, the dinosaurs had perished, with the sole exception of modern crocodiles, which are the only surviving members of these archosaurs, the 'ruling reptiles'.

THE EGG THAT CHANGED THE WORLD

Reptiles', and hence the dinosaurs', success on land is due to their ability to conquer their new environment. Life on land would have been impossible if reptiles did not evolve to lay eggs with shells. Life on land for tiny vertebrates is almost impossible: their body weight is too great for them to bear on their limbs, and they lose moisture from their bodies very rapidly. Amphibians developed a solution to this by having two stages to their life: the egg is laid in water and develops into larva, which then develops and grows into a miniature adult, fully formed and able to leave its watery birthplace for life on land.

THE AMNIOTIC EGG

Reptiles evolved a different, and ingenious, solution that freed them completely from laying eggs in the water: they took the water with them on to land in the form of amniotic eggs. Amniotic eggs have a semi-permeable shell that protects the embryo from drying out on land. Inside the egg, an internal membrane called the amnion surrounds the embryo. A second membrane surrounds the yolk from which the embryo gets its nutrition. A sac called the allantois stores waste material, while oxygen passes through the porous shell from the outside atmosphere to the embryo via a membrane called the chorion.

Female dinosaurs laid elongated, sausage-shaped eggs with tough, leathery shells that not only protected the developing embryos from drying out, but also offered protection from potential predators. Safe inside their own watery world of the amniotic egg, the baby dinosaurs only emerged when they had grown to a size that made them able to survive on land. As with today's reptiles, the incubation period – the time between the eggs being laid and the babies hatching out – for dinosaurs is likely to have varied by weeks, or even months, depending on the temperature of the eggs in the nest, which most likely were warmed by the heat of the sun.

NESTS AND NURSERIES

The first discoveries of fossilised dinosaur nests and hatchlings were made by Roy Chapman Andrews (1884–1960), who made many expeditions to the Gobi Desert in Outer Mongolia between 1919 and 1930.

In some instances, such as with the small herbivore *Orodromeus*, as soon as the young dinosaurs hatched from their eggs, they were left to fend for themselves. In recent years, scientists have found many dinosaur nesting sites that have shown that in some cases, the hatchlings – the newly hatched dinosaurs – stayed in their nests and were looked after by adults until they were old enough to leave.

Representations of a carnatosaur's nests.

The female *Maiasaura*, whose name means 'good mother reptile', appears to have cared for her young, which were in constant danger from predatory carnivores, in particular, tyrannosaurids. Fossilised nests discovered by John Horner in Montana during the late 1970s contained trampled eggshells, as well as the remains of hatchlings that are identifiable by their much shorter, juvenile heads. Some of the hatchlings had leg bones and joints that were not fully developed, which suggests that they were not quite able to move about and gather their own food – like baby birds, they needed to be fed by their parents. However, their teeth were worn, which suggests that they had been eating solid food for some time in their nests.

Oviraptor, whose name means 'egg thief', was also a devoted mother. When the dinosaur was first described in 1924 by its finder, George Olsen, it was believed that the *Oviraptor* had died while raiding a nest of *Protoceratops'* eggs. In remarkable finds at Ukhaa Tolgod, in Mongolia, by Mark Norrell and

Michael Novacek during the 1990s, more *Oviraptor* remains were found in nests, and in one lay the remains of eggs, one of which contained tiny bones of an *Oviraptor* embryo. Although the egg was a mere 7cm (3in) across, had it hatched, the baby would have grown to be around 2m (6ft 6in) long. Far from stealing eggs, in this case, the mother *Oviraptor* had died protecting her own.

It also appears that some dinosaurs, like *Maiasaura* and *Protoceratops*, bred in large colonies and occupied the same nesting sites every year, for scientists have found the remains of old nests on top of newer ones.

Maiasaura and her young.

Apatosaurus.

The female *Protoceratops* made nests that were shallow, bowl-shaped pits about 1m (3ft) in diameter, which were scraped into dry, sandy earth, with the bowls' contents arranged to form low, protective walls. Into this pit, the female laid a clutch of around 20 eggs, arranged neatly in a circle or spiral shape. It is likely that the eggs were then covered with earth to keep them warm. *Maiasaura*'s nests were similarly constructed in the earth, but these dinosaurs added a comfortable lining of twigs and leaves, on to which they laid around 25 eggs. From fossil remains, it appears that a young *Maiasaura* was about 30cm (12in) long when it hatched, but remained in the nest to be reared by perhaps both parents until it had grown to around 1.5m (5ft).

In 1998, scientists in Auca Mahuevo, in western Argentina, found the first sauropod fossil eggs. Thousands of crushed, round eggs about the size of ostrich eggs were scattered across a huge nesting ground. The fossilised egg remains contained tiny bones and skin, but the most significant discovery was of pencil-shaped teeth that identified the remains as sauropods, possibly *Titanosaurus*, the only sauropod to inhabit South America during the late Cretaceous period.

SIZE AND MATURITY

Calculating the weight of dinosaurs when they were alive offers a number of problems. Using reptiles, such as crocodiles, as comparisons, scientists estimate dinosaur weights using scaled-down models of skeletons that are fleshed out with muscles, inner organs and skin. The model is then immersed in water and its volume calculated, and then the model is mathematically scaled up to full size to estimate its possible live weight. The big problem that scientists have is that most dinosaurs are known from only a few bones, so they have to reconstruct dinosaurs using combinations of bones from similar dinosaurs. And even when there are lots of bones, as in the case of *Apatosaurus*, which is known from around 12 skeletons, giving scientists practically every bone in its body, and accurately estimating the size (about 21m/62ft) is possible, fleshed-out body weights still vary from 20,320kg (20 tons) to more than 50,800kg (50 tons).

No one really knows how fast dinosaurs grew, how long they took to reach their full size, or even how long they lived. Scientists can only estimate growth rates and ages by making comparisons with modern reptiles. Some living reptiles reach an optimum size at maturity, while others continue to grow in size during their lifetime, although the rate of growth does slow down with increasing age.

Scientists have offered some estimates: a fully grown *Tyrannosaurus* may have reached maturity aged around 20 years and lived until it was 50 years old. The giant sauropods, like *Diplodocus*, may have lived for up to 100 years. In each case, potential growth and life expectancy would have been dependent on a number of contributing factors, not least of which was diet.

DIET

Growth, health and age for dinosaurs, as for humans, would most likely have increased with a plentiful food supply. Just as scientists use the shape of dinosaurs' pelvic bones, and the arrangement of muscles that would have been attached to them, to work out how they would have walked, so, too, they can use jaws and teeth to work out how they ate their food. In the case of carnivorous dinosaurs, their teeth and jaws were designed for stabbing and biting off chunks of flesh, which were swallowed quickly and then digested in the stomach.

PROLIFIC PREDATOR OR SCAVENGER OF SCRAPS?

Tyrannosaurus had more than 50 dagger-like teeth – some more than 15cm (8in) long – set into a head that was an incredible 1.2m (4ft) long. Its jaw was hinged at the back of its head, which allowed it to open its mouth extremely wide, while powerful neck and jaw muscles allowed it to swing its head while it ripped and tore at its victim's flesh. *Tyrannosaurus* certainly needed a jaw of this design: because its arms were so small, food could not have been passed from hand to mouth. *Tyrannosaurus* may have been an active hunter, perhaps lying in wait to ambush passing prey and catching it after a short chase. But it may, as John Horner of the Museum of Rockies, in Montana, USA, has proposed, alternatively have been a scavenger that survived on carrion. When a dinosaur died – of natural causes or as the result of injury – its carcass would have given off a very powerful odour that would have attracted the giant meat-eaters from miles around.

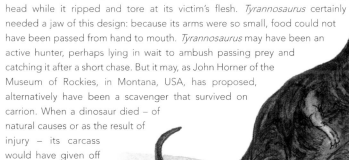

Tyrannosaurus.

COELOPHYSIS, THE CANNIBAL

Coelophysis was one of the earliest and most primitive dinosaurs. A fleet-footed carnivore, it probably dined on a varied diet of large and small insects, as well as smaller dinosaurs. In 1947, at a mass burial at Ghost Ranch, in New Mexico, palaeontologists found the remains of juvenile *Coelophysis* inside the ribcages of adults. At first, it was thought that the young skeletons were unborn infants, but this was impossible because it appears that all dinosaurs laid eggs, and these supposed embryos were also much too large and well formed to be from embryos within eggs. The shocking conclusion was that these juvenile *Coelophysis* were, in fact, the last meals of the adults of the same species.

Coelophysis.

GRAZERS AND GASTROLITHS

Herbivores faced a different problem: because plant food is far less nutritious than meat, far greater quantities of vegetable matter are needed to compensate for its lower nutritional value, and digestion of vegetable matter is a far longer process. Herbivorous dinosaurs would not only have needed to be constantly eating, but they would have had to pound away at the tough, fibrous material in order to release its goodness. Like modern cows, it is likely that many herbivorous dinosaurs had to chew the cud. Some herbivores were equipped with a sharp beak for snipping away twigs and leaves. Others had teeth, often in huge numbers, that were shaped for chopping, raking or crushing and chewing plant matter. Meanwhile, *Barosaurus* didn't even chew its food: it swallowed tough leaves and twigs whole. In part of its stomach were gastroliths, or gastric 'millstones'. These were stones that had also been swallowed by the dinosaur and that acted like millstones, grinding up the food in the stomach for digestion. As these gastroliths tumbled away inside the dinosaur's stomach, they became rounded, smooth and highly

polished. Some fossil remains show gastroliths as small as peas, and others the size of soccer balls.

It is important to remember, though, that during the Mesozoic era, many types of plants changed or evolved, just like the dinosaurs themselves. Like dinosaur fossils, plant fossils have given scientists an insight into the changes in life on Earth during the Mesozoic era.

Like modern cows, herbivorous dinosaurs probably chewed the cud.

During the Triassic period, early in the Mesozoic era, the main plants for herbivorous dinosaurs were conifer trees, gingkoes, cycads and the smaller seed-ferns, ferns, horsetails and club mosses. During this time, only the prosauropods were big enough, or had long enough necks, to reach tall cycad fronds and ginkgo leaves. During the warm, damp Jurassic period, new plant life evolved and covered land that had previously been barren: tall conifers, such as redwood trees and monkey-puzzle trees, were widespread, whose great heights required herbivorous dinosaurs to be incredible large and very long-necked. It was not until the middle of the Cretaceous period that flowering plants appeared, which, by the end of the period, included magnolias, maples and walnuts. But because they did not appear on Earth until 30–20 million years ago – long after the dinosaurs were extinct – no dinosaur ever ate grasses.

COPROLITES: DINO-DROPPINGS

Coprolites are fossilised droppings, or dung, and palaeontologists have discovered thousands at many fossil sites around the world. Believed to have been deposited by a *Tyrannosaurus*, one of the largest dinosaur coprolites to be found measured 44cm (17⅓in) long. Like other fossils, the once soft – and, no doubt, smelly – coprolites have become solid rock, and when they are cracked open, they sometimes reveal what the dinosaurs had recently eaten.

Huge piles of coprolites were found in Montana, USA, left apparently by a large herd of herbivorous hadrosaurs, the duck-billed *Maiasaura*. When examined, the coprolites were found to contain the remains of buds, cones and the needle-like leaves of the conifer trees on which they fed.

The coprolites of carnivorous dinosaurs often contain fragments of bone from their prey, which can be analysed under a microscope to determine the approximate age of the prey when it was devoured. It seems, from coprolite evidence, that many carnivorous dinosaurs were opportunists, preying on the very young and the very old. As they were the most vulnerable to attack, the very young and the old would have been easy pickings for a hungry carnivore in his (or her) prime

The prosauropods were the only dinosaurs tall enough to reach the tops of the trees.

HERD LIVING

The patterns of nests and quantities of coprolites found in one place have suggested that some dinosaurs lived in herds or colonies. The herding behaviour of some dinosaurs is also supported by footprint trackways, such as those found in Bandera County, Texas, which showed that more than 20 sauropods had been moving together across an open area in the same direction.

Patterns of footprints tend to support the theory that some dinosaurs lived in herds.

Living in a herd would seem logical for large sauropods. Fully grown adults reached immense sizes, which made them pretty much immune from attack by even the largest carnosaurs. Their young, however, would have been easy prey, so herding together as they moved off to a new feeding ground would have offered some degree of protection to their young. Some footprint tracks show larger footprints on the outer edges of the group, while smaller footprints belonging to juveniles are contained inside. Near Winton, in Queensland, Australia, more than 3,300 footprints show that 130 dinosaurs once walked across the earth in a herd.

Furthermore, the discovery of numbers of dinosaur remains of the same type suggests that they may have died in the same place if they had lived there as a group. At the Red Deer River area in Alberta, Canada, the fossils of over 1,000 *Pachyrrhinosaurus* suggest that a herd was caught in a flood. Many ceratopsians, the horned dinosaurs, appear to have been herding animals: remains have been found that suggest that the herd panicked and drowned during a river crossing, and that their bodies and bones were subsequently trampled and scavenged by theropods.

MIGRATION AND HIBERNATION

Using fossil evidence of skeletons, tracks, plants and knowledge of the positions of the continental plates at different times in the Earth's history, scientists have gained evidence to suggest that unlike living land reptiles, some dinosaurs appear to have migrated. In certain regions, cool winters would have meant that some plants would have died, forcing dinosaurs to move on to warmer parts to find food. In North America, huge herds of *Centrosaurus* are known to have migrated north to feed on the plants that grew during the short, sub-Arctic summer.

The same is true in very hot periods: fossilised evidence of plants shows that some stopped growing in summer, which would have forced the dinosaurs that fed on them to migrate to cooler climes.

Those dinosaurs that did not migrate may have instead gone into hibernation during sustained periods of cold weather, protected, perhaps, in a cave or a burrow. Many living reptiles today hibernate in colder winter months, or at least shift into extended periods of inactivity to conserve energy when outside temperatures drop. The small, herbivorous *Leaellynosaura* whose remains were found at Dinosaur Cove, on the coast near Melbourne, Australia, is believed to have hibernated as the site was much closer to the South Pole when the dinosaurs lived there some 120–100 million years ago. While there were no polar ice caps at this time, the Australian dinosaurs would have had to cope with longer, cooler – and much darker – winters, when fewer plants would have grown.

EXTINCTION

The extinction of animal and plant life, along with evolutionary lines, is a natural phenomenon, part of the history of life on Earth whereby the balance of the emergence and evolution of new life forms and species is maintained. Based on fossil evidence, scientists can demonstrate that extinctions occurred quite frequently and quite regularly: some dinosaurs lived in the Jurassic period (203–135 million years ago), but were extinct by the Cretaceous period (135–65 million years ago), although they took several million years to die out. There are also instances when, in a relatively short space of time, mass extinctions occurred. One such period was during the K-T boundary (the border between the Cretaceous and Tertiary periods, around 65 million years ago), when the dinosaurs became extinct, along with their cousins, the reptiles of the sea and air, although many animal groups, including fish, crocodiles, turtles, lizards, birds and mammals (which appeared during the Triassic period and lived alongside dinosaurs), survived. There are no dinosaur fossils since this time 65 million years ago, but there are many theories for their extinction.

One theory suggests that a massive meteorite, some 10km (6 miles) across, crashed to Earth: indeed, under seabed mud off the Yucatan coast of Mexico is the 200km- (120 mile-) wide Chixulub Crater, which could mark the place of impact of a meteorite crashing to Earth 65 million years ago. The impact would, no doubt, have triggered earthquakes and volcanic activity, including poisonous fumes, as well as throwing up vast quantities of dust that would have obliterated the sun and darkened the skies. A single year of darkness would have caused the death of many plants, and of the herbivores that fed on them, and thus of the carnivores at the top of the food chain. Supporting this cataclysmic theory is evidence provided by the American father-and-son team of geologists Luis (1911–88) and Walter (born 1940) Alvarez, who, in 1980, announced their discovery of worldwide deposits of rocks that contained abnormally high concentrations of rare metals like iridium, osmium and rhodium, which were present in the same proportions in meteorites.

Because modern methods of dating rock samples is accurate only to within a few hundreds of thousands of years, it remains uncertain whether the extinction of the land-living dinosaurs and the extinction of marine and flying reptiles took place exactly at the same time. We know that, for example, ichthyosaurs became extinct before the end of the Cretaceous period, and it seems that plesiosaurs, pterosaurs and dinosaurs themselves were less common towards the end of that period. This suggests to some that more gradual changes in the environment were taking place worldwide. During the Cretaceous period, sea levels dropped, and, as a result, the average air temperature also dropped and the climate became more variable worldwide. These gradual climate changes could have been the cause of the gradual decline of dinosaurs, especially if they were exothermic – cold-blooded – animals that relied on the heat outside their bodies to keep them warm. Climate change would have also encouraged the evolution of new plant species, which may have been poisonous: herbivores that ate these plants would have died, and the carnivores would also have died later as their own food became less available. The carnivorous *Tyrannosaurus* was one of the last dinosaurs to become extinct.

Whichever theory is adopted – the cataclysmic mass extinction or the gradual decline and demise – to explain the extinction of the dinosaurs, one great puzzle remains: why did some very similar reptiles, like crocodiles, lizards and turtles, survive?

CHAPTER 4
EARLY DINOSAURS

EARLY THEROPOD DINOSAURS

(See pages 55 to 61)

The first-known dinosaurs appeared about 230–225 million years ago, in the latter part of the middle Triassic period. Fossils from Argentina and Brazil, in South America, part of what was once the continent of Gondwana, show that many of these primitive dinosaurs were small-to-medium-sized saurischian (lizard-hipped) therapods ('beast-feet'): carnivorous predators that hunted small animals, such as lizards, insects and mammals, which were around at the same time as the dinosaurs. They were armed with sharp teeth and clawed, four-toed feet – the first toe short and high – and they ran on their muscular hind legs.

Coelophysis.

EARLY ORNITHOPOD DINOSAURS

(See pages 62 to 66)

Ornithopods, or 'bird feet', were a suborder of bipedal and bipedal/quadrupedal herbivorous ornithischian (bird-hipped) dinosaurs. They had feet that were rather like a bird's, leaf-shaped cheek teeth, a backwards-pointing pubic bone and bony tendons that stiffened their tails to counterbalance their bodies while feeding or running. Some scientists believe that the earliest ornithopod was *Pisanosaurus* ('Pisano's lizard'), from the late Triassic period in Argentina, several million years before any other bird-hipped dinosaurs appeared, although evidence is still very fragmentary. It is generally accepted that the earliest-known ornithopods date back to the early Jurassic period, some 200 million years ago. In appearance, they were small and lizard-like, but they ran upright on their slender back legs. Superficially, they looked like the smaller carnivorous theropod dinosaur,s such as *Coelophysis*, but ornithopods were exclusively herbivores. All ornithischian dinosaurs, including the late Cretaceous giant *Edmontosaurus,* were descended from long-legged bipedal ancestors, such as *Lesothosaurus.*

Lagosuchus.

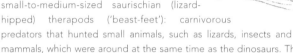

EORAPTOR

Pronounced: 'EE-oh-RAP-tor'

Eoraptor is believed to have lived some 228 million years ago in Argentina, where, in 1992, a near-complete skeleton was discovered and named by Paul Sereno, an American palaeontologist from the University of Chicago who is famous for his fieldwork in South America, Asia and Africa, and for his research into early dinosaurs. It is thought that *Eoraptor* is very close to the common ancestor of all of the dinosaurs. *Eoraptor* was a small, primitive therapod, about the size of a large dog. Though small in size, *Eoraptor* was a fierce predator, with long hind legs and a crocodile-like skull, with sharp, curved teeth able to rip the flesh of lizards and small mammals. Although it resembled later theropods, *Eoraptor's* remains indicate that it was smaller and more lightly built. It also retained some more primitive features, in particular, fewer vertebrae supporting the hips, and compared to *Herrerasaurus*, another primitive therapod found in South America (see page 55), *Eoraptor* had shorter grasping hands and, significantly, four fingers. The number of fingers indicates the primitive nature of *Eoraptor*: the trend in the more advanced dinosaurs was to have fewer fingers (and toes).

NAME MEANS
'Early plunderer'

TIME
Late Triassic
(250–203 MYA*)

LOCATION
Argentina,
South America

SIZE
1m (3ft 3in) long

WEIGHT
11kg (24lb)

DIET
Carnivore

*MYA = million years ago

HERRERASAURUS

Pronounced: 'eh-ray-rah-SORE-us'

NAME MEANS
'Herrera's lizard'

TIME
Late Triassic
(250–203 MYA)

LOCATION
Argentina,
South America

SIZE
3–5m (10–17ft) long

WEIGHT
90–100kg (200–220lb)

DIET
Carnivore

Herrerasaurus lived at the same time, and in the same place, as *Eoraptor* (see page 55): around 228 million years ago in Argentina, South America. The first *Herrerasaurus* bones were discovered in the 1960s by a goat herd, Victorino Herrera, who gave the dinosaur its name. These first, fossilised fragments were the only bones known to scientists until 1988. It had sharp teeth, short arms (less than half the length of its hind legs) and three-fingered hands, with curved claws; the fourth and fifth fingers were mere stubs, and were clawless.

Like most theropods – and birds – *Herrerasaurus* had a small hallux (first toe) that pointed backwards, instead of forwards. But *Herrerasaurus* also had seemingly primitive leg and feet bones, which at first led scientists to think that *Herrerasaurus* was more primitive than any dinosaurs in the two main groups of saurischians and ornithischians.

In the 1980s, further excavations were made in the Valley of the Moon, in the foothills of the Andes Mountains, which revealed near-complete skeletons, including one with a skull. The skull, which was long and narrow, with small nostril holes, showed that *Herrerasaurus* had a sliding lower jaw joint: the front half of the jaw was able to move against the rear half and provide a grasping bite, in the same way that some living lizards bite and overcome their prey. Because this flexible mandible was common to some other theropods, in 1992, Paul Sereno, working with Fernando Novas, proved that *Herrerasaurus* was, in fact, an early theropod and one of the most primitive dinosaurs.

An early bipedal, predatory dinosaur, *Herrerasaurus* was about the size of a small car and weighed about the same as a small pony. Even with relatively few species of predatory dinosaurs around in the late Triassic period, their upright stance and long hind legs meant that *Herrerasaurus* and its relatives, like *Eoraptor*, were fast and effective killers. Its diet may have included the

small, bipedal, herbivorous dinosaur *Pisanosaurus*, but reptiles, such as the tusked, pig-like rhynchosaurs, would probably have formed its main diet.

COELOPHYSIS

Pronounced: 'SEEL-oh-FIE-sis'

NAME MEANS
'Hollow form'

TIME
Late Triassic
(250–203 MYA)

LOCATION
Arizona and New Mexico,
North America

SIZE
3m (10ft)

WEIGHT
27kg (60lb)

DIET
Carnivore

One of the earliest, and best-known, dinosaurs, was *Coelophysis,* which had some features that were bird-like and others that were reptilian. It was built like a large, slender bird, with a narrow, stork-like head on an 'S'-shaped neck, a slim body, a long, bony, yet flexible, tail – which made up about half the length of its body – and almost bird-like legs. Like a bird, it also had hollow, thin-walled bones and fused bones of the pelvis (hips) and sacral vertebrae (spine), as well as fused tarsals (ankle bones) and metatarsals (upper feet). A ferocious hunter, *Coelophysis* was lightly built for speed. Its bird-like feet had three walking toes, with sharp claws, while its primitive, clawed hands had four fingers, although only three were strong enough to grasp prey. Its long, narrow jaw was equipped with sharp, serrated teeth.

The first remains of *Coelophysis* were found by amateur fossil hunter David Baldwin in Abiquiu, New Mexico, in 1881, and were identified by Edward D Cope. The early finds consisted of various vertebrae, leg, pelvis and rib bones and remained all that was known of this early dinosaur until 1947, when the American Museum of Natural History organised a expedition to the area around Ghost Ranch in New Mexico. Excavating a section of hillside, scientists found a 'graveyard' of dinosaurs: dozens of skeletons, some of which were complete, ranging from the very young to the old and ranging in length from 1–3m (3–10ft), were found lying across one another, all killed at the same time, perhaps in a flash flood. Finding so many specimens together suggested that *Coelophysis* lived in a herd, roaming the upland forests of Arizona and New Mexico, hunting in packs along the banks of streams and lakes, searching and killing lizards and the small, shrew-like animals that evolved during the late Triassic period.

Significant among the remains at Ghost Ranch were the tiny bones of hatchling *Coelophysis* that were discovered inside the ribcages of adults:

since dinosaurs did not give birth to live offspring, but laid eggs, and the bones were too large and too well formed to be from embryos within eggs, it appears that *Coelophysis* was not only a carnivore, but also – at least on occasion – a cannibal.

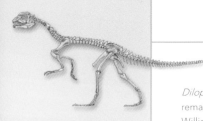

DILOPHOSAURUS

Pronounced: 'die-LOAF-of-SORE-us'

NAME MEANS
'Two-ridge lizard'

TIME
Early Jurassic
(208–144 MYA)

LOCATION
Arizona, USA;
Yunnan, China

SIZE
6m (20ft)

WEIGHT
500kg (1,100lb)

DIET
Carnivore

Dilophosaurus is the earliest of the larger theropods that is well known from remains found first in 1942, in Arizona, by Navajo Native American Jesse Williams. At first, though, palaeontologist Samuel Welles believed that the remains belonged to a *Megalosaurus*, and it was not until 1977 that Welles named 'the terror of the Jurassic age' *Dilophosaurus*. In the late 1980s, scientists made further discoveries in Yunnan Province, China.

Its name means 'two-ridge lizard', and it was given it because of the unique, tall crest made up of a pair of parallel, bony ridges that stood like two halves of dinner plates on its head. Wafer thin in places, these crests were strengthened by vertical struts of bone. At the back of the head, the tips of each crest narrowed into a spike. The function of these crests remains a mystery. Some scientists believe that they were for sexual display, and that only males sported them. This theory is supported in part by the fact that not all specimens had these crests. In fact, none were ever found on the first few fossil remains (which led Welles to suspect that they were *Megalosaurus*), and none of the crests have ever been found attached to the skull, but were instead lying nearby.

Dilophosaurus was a lightly built carnosaur (flesh lizard); some of the largest ever terrestrial carnivores, such as *Tyrannosaurus,* belonged to the carnosaur group. *Dilophosaurus* had a very large head – a typical feature of carnosaurs. But it was also light-boned, and had a long, slender, but powerful and flexible, neck; a tail that was as long as its whole body; and short arms, which were typical of the small, lightweight theropods called coelurosaurs, the 'hollow-tailed lizards'.

The jaws of *Dilophosaurus* give clues to its lifestyle: the lower jaw was strong and full of long, sharp, thin teeth. Like *Coelophysis* (see page 58),

Dilophosaurus had a kink in its upper jaw called the subnarial gap: this gap separated a cluster of teeth at the front of the upper jaw from the rest of the teeth, a type of arrangement that can be seen today in the jaws of a modern crocodile. While it had a large head and very strong jaws, *Dilophosaurus* would not have killed its prey by biting it: its thin teeth and apparently delicate head crests would have been too vulnerable in a fight. It is instead more likely that *Dilophosaurus* ripped at its prey – perhaps the remains of corpses killed by larger and stronger carnosaurs – with its sharply clawed fingers (the first three of its four fingers bore these claws) and its feet because its hind limbs were long and powerful and ended in three forward-facing, sharp-clawed toes.

LESOTHOSAURUS

Pronounced: 'le-SOO-too-SORE-us'

NAME MEANS
'Lesotho lizard'

TIME
Early Jurassic
(203–135 MYA)

LOCATION
Lesotho Mafeteng,
Southern Africa;
Venezuela,
South America

SIZE
1m (3ft 3in)

WEIGHT
11kg (24lb)

DIET
Herbivore

Small and lithe, *Lesothosaurus* was no larger than a dog, and ran from its enemies on its back legs across the hot, arid plains of southern Africa and South America, but rested on all fours when grazing on low-growing plants. Like a small ornithopod, *Lesothosaurus* had strong, but short, arms, and hands with five fingers (the fifth shorter than the rest), but very long legs designed for sprinting – the shins, in particular, were elongated and 25 per cent longer than its thighs – and its three-toed feet were the same length as the shins. Bony tendons stiffened its tail and counterbalanced its body at the hips. A herbivore, without sharp teeth or claws with which to defend itself, *Lesothosaurus* depended on its speed and agility for survival.

Lesothosaurus' skull was small, short and rather flat faced – a little like a modern iguana. It had very large eye cavities and a fairly large opening in front of the eye, which may have been for a salt gland. The lower jaw was tipped by a horn-covered, predentary bone – a useful device for chipping off foliage.

The teeth were pointed and shaped like arrow heads, with grooved edges, the upper teeth fitting alternately between the lower teeth. This meant that when it was chewing, instead of using a rotating movement that ground up leaves, *Lesothosaurus* used a more primitive, and less efficient, up-and-down, chopping action, which sliced leaves before they were swallowed.

It is possible that *Lesothosaurus* lived in herds: a pair of skeletons was found together in southern Africa. Their bodies were curled up and surrounded by worn, discarded teeth, although the skulls of both animals contained full sets. This led some palaeontologists to surmise that these small dinosaurs may have aestivated, or slept through the hottest and driest parts of the year, in underground burrows or chambers. The worn teeth scattered around them may possibly have been shed while they slept and grew new ones.

In 1964, a fragment of jaw and a few teeth were found in southern Africa and were named *Fabrosaurus australis* ('Fabre's southern reptile'), for a dinosaur that eventually gave its name to the family of fabrosaurs. In 1978, remains of a small animal were found in Lesotho that appeared to be very similar to *Fabrosaurus*. But because there was so little fossil evidence in the earlier find to make more accurate comparisons with the later find, the new skeleton was renamed *Lesothosaurus*. If the two sets of fossil bones do, in fact, turn out to be from the same dinosaur, then *Lesothosaurus* will be renamed *Fabrosaurus*. This is because in cases of duplicate identification, the name first given to an animal (or plant) takes priority over any names given later.

LAGOSUCHUS

Pronounced: 'lah-go-su-chus'

NAME MEANS
'Rabbit crocodile'

TIME
Middle Triassic
(250–203 MYA)

LOCATION
Argentina,
South America

SIZE
30cm (1ft)

WEIGHT
90g (⅜oz)

DIET
Insectivore, possibly
also carnivore

The earliest dinosaurs appeared on Earth during the middle Triassic period, around 220–235 million years ago, so their ancestors, scientists assume, were around for some time before this. Many believe that the thecodonts, or 'socket-toothed' group of reptiles (so called because their teeth grew from roots fixed into pit-like sockets in the jaw bones), may have been the dinosaurs' ancestors as they both shared the same dental structure. The thecodonts are grouped into five suborders: *Proterosuchia*; *Rauisucha*; *Phytosauria*; *Aetosauria*; and *Ornithosuchia*. It is this last subgroup, the *Ornithosuchia*, which became extinct by the end of the Triassic period, that many palaeontologists regard as the ideal intermediaries between four-legged, lizard-like thecodontians and two-legged dinosaurs.

Lagosuchus was one of the most dinosaur-like of the thecodontians, and many regard it as the ancestor of the dinosaur as all shared a common feature: a diapsid skull. The subclasses of reptiles are recognised by the patterns of skull openings behind the eye socket: the synapsids (the reptilian ancestors of mammals) have a single hole – the temporal fenestra – low down on the side of the skull; the euryapsids (the extinct marine reptiles like the plesiosaurs) also have one temporal fenestra, but in a higher position on the skull.

Anapsids (the earliest reptiles, but also the chelonians, today represented by turtles, tortoises and terrapins) have no temporal fenestra, while diapsids – dinosaurs (as well as crocodiles, snakes, lizards and birds) and pterosaurs (see page 205), the flying reptiles of the late Triassic period – had two temporal openings on each side of the skull behind the eye socket.

Lagosuchus was a reptile about 30cm (1ft) long, with extremely long, slender limbs, and was possibly able to run quite swiftly on its hind legs as these limbs were much longer than its forelimbs: the shin bones were almost twice the

length of the thigh bones, which is a feature of running animals, and is
particularly evident in the later bidepal dinosaurs.

STAURIKOSAURUS

Pronounced: 'stor-IK-oh-SORE-us'

NAME MEANS
'Southern Cross lizard'

TIME
Late Triassic
(250–203 MYA)

LOCATION
Brazil, South America

SIZE
2m (6ft 6in)

WEIGHT
30kg (66lb)

DIET
Carnivore

Named after the Southern Cross constellation, *Staurikosaurus* was a small, early therapod found in Brazil. So far, scientists have only incomplete skeletal remains with which to work, but it seems that *Staurikosaurus* shared many of the physical features found in its larger relative, *Herrerasaurus* (see page 56), and that were common to therapods – the group that all other known carnivorous dinosaurs belong to. Therapods had three weight-bearing toes on the foot as the first toe, the hallux, did not reach the ground. This was some way up the foot and pointed backwards. The middle toe was the longest and bore most of the body's weight.

The primitive theropod *Staurikosaurus* perhaps had five-toed feet, but again, only three toes would have carried its weight. Like *Herrerasaurus*, *Staurikosaurus* had a slim, curved neck, a large head, with tooth-lined jaws, and a long, stiff tail that acted as a counterbalance to the front of the body. Bipedal, it had long, strong, yet slender, bird-like hind legs and it is also likely that it had four fingers on each hand. *Staurikosaurus* was more lightly built than *Herrerasaurus*, measuring about 2m (6ft 6in) long and weighing only around 30kg (66lb). Able to run swiftly on its rear legs, *Staurikosaurus* could easily have outrun the smaller-moving, four-legged prey on which it fed.

CHAPTER 5
SAURISCHIAN DINOSAURS I

THEROPODS

The saurischian, or 'lizard-hipped', dinosaurs were one of the two great groups of dinosaurs and comprised both herbivores and carnivores. The saurischians inherited their primitive, forward-pointing pubis bone from their early ancestors. This pelvis – and the way that their back legs were articulated from it – meant that they were able to walk on their hind legs, allowing them to become swift and efficient killers.

The saurischian dinosaurs are subdivided into two distinct groups: theropods ('beast feet') and sauropodomorphs ('reptile-like feet'). The theropods tend to be bipedal carnivores of a variety of shapes and sizes, but are grouped together because of their associated skeletal structures and their predatory lifestyle. Other key saurischian features include a long second finger, cavities in their bones, which housed air sacs connected to their lungs, and elongated necks.

CARNOSAURS

(See pages 72 to 78)

The carnosaurs are one major group of theropod dinosaurs and were typically large – 6m (20ft) or more in length – heavily built and stood on stout, strong, pillar-like hind legs. Their forearms were short and relatively weak and they had large heads supported by a sturdy neck. The carnosaurs are well represented – although in many instances, in very incomplete forms – in fossil finds from rocks from North America, China and Africa dating from the late Jurassic period (203–144 MYA). The oldest-known carnosaur is *Piatnitzkysaurus*, from the Jurassic period, but most carnosaur species existed during the last 10 million years of the Cretaceous period (144–65 MYA).

TYRANNOSAURIDS

(See pages 79 to 83)

Some of the largest terrestrial carnivores that ever lived belonged to this family of 'tyrant lizards'. The fiercest predators in western North America and Asia in their time, the family Tyrannosauridae as a whole was a small group. There are four well-established species of tyrannosaurids: the famous *Tyrannosaurus rex*, *Daspletosaurus torosus* and *Albertosaurus libratus*, which come from Canada; and *Tarbosaurus bataar*, which comes from the Nemeght Basin in Mongolia. Though small, it was a highly specialised group, and one that has given rise to the popular notions of what flesh-eating dinosaurs looked like, and how they behaved. They were also a remarkably short-lived group: the tyrannosaurids first appeared on Earth around 80 million years ago, and were among the last dinosaurs to become extinct at the end of the Cretaceous period, around 65 million years ago.

ORNITHOMIMIDS

(See pages 84 to 87)

The so-called 'bird mimics' were a rather specialised offshoot of the coelurosaurs – the 'hollow-tailed lizards' that were the lightweight predators among the theropods. The ornithomimosaurs were about the same height and proportions as a modern ostrich, but had the dinosaur features of clawed hands and a long, bony tail.

Carnotaurus.

All were long-necked and long-legged sprinters – perhaps capable of speeds of up to 70km/h (43mph) – and probably travelled in herds over the opens plains of North America, Europe and east Asia in the mid-Cretaceous period, but appear to have died out before the end of that time. Unlike most other dinosaurs, but like the oviraptosaurs (see below), ornithomimosaurs did not have teeth. Instead, they had a horny, bird-like bill, but their wide mouth allowed them to snap up sizeable prey, such as small mammals and lizards, as well as insects and fruits. Other distinguishing features were exceptionally large eyes and very big brains – features that suggest that they were well-co-ordinated predators.

OVIRAPTOSAURS

(See pages 88 to 91)

This small family of toothless, bipedal, bird-like theropods lived during the late Cretaceous period in eastern Asia, and were named the 'egg thieves' on account of their suspected diet. The first remains of fossils of these extraordinary creatures, which appear to have been the dinosaurs that are the most closely related to birds, were discovered during the American Museum of Natural History's Mongolian expedition in the early 1920s, which set out to find the remains of early humans and instead discovered dinosaurs. The remains consisted of a partial skull preserved in the sandstone of Shabarakh Usu, in southern Mongolia, which is notable for the curious prong on the tip of its snout. They differed further from their relatives, the ornithomimids, or 'ostrich dinosaurs' (see above), in that oviraptosaurs had larger heads, with short, stumpy beaks, and hands with 'thumbs' shorter than the fingers, with strongly curved claws.

Oviraptor.

TROODONTIDS

(See pages 92 to 94)

Towards the end of the Cretaceous period, a rare group of dinosaurs appeared. Their body design was similar to the ornithomimosaurs (see above), and at first scientists believed their remains to belong to a large lizard, such as a monitor lizard. The first discovery of troodontid remains consisted of a single tooth found by Ferdinand Hayden in the Judith River beds of Montana, USA, and described by Joseph Leidy in 1856. The tooth was flattened and serrated along its edge and was named Troodon or 'wounding tooth'.

In the early 1900s, more remains were found in Wyoming and in Alberta, Canada, but again, scientists attributed them to a pachycephalosaur, or 'bone-headed dinosaur'. By the 1980s, a much fuller picture was finally beginning to emerge, when the teeth were matched with other bones that showed that Troodon was a bird-like theropod, with a much bigger brain proportionally for its body size than any other dinosaur. Consequently, the new family name of Troodontidae was applied to this, and to its possibly related genera, *Saurornithoides* and *Bambiraptor*. These were 'small-game' hunters, perhaps preying on hatchlings and juvenile dinosaurs, and belonged to the maniraptoran ('seizing-hand') dinosaurs – the theropod group to which birds also belong. Like *Caudipteryx*, it is also likely that down or feathers covered the North American theropods *Troodon* and *Bambiraptor*.

DROMAEOSAURIDS

(See pages 95 to 98)
The dromaeosaurids are very restricted in their time of appearance in the fossil records: the earliest-known, *Phaedrolosaurus*, appears as fossil remains in rocks dating from 130 to 120 MYA. The later species, like *Deinonychus*, are known from rocks only a mere 10 million years younger, and were followed very closely by *Velociraptor* and *Dromaeosaurus*.

Although they were no larger than any of the other carnivores around in the period, the members of this family of dinosaurs, the so-called 'running lizards', were among some of the most fearsome predators of the Cretaceous period in North America and Asia. Armed with a particularly large and lethal, sickle-shaped claw on the second toe of each foot – rotatable through 180 degrees – structurally, however, the dromaeosaurids seem to have been an intermediate group of dinosaurs, having the light and speedy body of the coelurosaurs (the 'hollow-tailed lizards', see below) and the large head of a carnosaur (see page 68). They also had very sharp, pointed teeth and grasping, clawed hands. With large brains, it is also possible that they hunted in packs.

Velociraptor.

COELUROSAURS

(See pages 99 to 100)

The coelurosaurs, or 'hollow-tailed reptiles', were an odd mix of small, generally lightweight, theropods, who were fast-running predators, with small heads lined with small, sharp teeth, long, flexible necks and long arms with sharply clawed, grasping hands. They appear to have been very abundant throughout the 140-million-year reign in which dinosaurs ruled the Earth, but because they were lightly built and small, their chances of being preserved as fossils were greatly diminished as small animals tend to decay more quickly, with their bones being scattered or completely destroyed. We have already encountered *Coelophysis*

Ornitholestes.

('hollow form') on page 58. Two of the best-known, and possibly related, species are *Compsognathus,* whose remains have been found in France and Germany, and *Ornitholestes,* from Wyoming, USA.

BARYONYX AND SUCHOMIMUS

(See pages 101 to 102)

As we can see, there is a huge variety of theropods, and most have been put into family groups. There are some, however, that are unique and don't fit into any of the established family groupings. The family of Baryonychidae – of large, long theropods – was created in 1986 to cover just one single member, *Baryonyx,* 'heavy claw', a skeleton of which was discovered by amateur fossil hunter William Walker in 1983 in a clay pit in Sussex, southern England. This unique specimen of a hitherto unknown dinosaur was also the best-preserved example of any dinosaur dating from around 130 million years ago. Unlike other dinosaurs, *Baryonyx* had a peculiar skull and forelimbs.

Baryonyx.

Also included in this section (because it may be related to *Baryonyx*) is *Suchomimus*. Some palaeontologists believe that this tetanuran (stiff-tailed) theropod was a larger example of *Baryonyx*. In other instances, scientists group both dinosaurs into the special group of tetanuran (stiff-tailed) theropods, the spinosaurs (see *Spinosaurus,* page 73). While neither *Baryonyx* nor *Suchomimus* have the tall skin 'sail' on their backs, they do share *Spinosaurus'* long, low skull and kinked snout.

ALLOSAURUS

Pronounced: 'al-oh-SORE-us'

NAME MEANS
'Other lizard'

TIME
Late Jurassic
(203–144 MYA)

LOCATION
Colorado, Montana,
New Mexico, South
Dakota, Utah, Wyoming,
USA; Mtwara, Tanzania;
Victoria, Australia

SIZE
11m (36ft)

WEIGHT
1,524–2,032kg
(1½–2 tons)

DIET
Carnivore

The allosaurs, which include *Allosaurus* and *Yangchuanosaurus* (which was found in Szechwan Province, in China, in the 1970s), were among the largest carnosaurs around during the late Jurassic times. *Allosaurus* was named in 1877 after it was first discovered in Colorado, USA, by Benjamin Mudge, who was working for O C Marsh. It was by far one of the largest and most fearsome of predators. It was a close relative of its contemporary, *Megalosaurus* (see page 78), but was bigger, and had two bony bumps above its eyes and a narrow, bony ridge running between the eyes, down to the tip of its snout. Its head was huge, but not heavy, as its skull consisted mainly of bony struts, or load-bearing bars that made a framework of openings, or 'fenestrae', that surrounded the eyes, nostrils and muscles. The strongest bones were in the jaw: *Allosaurus* was able to open its jaws far apart and then expand the width of the gape by sliding its skull back over its lower jaw. This meant that its narrow, knife-like teeth sliced through flesh as *Allosaurus* bit into its victims.

Pillar-like legs supported the squat body, which was counterbalanced over the hips by the massive tail. The high-ankled, scale-covered foot looked like a giant, flightless bird's: three large toes bore the body weight, while the hallux, the first toe, was placed higher, off the ground, on the inside of the leg and facing backwards. The toes bore curved, narrow claws made up of a bony core, covered in horn. The short neck was strongly curved so that the head was held almost over its shoulders. The fore limbs were quite short, but equipped with three viciously curved claws.

SPINOSAURUS

Pronounced: 'SPINE-oh-SORE-us'

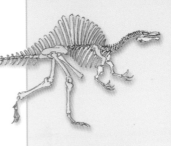

Spinosaurs were a group of large theropods that may have evolved from the megalosaurs in the Cretaceous period. Spinosaurs had a particular feature: an elongation of the back vertebrae that produced a pronounced ridge down the centre of the backbone. *Spinosaurus* was the most spectacular: it was as big as the largest carnosaurs, but its ridge was a large 'sail' down its back, which alone was taller than the average man. The 'sail' was formed by a row of broad, club-like 'spines' about 2m (6ft 6in) tall, which projected from the backbone and would have been covered with skin. What the sails' function was is unknown; perhaps it was a 'solar panel' that regulated the dinosaur's body temperature, or, perhaps, a highly visible sign used to attracted females and warn off competing suitors.

The forearms of *Spinosaurus* were larger than those of other theropods, which suggests that it may have spent some time on all fours, an unusual posture among the bipedal carnosaurs. A fossilised maxilla (upper jaw bone) found in Morocco and examined by French paleontologist Eric Buffetaut is thought to be from *Spinosaurus,* and suggests that it had a long, narrow snout and crocodile-like teeth designed more for eating fish than other dinosaurs. It may

have stood on a river or lake bank and grabbed fish with its jaws, like a heron, or it may have waded into shallow water and grabbed them with its claws (although no claws of *Spinosaurus* have been found). The finest fossilised remains of *Spinosaurus* were found in an oasis in Egypt in 1912 and examined by German palaeontologist Ernst Stromer von Reichenbach in 1915. However, an Allied bombing raid over Germany during World War II destroyed the best fossil finds, leaving only fragmentary evidence.

NAME MEANS
'Thorn lizard'

TIME
Middle Cretaceous
(144–65 MYA)

LOCATION
Marsa Matruh, Egypt;
Taouz, Morocco; Tunisia;
Niger, Africa

SIZE
15m (49ft)

WEIGHT
38,608km (3.8 tons)

DIET
Carnivore

CARNOTAURUS

Pronounced: 'kar-noh-TORE-us'

NAME MEANS
'Carnivorous bull'

TIME
Late Cretaceous
(144–65 MYA)

LOCATION
Chubut, Argentina

SIZE
12m (40ft)

WEIGHT
1,016kg (1 ton)

DIET
Carnivore

The discovery of this big, powerful dinosaur was only made in 1985, by Argentinian palaeontologists Jose Bonaparte and Fernando Novas, from digs in the Chubut region of Argentina, South America. The near-complete finds – lacking only half of the tail and parts of the feet, but including detailed fossilised skin impressions – revealed a dinosaur like nothing seen before. *Carnotaurus* had a deeper (taller from top to bottom), shorter (from front to back) and more 'snub-snouted', or 'bull-like', head than other theropods. Its very short, 'dwarfed' arms could not reach its mouth and would have been almost useless; it had forward-facing eyes and thousands of non-overlapping, disc-shaped scales covering its body, with rows of extra-large, semi-conical scales along its back and sides. Underneath its skin, bony wings projected from the top of some of its vertebrae. Even more extraordinary were the two pointed horns above its eyes.

Carnotaurus proved to belong to a group of theropods that the scientists called Abelisauridae, which take their name from *Abelisaurus* ('Abel's lizard'), named after Roberto Abel, who discovered it in 1985. Because there were similarities with *Ceratosaurus*, which had a small horn on its snout, scientists

believed the newly discovered abelisaurids to be a previously unknown group of ceratosaurs ('horned lizards'). Soon more discoveries were made: *Indosaurus* and *Indosuchus* were found in India; *Majungatholus* was found on the island of Madagascar, off Africa; and *Xenotarsosaurus* ('strange-ankle lizard') was found in Argentina. The global distribution of the abelisaurids suggested that they had spread across the southern supercontinent of Gondwana (which included South America and India) after it had separated from Laurasia.

GIGANOTOSAURUS

Pronounced: 'GIG-ah-noh-toh-SORE-us'

Some of the earliest dinosaurs, such as *Eoraptor* (see page 55), and some of the latest dinosaurs, such as the sauropod *Saltasaurus* (see page 126), as well as the biggest of all of the dinosaurs – the giant, herbivorous sauropod *Argentinosaurus* and the huge, carnivorous theropod *Giganotosaurus* – come from South America.

Giganotosaurus, from late Cretaceous Argentina, was the largest carnivore ever to walk the Earth. More massive than *Tyrannosaurus rex* (see page 82), *Giganotosaurus* was a tetanuran, theropod (stiff-tailed, beast-foot) dinosaur that was a close relative of *Allosaurus* (see page 72) and shared its deep skull, distinctive bones and weight-saving 'fenestration' (although its head was twice as large as that of *Allosaurus*). Its jaws were immense, with narrow, blade-like, saw-edged teeth 20cm (8in) long. On its head were bony ridges running down its snout. Short, but strong, arms ended in sharp claws on the three-fingered hands, powerful enough to rip flesh – from living sauropods or from carcasses of the dead. Each enormous foot, capable of supporting up to 3,556kg (3.5 tons) of body weight (about the same as around 75 adults), had three immensely strong, clawed toes.

Giganotosaurus lived around 90 MYA, and like all of the allosaurids, seemed to have died out before the end of the Cretaceous period. They were superseded by abelisaurids (see *Carnotaurus* at left) and tyrannosaurids (see page 68).

NAME MEANS
'Giant southern lizard'

TIME
Late Cretaceous
(144–65 MYA)

LOCATION
Southern South America

SIZE
15-16m (50–52ft)

WEIGHT
7,112–7,620kg
(7-7.5 tons)

DIET
Carnivore

EUSTREPTOSPONDYLUS

Pronounced: 'yoo-STREP-toh-SPON-die-lus'

NAME MEANS
'Well-curved vertebrae'

TIME
Late Jurassic
(203–144 MYA)

LOCATION
Wolvercote, Oxfordshire,
England

SIZE
7m (23ft)

WEIGHT
220kg (485lb)

DIET
Carnivore

Many of the later theropods are known as tetanurans, which means 'stiff tails'. In early therapods, the muscles of the thighs were linked to the middle of the tail, which allowed it to wave from side to side as the dinosaur walked. Later theropods, like *Eustreptospondylus,* had evolved much shorter tail-to-thigh muscles, which meant that their tails were much less mobile. In time, some tetanurans would lose their tails completely.

The first-known tetanurans included *Eustreptospondylus,* which lived in southern England around 170 million years ago. A fairly complete skeleton, missing only a few parts of the skull, was found near Wolvercote, in Oxfordshire, in the 1850s, but was named *Megalosaurus* (see page 78) because of other finds in the region. At this time, very few dinosaurs had been discovered and identified, and many scientists believed that during the Jurassic period in western Europe, only one large, predatory dinosaur was living, to which they gave the conceptual name *Megalosaurus* ('great lizard'). In 1964, British palaeontologist Dr Alice Walker was able to show that the Wolvercote fossil specimen was a completely different animal, and it was given the new genus name of *Eustreptospondylus,* with the species name *oxoniensis* ('from Oxford').

Eustreptospondylus was a large, carnivorous dinosaur with short arms and three-fingered hands, thick legs and a stiff tail. Despite its size – up to 7m (23ft) – *Eustreptospondylus* was lightly built and had weight-saving 'fenestration' (the window-like holes) in its skull. The jaws were armed with a number of small, blade-like teeth, which, in commom with other tetanurans, grew only in the jaw areas in front of their eyes. A carnivore, *Eustreptospondylus* may have preyed on herbivorous sauropods like *Cetiosaurus* (see page 114) that also roamed the region at the time.

The fossil of *Eustreptospondylus oxoniensis* is the only example of this dinosaur to be found so far. Now mounted in the University Museum of Oxford, it remains the best-preserved specimen of any European carnosaur discovered to date.

MEGALOSAURUS

Pronounced: 'MEG-ah-loh-SORE-us'

NAME MEANS
'Great lizard'

TIME
Middle Jurassic
(203–144 MYA)

LOCATION
Western Europe:
Stonesfield, Oxfordshire,
England; France; Portugal

SIZE
9m (30ft)

WEIGHT
1,016kg (1 ton)

DIET
Carnivore

The first dinosaur bone on record, which was discovered in England in 1676, most likely belonged to *Megalosaurus*. *Megalosaurus* (or 'great lizard') is neither the biggest nor the heaviest dinosaur, but it can claim to be the first ever to be found, and the first dinosaur to be given an official scientific name, even though the term 'dinosaur' was yet to be invented by Richard Owen (he did so in 1841). In 1819, William Buckland (1784–1856), a clergyman (later dean of Westminster Abbey) and geologist, discovered part of the lower jaw, several vertebrae and parts of the pelvis and hind limbs in a quarry at Stonesfield in Oxfordshire, which he described and named *Megalosaurus* (it was later known as *Megalosaurus buklandi* in his honour).

Although no complete skeleton has yet been found, from the fragments available (found in England, France and Portugal), scientists have surmised that *Megalosaurus* was probably longer and stronger than *Eustreptospondylus* (see page 76), but shared the body of the typical carnosaur, with a large head, a jaw set with great, curved teeth (Buckland's jaw fragment shows new teeth beginning to grow, ready to replace old ones when they fell out or lost them in the flesh of their victims), a thick neck and long, powerful legs. The three digits on each hand, and the three weight-bearing toes, also bore long, sharp claws, making them well equipped to attack, kill and feast off the large, long-necked plant-eating dinosaurs of the day. Track marks left by *Megalosaurus* in the limestone rocks of southern England show how these heavy bipeds walked upright on their two hind legs, their toes pointing slightly inwards, and perhaps moving their long, stiff tails from side to side with each step.

DASPLETOSAURUS

Pronounced: 'das-PLEET-oh-SORE-us'

Daspletosaurus came from the Red Deer River, near Steveville, Alberta, Canada, and was a large, bipedal carnivore resembling *Tyrannosaurus rex* (see page 82). Most of the skeleton was found in 1921 by C M Sternberg. It was smaller than *Tyrannosaurus,* but with a body length of around 9m (over 29ft), it was still a fearsome carnivore – and it had larger teeth than any other tyrannosaur. Although they were fewer in number, each tooth was razor sharp, curved and saw-edged. The forearms, while quite small, as in all of the tryannosaurids, were larger than those of all of the other known species. Its massive head and strong jaws suggest that it may have preyed on the quadrupedal armoured and horned ceratopsians, sinking its teeth into the unprotected flanks of its prey. Once *Daspletosaurus* had locked its curved jaws together, the victims were unlikely to have been able to escape – especially if they were pinned to the ground, with one or both of its clawed feet – and would have died of blood loss.

As well as spending only a short time on Earth, the tyrannosaurids seem to have had a very limited distribution across it, with fossil remains largely confined to North America and Asia, although a number of fragmentary fossil finds have been attributed to the family. They appear to have replaced the earlier carnosaurs (see page 68) as the main predators, and while it is possible that they were in existence earlier than 80 million years ago, fossil evidence has yet to be found to support this.

NAME MEANS
'Frightful lizard'

TIME
Late Cretaceous
(135–65 MYA)

LOCATION
Alberta, Canada

SIZE
8.5–9m (28–29½ft)

WEIGHT
4,064kg (4 tons)

DIET
Carnivore

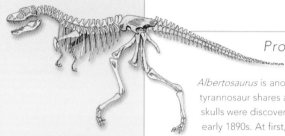

ALBERTOSAURUS

Pronounced: 'al-BERT-oh-SORE-us'

NAME MEANS
'Alberta lizard'

TIME
Late Cretaceous
(135–65 MYA)

LOCATION
Alberta, Canada

SIZE
8–9m (26–29½ft)

WEIGHT
3,048–3,556kg
(3–3½ tons)

DIET
Carnivore

Albertosaurus is another North American tyrannosaurid, and this 'small' tyrannosaur shares all of the features common to the family. Two partial skulls were discovered on the Red Deer River in Alberta, Canada, in the early 1890s. At first, the species was attributed by E D Cope in 1892 to *Laelaps,* an early name that had also been given to *Tyrannosaurus.* Later, the pioneering Canadian palaeontologist Lawrence Lambe (1863–1919) transferred it to the genus *Dryptosaurus* ('wounding reptile'), but in 1905, the remains of these large theropods were reviewed by H F Osborn, who subsequently renamed both *Tyrannosaurus* and *Albertosaurus.*

Understanding of *Albertosaurus* was further enhanced in 1913, when C H Sternberg discovered a well-preserved skeleton at Berry Creek, on the Red Deer River, although this was named *Gorgosaurus libratus* ('free dragon lizard'). While the majority of theropods had a three-fingered hand, *Gorgosaurus,* it was noted, had only two quite small fingers. The small forelimb and the two fingers are now characteristics that distinguish the tyrannosaurids as a whole. Even so, in 1917, *Gorgosaurus* was not 'related' to *Tyrannosaurus* because Osborn had reconstructed the latter with three fingers! It was not until 1970 that Dr Dale Russell was able to untangle all of the threads and confirm *Albertosaurus* as a genus in its own right.

Like *Tyrannosaurus, Albertosaurus* was a large, massively built theropod, with a big head and a short body that was balanced at the hips by a long, strong tail. Like other tyrannosaurs, *Albertosaurus* had a large 'foot' on the pubis and a well-developed second set of ribs on the underside of its body. A possible explanation for these is that they could have been adaptations for lying prone on the ground. The innards would have been supported by the extra ribs and would not have been crushed by the great body weight.

When *Albertosaurus* rose to its feet, its tiny, but strong, arms would have stopped it from sliding forwards. The body would then have been steadied by the forearms as the rear legs were straightened. By tilting its head and upper body backwards, *Albertosaurus* may have been able to raise itself upright, on to its back feet.

TYRANNOSAURUS REX

Pronounced: 'tie-RAN-oh-SORE-us recks'

Until the discovery of the mighty *Giganotosaurus* in Argentina in the late 1980s, scientists believed that *Tyrannosaurus rex* was the largest carnivorous animal ever to walk on Earth. In spite of this discovery, *Tyrannosaurus* was still a remarkable – and very impressive – creature. *Tyrannosaurus* is not only one of the best-known dinosaurs, it also one about which scientist know a lot as discoveries have yielded fossilised bones, teeth, entire skeletons and other remains. Living at the very end of the 'age of the dinosaurs', about 68–65 million years ago, *Tyrannosaurus'* time on Earth was very short lived: only about 15 million years.

When fully grown, the 'king of the tyrant lizards' was as long as the width of a tennis court, as tall as a double-decker bus and weighed about the same as a modern, adult, African bull elephant. Its head alone was around 1.25m (4ft) long, and its jaw was armed with more than 50 teeth that were serrated on both the front and back sides, which left very distinctive marks in the flesh of it prey. The longest fangs measured an impressive 18cm (7in). Its mighty jaws were powerful and big – big enough to swallow an adult whole – because the lower jaw was hinged at the rear of the head, allowing for a huge gape when the mouth was open. The upper and lower jaws were curved, so that when *Tyrannosaurus* closed its mouth, all of the great teeth met.

Its massive head – nearly half the length of its backbone between its hips and legs – with its short, deep snout, was carried on a strong, thick, but flexible, neck, supported by short, wide vertebrae and immensely powerful muscles. Thick, strongly boned legs bore its enormous weight, and three large, clawed toes touched the ground, but two-fingered claws ended its ridiculously short, but nevertheless very powerful, forearms. The arms and hands were so small that it would have been impossible for *Tyrannosaurus* to pass food to its mouth with them. With large areas of its (relatively small) brain devoted to the

NAME MEANS
'King of the tyrant lizards'

TIME
Late Cretaceous
(135–65 MYA)

LOCATION
North America: Colorado,
Montana,
New Mexico, Texas,
Wyoming, USA; Alberta,
Saskatchewan, Canada;
Asia: Mongolia, China

SIZE
13–15m (46–50ft) long, up
to 6m (20ft) tall

WEIGHT
6,096–6,604kg
(6–6½ tons)

DIET
Carnivore

senses of sight and smell, and with possibly binocular vision, *Tyrannosaurus,* it seems, was an active predator of the herds of hadrosaurs (duck-billed dinosaurs) that roamed the forests of North America.

DROMICEIOMIMUS

Pronounced: 'droh-MEE-see-oh-MEEM-us'

NAME MEANS
'Emu mimic'

TIME
Late Cretaceous
(135–65 MYA)

LOCATION
Alberta, Canada

SIZE
3.5m (11ft) long,
2m (6ft) high

WEIGHT
150kg (330lb)

DIET
Carnivorous (insects,
small mammals, eggs
and lizards), possibly
fruit and leaves

The first ornithomimosaur remains were of a partial foot found by George Cannon in 1889, in rocks near Denver, Colorado, USA. Later fragments found in Montana, including fragments of a pelvis, were described by Marsh in 1892, and he recognised that the remains were not ornithopods (bipedal, herbivorous, ornithischian – 'bird-hipped' – dinosaurs) as first suspected, but theropods: carnivorous, 'beast-feet' dinosaurs. In the 1920s, two specimens found on the Red Deer River in Alberta, Canada, were originally described as *Struthiomimus breviterius* and *Struthiomimus samueli* by William Parks. In 1972, Dr Dale Russell, in Ottawa, reassessed the various species proposed since the late 19th century and revealed that there were three genera of ornithomimosaurs in the late Cretaceous period in North America: *Ornithomimus*, *Struthiomimus* and *Dromiceiomimus*, or 'emu mimic', of which Parks' specimens were a part.

All ornithomimids had long, slender legs: their tibias (shin bones) were on average about 20 per cent longer than their femurs (thigh bones), but *Dromiceiomimus* had even longer shins than average, indicating that it was a very fast runner. Only its toes touched the ground – the foot bones were locked into a single, bird-like extension of the tibia. The 10 neck vertebrae made a very flexible stem on which its head was mounted. The size of the brain cavity and eye sockets in its skull show that *Dromiceiomimus* had an exceptionally large brain – proportionally larger than a modern ostrich – and enormous eyes. *Dromiceiomimus* was in all likelihood a nocturnal hunter of small mammals and lizards in the forests of North America and Canada.

STRUTHIOMIMUS

Pronounced: 'STRUTH-ee-oh-MEEM-us'

NAME MEANS
'Ostrich mimic'

TIME
Late Cretaceous
(135–65 MYA)

LOCATION
New Jersey, USA;
Alberta, Canada

SIZE
4m (12ft 6in) long,
2m (6ft) tall

WEIGHT
Unknown

DIET
Carnivorous (insects,
small mammals, eggs
and lizards), possibly
fruit and leaves

Struthiomimus, the 'ostrich mimic', is the best-known of North America's fast-running, bird-like dinosaurs. Its tail counterbalanced the front part of its body, but the stiffened aspect of the tail – long prongs of bone joined the vertebrae together and restricted movement – also meant that it acted as a stabiliser when it changed direction. Pretty well defenceless, apart from perhaps being able to deliver power-kicks to drive away small, predatory theropods, *Struthiomimus* had to rely on its speed and agility to escape. The feet bear a resemblance to those of modern running birds, such as ostriches: the claws are narrow and flattened to provide traction with the ground and stop the foot slipping as it was pushed backwards during running.

The neck was long, slender and presumably highly mobile if *Struthiomimus* was always alert for danger, scanning the landscape with its huge eyes. The vertebrae of the back, however, appear to have been held stiffly in place by very strong ligaments. Belly ribs, or gastralia, are found in many reptiles, but not in mammals, and no one really knows what their function is: they may perhaps help to support the abdomen in some way. The long and slender, toothless jaw was probably covered with tough horn, and the thin, light bones suggest that they may have been flexible, allowing movement in the skull and offering a greater degree of precision in manipulating food in the mouth (as with modern parrots, which can hold a nut in their jaws, move their upper and lower beaks and tongue in unison and quite deftly remove the shell). The forelimbs were very slender and quite long, ending in three very long, clawed fingers. These may have been used to hook and pull down leafy branches towards its mouth, or to scrape into the earth in order to uncover eggs on which to feast.

GALLIMIMUS

Pronounced: 'gal-lee-MEEM-us'

Gallimimus, or 'chicken mimic', is an Asian ornithomimosaur and comes from the late Cretaceous period in Mongolia, Asia. Over twice the length of a modern ostrich, *Gallimimus* was the largest of the lightly built, bird-like theropods. Remains found in the Gobi Desert include two near-complete skeletons, a complete skeleton except for the skull, a skull and fragments of a skeleton and fragments of different skeletons. From this range of material, scientists have deduced that *Gallimimus* differed from the North American ornithomimids not only in size – it was the largest ostrich–dinosaur discovered to date – but in the shape of its skull and the proportions of its limbs. The slender hind limbs were shorter than *Struthiomimus'*, and its small, lightweight head was long and narrow, the snout ending in a broad, flat-tipped, horny beak. Its jaws also appear to have been weaker than other ornithomimids'. The hands of *Gallimimus* were also proportionally shorter than other species', and seem poorly designed for grasping, although its claws were more curved. This is probably because *Gallimimus* lived much deeper inland, in more arid and drought-prone regions than its North American cousins. No doubt the more curved claws were better suited to scratching into the earth in search of eggs.

NAME MEANS
'Chicken mimic'

TIME
Late Cretaceous
(135–65 MYA)

LOCATION
Omnogov, Mongolia

SIZE
6m (19ft 6in) long,
3m (9ft) high

WEIGHT
400kg (880lb)

DIET
Carnivorous (insects,
small mammals, eggs
and lizards), possibly
fruit and leaves

OVIRAPTOR

Pronounced: 'OHV-ih-RAP-tor'

NAME MEANS
'Egg thief'
(*philoceratops*: 'fond of
ceratopsian eggs')

TIME
Late Cretaceous
(135–65 MYA)

LOCATION
Shabarakh Usu,
southern Mongolia

SIZE
2m (6ft 6in)

WEIGHT
33kg (72lb)

DIET
Eggs, molluscs

The circumstances of preservation of the original remains of the 'egg thief' provide the reason for its name, *Oviraptor philoceratops* ('egg thief, fond of ceratopsian eggs'): its skull and skeleton were found in 1923 by George Olsen at the *Protoceratops* site in Shabarakh Usu, in southern Mongolia, lying on top of a clutch of *Protoceratops* eggs. It's possible that *Oviraptor* had died while in the process of raiding the nest, its skull crushed by an angry parent. It is possible that *Oviraptor* did feast on eggs, cracking them open with its horny beak and supplementing its diet by scavenging for berries, insects and on the carcasses of dead dinosaurs in the arid, semi-desert conditions. In the 1990s, further *Oviraptor* remains were found on top of an egg-filled nest; this time, however, the tiny bones in the embryos proved to be those of hatchling *Oviraptors*. Rather than stealing the eggs of other dinosaurs, this devoted mother had died protecting her own.

Oviraptor's toothless-jawed skull was deep, but lightweight, with many of the bones acting as struts surrounding windows for the eyes, nostrils and jaw muscles. The jaw ended in a horny beak, but inside the mouth, jutting down from the roof, were two bony prongs that could have been used for egg-crushing. As with other theropods, *Oviraptor* had a pubis bone that ended in a 'foot', and as with other swift-running dinosaurs, its tibias (shin bones) were elongated and there were three weight-bearing toes on each foot, with a backwards-facing hallux (first toe). The long tail core, used to counterbalance the body weight and perhaps as a steering rudder when running at speed, consisted of 40 caudal vertebrae.

One of the most distinguishing features of *Oviraptor* was the head crest: two species, *O. philoceratops* and *O. mongoliensis,* appear to have had crests sheathed in horn, perhaps brightly or differently coloured. The bony crests resemble the casque on the head of the modern cassowary, the large

(2.5m/5ft high) flightless bird of Australia, New Guinea and adjacent islands. The cassowary uses its bony helmet to butt its way head first through forest undergrowth. Different oviraptosaurs appear to have had different-shaped crests: *O. mongoliensis* had a tall, domed crest much larger than that of *O. philoceratops*, while *O. ingenia* may have been crestless and have had brightly coloured skin on its head instead. In 1971, a Polish–Mongolian expedition, followed by a Soviet–Mongolian expedition, both recovered further *Oviraptor* remains, which revealed a wider range of skull and crest shapes and crest development than had been expected. It is possible that many of the differences may be due to the specimens' degree of maturity.

CAUDIPTERYX

Pronounced: 'caw-DIP-ter-icks'

Of all of the recent discoveries, none is more amazing than *Caudipteryx*, from China. For centuries, dinosaur fossils found in China were identified as the dragons of traditional folklore, and it was not until the 1920s and 1930s that fossil finds in China were first studied scientifically. Since the 1980s, fossil finds from the country – including some remarkable hoaxes – of dinosaurs, non-bird dinosaurs and birds, have been causing scientists across the world to rethink many theories about dinosaurs, their interrelationships and their descendants.

Caudipteryx was a long-legged, bird-like creature, about the size of a turkey. What is unusual is that it had both dinosaur and bird features. Its dinosaur features included sharp, buck teeth at the front of its beak and a pubis bone that pointed forwards, the caudal or tail vertebrae also hinting that it was a close relative of *Oviraptor*. Long legs and bird-like toes – some scientist claim that it had a reversed big toe like a bird, although this is, as yet, unproven – indicate that it was capable of running quite fast. It also had short forearms (although shorter than those of other advanced theropods), with long, three-fingered hands ending in claws to mark it as a non-bird, theropod dinosaur.

Caudipteryx seems to have been covered in feathers: short down feathers for insulation suggest that it was warm-blooded, while longer feathers, with 20cm- (8in-) long quill shafts, sprouted from the arms, fingers and tail. Yet *Caudipteryx* was not able to fly: its 'wing' feathers were symmetrical in shape, not asymmetrical, as in flying birds. The feathers may have been camouflage or displayed for mating purposes.

NAME MEANS
'Tail feather'

TIME
Early Cretaceous
(135–65 MYA)

LOCATION
China, eastern Asia

SIZE
75cm (2ft 6in) tall

WEIGHT
10kg (22lb)

DIET
Possibly carnivorous

THERIZINOSAURUS

Pronounced: 'THER-ih-ZINE- oh-SORE-us'

In 1948, a large amount of dinosaur material was collected by a Soviet–Mongolian expedition to the Gobi Desert, which included some extremely large, bony claws – one was 70cm (28in) long, and this does not include the horny part of the claw, which would have made it even longer! The other two claws were shorter, but no less impressively curved, like scythe blades, flat-bladed and gently tapering to a very narrow point. The claws were so long that scientists suspected that 'scythe lizard', as it was named, would have had to walk on its knuckles if it went down on all fours. Later, in 1957, 1959 and 1960, more huge claws were discovered in Kazakhstan, Transbaykalia and Inner Mongolia, along with a partial forelimb, incomplete hind limbs and a tooth. These remains demonstrated that *Therizinosaurus* was not a huge turtle (as many originally thought), but a large theropod, and yet another remarkable late Cretaceous period dinosaur from China. The wrist bones of the forelimb remains and the toe bones of the hind limb remains show that *Therizinosaurus* was a tetanuran (stiff-tailed) theropod related to *Oviraptor* (see page 88).

From various finds, scientists have suggested that *Therizinosaurus* had a small head supported on a long, flexible neck and was largely bipedal. Despite their immense size, the claws do not appear particularly well suited to aggression, especially when compared to the claws of the dromaeosaurids (see page 70). This has led some scientists to suggest that *Therizinosaurus* did not use them for slashing skin, but for raking the ground and tearing open termitaria (anthills). Others, however, find it difficult to believe that such a large dinosaur could sustain itself on termites, unless they themselves were very large.

NAME MEANS
'Scythe lizard'

TIME
Late Cretaceous
(135–65 MYA)

LOCATION
Mongolia, China

SIZE
Up to 12m (39ft) long

WEIGHT
Unknown

DIET
Possibly
carnivore/insectivore,
possible herbivore

NAME MEANS
'Wounding tooth'

TIME
Late Cretaceous
(144–65 MYA)

LOCATION
Montana, Wyoming, USA;
Alberta, Canada

SIZE
2m (6ft 6in) long

WEIGHT
50kg (110lb)

DIET
Carnivore

TROODON

Pronounced: 'TROH-oh-don'

Named for its small, triangular, saw-edge tooth, which was flattened from side to side like the blade of a knife, *Troodon,* or 'wounding tooth', had up to 25 teeth on each side of its upper jaw, with exactly 25 teeth on each side of its lower one. It flourished in North America about 70 million years ago, right at the end of the 'age of the dinosaurs', the Mesozoic era. The long, bird-like head had very large, partially forward-facing eyes. Scientists believe that the overlapping visual fields of the two eyes may have allowed *Troodon* to judge distances accurately and enable it to pounce on fast-moving, small prey. Its slim, elongated legs certainly allowed it to run very fast on its three weight-bearing, clawed toes. However, the second toe appears to have been held above the ground, and was also articulated so that it could swivel around, and this, too, was armed with a long, deep, switch-blade-like claw, a little like that of *Deinonychus* (see page 98). Nevertheless, this toe claw would not have been sufficient for *Troodon* to attack and kill large prey, although it could have seized it with its sharply curved claws on the ends of three-fingered hands.

SAURORNITHOIDES

Pronounced: 'sore-OR-nith-OID-eez'

In 1923, Henry Fairfield Osborn described the incomplete remains of a bird-like, theropod dinosaur found in rocks at Shabarakh Usu, in the Gobi Desert of Mongolia. This dinosaur was named *Saurornithoides mongoliensis* ('bird-like reptile from Mongolia'), and at first was thought to be an early toothed bird because its skull had a long, narrow, bird-like muzzle. The skull housed a large brain and large eyes, which may suggest nocturnal habits. It had 38 teeth in the upper jaw, which were unusual in that only their back edges were serrated. An incomplete back foot showed that the toes were articulated in a typical theropod fashion, with a small, spur-like first toe and three longer, 'walking toes'. Like *Troodon*, *Saurornithoides* had a second toe that was jointed in such a way that it could have been raised clear of the ground. While *Troodon* was native to North America, *Saurornithoides* has been found only in Mongolia. The two may be related, having spread across the northern hemisphere by way of the land bridge across the Bering Straits, and could then have evolved differences to suit the different environment.

In 1974, more finds were discovered in Bugeen Tsav, Mongolia. These were described by Rinchen Barsbold and named *Saurornithoides junior* ('younger bird-like reptile'). It was found in slightly earlier rocks, was around a third larger than Osborn's specimen and had a greater number of smaller teeth, which were only serrated along their back edges. The well-preserved skull also showed strange, swollen areas around the ears and on the floor of the brain case. These differences led Barsbold to propose that *Saurornithoides* should be placed not with the troodontids, but in a family of its own, the saurornithoides.

NAME MEANS
'Bird-like lizard'

TIME
Late Cretaceous
(144–65 MYA)

LOCATION
Mongolia, Asia

SIZE
2m (6ft 6in) long

WEIGHT
15–20kg (32–50lb)

DIET
Carnivore

BAMBIRAPTOR

Pronounced: 'BAM-bee-RAP-tor'

NAME MEANS
'Bambi raider'

TIME
Late Cretaceous
(144–65 MYA)

LOCATION
Montana, USA

SIZE
1m (3ft 3in) long

WEIGHT
15kg (32lb)

DIET
Carnivore

Bambiraptor is one of the most recent dinosaur discoveries. The remains, discovered only in 1994, in Montana, USA, made one of the most complete fossil skeletons of the bird-like, but non-avian, North American dinosaurs. At only 1m (3ft 3 in) long, it appeared that this specimen of *Bambiraptor* was a juvenile, and not yet fully grown. While some of its bones contained air sacs that were linked to its lungs, as in a bird, and provided extra oxygen to the body when the animal was active, *Bambiraptor* also shared some of the features of *Troodon*, such as elongated shins and huge eye sockets. Its much larger head also displayed a rather deeper snout, with much bigger teeth, giving *Bambiraptor* a far less bird-like appearance. The skull size also indicates that *Bambiraptor* had the largest brain for the size of its body of any other dinosaur. The wrist bones were articulated to allow it to fold its hands 23cm (9in), in the same way that a bird folds its wings, while the wishbone and shoulders allowed it to swing out its long arms to grab at its prey. The stiffened tail would have acted to counterbalance the weight over the hips and probably swung from side to side as it ran. It is also thought that *Bambiraptor* may have been warm-blooded and covered with a downy feathering to help maintain its body heat.

DROMAEOSAURUS

Pronounced: 'droh-Mee-oh-SORE-us'

Dromaeosaurus, discovered in 1914, in Alberta, Canada, was the first of the sickle-clawed dinosaurs to be discovered, and it gave its name to the entire family. But it was not until 1964, when *Deinonychus* was discovered, that scientists were able to understand the species more fully. Until that time, *Dromaeosaurus* was considered either a large coelurosaur or a small carnosaur. Although it is only known from its skull and fragments of its arms and legs, palaeontologists have been able to piece together a picture of *Dromaeosaurus* as a small, but agile, predator. The head had a deep, rounded snout, but regarding the rest of it, it is assumed that *Dromaeosaurus* was similar to, but smaller than, *Velociraptor* (see page 96) and *Deinonychus* (see page 98) at just under 2m (6½ft) long.

The relationship of the dromaeosaurids to other carnivorous dinosaurs is still hotly debated. Some claim their nearest relatives to be the saurornithoides or troodontids (see pages 69 to 70), as these also have the same peculiar, sickle-shaped toe claw, but they do not have the same hip structure.

NAME MEANS
'Running lizard'

TIME
Late Cretaceous
(144–65 MYA)

LOCATION
Montana, USA;
Alberta, Canada

SIZE
1.8m (6ft) long

WEIGHT
15kg (33lb)

DIET
Carnivore

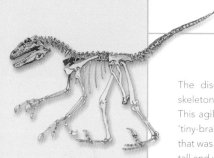

DEINONYCHUS

Pronounced: 'die-NON-i-kus'

The discovery, in 1964, in Montana, USA, of near-complete, fossilised skeletons of *Deinonychus* showed a dinosaur built for the chase and the kill. This agile killer really undermined the long-held notion that dinosaurs were 'tiny-brained', slow-moving reptiles. *Deinonychus* had the lightweight body that was characteristic of the coelurosaurs, stood on average around 1.8m (6ft) tall and weighed around 68kg (150lb). All in all, *Deinonychus* was about as tall as a man and weighed about the same. The head, however, was typical of the carnosaur: large and well equipped with numerous flesh-tearing, backward-curving teeth with serrated edges. Its jaws opened wide and would then clamp on to its prey; by tugging its head backwards, it could slice through its victim's flesh. Its long tail stood out from its body because all of the caudal vertebrae (tail bones), except for the ones closest to its body, were locked together by overlapping, bony, chevron-shaped tendons. As it ran, the body was most likely held horizontally, with the tail counterbalancing the weight of the body in front of the hips.

The legs were slender, with long shin bones designed for running, and each foot had four toes. The first toe was tiny and non-functioning – as in most of the later theropods – while the third and fourth toes carried the weight. The second toe on each foot gave *Deinonychus* its most lethal weapons: both bore a huge, hinged, sickle-shaped claw up to 15cm (6in) long. The arms were unusually long for a theropod – but still much shorter than the hind legs – and ended in long, clawed, three-fingered hands. These strong arms – the humerus (upper arm bone) is very broad and has roughened areas for the attachment of powerful arm and chest muscles – suggest that *Deinonychus* used its arms actively to grasp its struggling prey.

NAME MEANS
'Terrible claw'

TIME
Early Cretaceous
(144–65 MYA)

LOCATION
Montana, USA

SIZE
3–4m (10–13ft) long,
1.8m (6ft) tall

WEIGHT
68kg (150lb)

DIET
Carnivore

To overcome their prey, scientists suggest that the highly intelligent *Deinonychus* hunted in predatory packs, first harassing a potential victim, perhaps slowing it down by grasping its tail, exhausting it and then finishing it off with lethal blows with their feet claws to their prey's unprotected flanks or underbelly.

VELOCIRAPTOR

Pronounced: 'vel-O-see-RAP-tor'

Living some 75–70 million years ago in central Asia, *Velociraptor* had all of the fearsome features of the dromaeosaurids, including the 'terrible claw' on each second toe. The fossil remains of *Velociraptor* have been largely confined to finds in the Djadochta rock formation in Shabarakh Usu, in Mongolia, and the first finds were discovered by teams led by the American naturalist and explorer Roy Chapman Andrews, on expeditions dating up to 1930.

Although it was about the same size as *Deinonychus*, it can be distinguished from other dromaeosaurids by its very low, narrow head, which may be accounted for by dietary differences. One of the most dramatic fossil finds in Mongolia was of two skeletons found in 1971: a *Velociraptor* locked in mortal combat with the horned dinosaur *Protoceratops*. *Velociraptor* was found grasping the great head shield of *Protoceratops* with its clawed hands, while at the same time it ripped into its belly and throat with its long, sickle-clawed feet. But *Protoceratops* had also mortally wounded its attacker by caving in *Velociraptor*'s chest, perhaps with its horny beak.

Although no evidence has yet been found related to this particular species, it is also possible that *Velociraptor* and other dromaeosaurids, especially those from China and Mongolia, may have had a body covering of feathers rather than scales. The recent discoveries of other small theropods, including the dromaeosaurids *Sinornithosaurus* ('Chinese bird lizard') and *Microraptor* ('tiny robber'), which were found in the 1990s, also revealed fossil feathers.

NAME MEANS
'Quick plunderer'

TIME
Late Cretaceous
(144–65 MYA)

LOCATION
East Asia: Mongolia
and China

SIZE
1.8m (6ft) long

WEIGHT
15kg (33lb)

DIET
Carnivore

ORNITHOLESTES

Pronounced: 'Or-nith-oh-LEZ-teez'

This type of coelurosaur was discovered in 1900 at Bone Cabin Quarry, near Como, Wyoming, and the fossil remains consist of a partial skeleton, including the jaws, skull and other small fragments. It was first described and named by its discoverer, H F Osborn, in 1903 (and again in more detail in 1916), and apart from an incomplete hand of another individual, it remains the only example of *Ornitholestes*, the 'bird robber', so far discovered.

Like its relatives, *Coelophysis* (see page 58) and *Compsognathus* (see page 100), *Ornitholestes* had a body similarly balanced at the hips by a long tail held clear of the ground, and a slender, flexible, 'S'-shaped neck. It did, however, have a stronger, deeper skull than the two other theropods, and some scientists believe that it could also have had a bony crest at the end of its shorter snout. The teeth were also numerous and quite large; the front ones were almost conical, while those further along the jaw were small and curved. This suggests that *Ornitholestes* had a more powerful bite than either of the other species, and was perhaps more capable of tackling larger, and more active, prey. Although named 'bird robber', *Ornitholestes* more likely preyed on the eggs and hatchlings of other dinosaurs, as well as small lizards and mammals. The forearms were long in proportion to those of *Coelophysis* and *Compsognathus*, and the hands were also unusually proportioned: the second and third fingers were long and slender and almost equal in length, while the first finger or 'thumb' was much shorter. These features suggest that *Ornitholestes* had a much greater ability to reach and grasp its prey.

NAME MEANS
'Bird robber'

TIME
Late Jurassic
(208–144 MYA)

LOCATION
Como, Wyoming, USA

SIZE
2m (6ft 6in) long

WEIGHT
12.5kg (28lb)

DIET
Carnivore

NAME MEANS
'Pretty jaws'

TIME
Late Jurassic
(108–144 MYA)

LOCATION
Var, France; Bavaria,
Germany

SIZE
70cm–1.4m
(2ft 4in–4ft 6in) long

WEIGHT
3kg (6½lb)

DIET
Carnivore, possibly
insectivore

COMPSOGNATHUS

Pronounced: 'komp-soh-NAY-thus'

One of the smallest-known dinosaurs (the German example stood no taller than a chicken, although the French specimen was as large as a turkey), we also know *Compsognathus* – whose unlikely name means 'pretty' or 'elegant jaw' – as a swift-footed, bipedal predator of insects and small animals of various types. This is because, like *Coelophysis* (see page 58), the skeletal remains of *Compsognathus'* last meal of a small lizard named *Bavarisaurus* have been preserved in its ribcage. In order to have caught such a fast-moving animal, *Compsognathus* must have had very keen eyesight, been able to accelerate very quickly and have kept up a high speed, while all the time manoeuvring its body through undergrowth and around rocks. For such a small theropod, *Compsognathus'* skull was large and narrow, lightly constructed, with huge openings for the orbits (eye sockets) and tapering to the snout. The teeth were sharp, curved and widely spaced along its upper and lower jaws. Typical of the fast-running dinosaurs, *Compsognathus* had long hind legs, with elongated tibias (shin bones) and feet, running on its second, third and fourth toes. (The tiny first toe pointed backwards.) Uniquely, the short forearms appear to have borne two-fingered and clawed hands, much like the huge tyrannosaurids of

the late Cretaceous period. It is because of this two-fingered hand that some scientists classify *Compsognathus* as the sole known member of its own family, the Compsognathidae.

BARYONYX

Pronounced: 'bar-ee-ON-icks'

Two unusual features distinguished this large theropod from others: firstly, it had an enormous, curved claw about 30cm (12in) long, hence its name, *Baryonyx*, which means 'heavy claw'. Unfortunately, the claw became detached from the skeleton when fossil hunter William Walker's geological hammer hit it, so it is not known whether the claw was part of the hind or forelimbs, although most scientists know it as the 'thumb claw' and presume that it belonged to the forelimbs as these bones were unusually thick and powerful for a theropod.

The second peculiar feature of *Baryonyx* was its skull, which was long – about 1.1m (3ft 7in) – and narrow. In appearance, *Baryonyx*'s skull was more like that of a modern crocodile than a carnivorous dinosaur. The jaws (the upper one was kinked at the front) were lined with a vast number of small, pointed teeth (twice as many as other theropods') and there was evidence of a small, bony crest on top of the head. The long, stiff tail counterbalanced the body weight at the hips as the longer and straighter neck and head were held low and jutting forwards. This again was an unusual feature, as most theropods had a more curved, flexible, 'S'-shaped neck. The arms were powerfully built, and we have a picture of a huge animal, craning its neck over water and grabbing at fish with its giant hooks of thumb-claws. That *Baryonyx* ate fish is certain: palaeontologists found the scales of the 1m-/3ft 3in-long fish *Lepidotes* in its ribcage, while in its stomach cavity were half-digested bones of a young *Iguanodon*.

NAME MEANS
'Heavy claw'

TIME
Mid-Cretaceous
(144–65 MYA)

LOCATION
Sussex,
southern England

SIZE
10.5m (34ft) long,
3m (10ft) tall

WEIGHT
2,032kg (2 tons)

DIET
Fish, carrion

SUCHOMIMUS

Pronounced: 'soo-CHO-meem-us'

NAME MEANS
'Crocodile mimic'

TIME
Early Cretaceous
(144–65 MYA)

LOCATION
North Africa

SIZE
11m (36ft) long

WEIGHT
5,080kg (5 tons)

DIET
Fish, carrion

Suchomimus, 'crocodile mimic', was discovered only in 1997, in the Sahara Desert in North Africa. The fossilised remains show a creature 11m (36ft) long, but scientists believe that this specimen was not fully grown when it met its death. *Suchomimus* had a long, narrow head that ended in a flattened, paddle- or spoon-shaped tip. Inside the jaw were numerous small, sharp teeth, ideal for catching slippery fish. Its naris (nostrils) were placed far back along the head like a crocodile's, so perhaps *Suchomimus* could lie almost completely submerged in water as it waited for its prey. But *Suchomimus* was also well armed with powerful forelimbs and hooked thumb claws, which suggest that it was equally adept at fishing from the banks of rivers and lakes by hooking its prey out of the water. It is also possible that these claws used to rip at the flesh of corpses of already dead animals on which *Suchomimus* may have scavenged.

While very similar to *Baryonyx* (in fact, some scientists suggest that they are one and the same species), *Suchomimus* did appear to have one distinguishing feature: it had a low ridge running from the top of its head down its back, with the highest ridges above its hips.

CHAPTER 6
SAURISCHIAN DINOSAURS II

SAUROPODOMORPHS

The second suborder of the saurischian (lizard-hipped) dinosaurs was the sauropodomorphs (lizard-foot forms). Their lifestyle was completely different to that of their contemporaries, the theropods. Although both were saurischians, the theropods were bipedal carnivores, while the sauropodomorphs were largely quadrupedal herbivores. Sauropodomorphs inherited large thumb claws from their bipedal ancestors and had small heads and teeth that were shaped for cropping and chewing plants. Their necks were long – which allowed them to browse for tender shoots in tall trees – and their bodies were often enormous because they needed the extra room to process enough nutrition from tree leaves and ferns.

By late Triassic times (250–203 million years ago), there were two types of sauropodomorphs grazing across the Earth: prosauropods ('before the lizard feet'), which ranged from small, bipedal forms to enormous, quadrupedal monsters, and sauropods ('lizard feet'), gigantic herbivores supported on four pillar-like legs. The prosauropods died out during the Jurassic period, but the sauropods lived on right through to the end of the 'age of the dinosaurs'.

PROSAUROPODS
(See pages 108 to 112)

Although the prosauropods, as their name implies, lived 'before the sauropods', current theory rejects the once-held notion that the prosauropods were the direct ancestors of the sauropods. Instead, they are now regarded as a side branch of the sauropod family tree. The prosauropods lived in the late Triassic period and are themselves thought to have evolved from theropod-type ancestors – possibly *Staurikosaurus* (see page 66), from the mid-Triassic period, or *Herrerasaurus* (see page 56), from the late Triassic period, both of which were from South America. Scientists drew up a list of prosauropod features in 1990 that included: small, 'saw-edged', leaf-shaped teeth; a jaw that was hinged below the level of the upper teeth; paired pubic bones, which formed a sort of 'apron'; a skull that was half as long as the thigh bone; large, pointed thumb claws; and traces of a very small fifth toe on each foot.

Riojasaurus.

SAUROPODS

Between 200 and 65 million years ago, the largest herbivores – in fact, the largest creatures ever to have lived on land – were the giant, four-legged, long-necked sauropods. In order to support their immense bodies, they evolved some adaptations to their skeletons: firstly, great hollows were carved out of their vertebrae, lightening the load of their enormous bones while maintaining the structural strength, and, secondly, their massive hip girdles were fused to their backbone by four (and later by five) sacral vertebrae to form a solid support for the body and the massive tail.

The *infra*-order of sauropods includes some nine families of these very large quadrupeds, some of which weighed 49,784kg (49 tons) or more, although some of the various family relationships still remain unclear: Vulcanodontidae, Barapasauridae, Cetiosauridae, Brachiosauridae, Titanosauridae, Camarasauridae, Euhelopodidae, Dicraeosauridae and Diplodocidae. The sauropods survived as a group for some 50 million years, evolving during the late Triassic/early Jurassic period and reaching their peak during the late Jurassic period. Like all of the dinosaurs, they were extinct by the end of the Cretaceous period, around 65 million years ago.

FAMILY VULCANODONTIDAE
(See page 113)
While there are a number of distinct sauropod families, there are also a number of less well-known early sauropods, including *Vulcanodon*, which lived 208–144 million years ago in early Jurassic Zimbabwe. This dinosaur probably existed alongside later sauropods, such as cetiosoaurs. The fossil remains are missing skulls, and until more evidemce is found and they are reassigned to another family, *Vulcanodon* are termed part of the family Vulcanodontidae.

Shunosaurus.

FAMILY CETIOSAURIDAE
(See pages 114 to 115)
These early sauropods lived worldwide during the Jurassic period and into the Cretaceous. Their name means 'whale lizard': this relates to their enormous size, not to a marine lifestyle. Members of the cetiosaur family retained two primitive features: their vertebrae were only partially hollowed out, so their body would have been quite considerable; and, their hips were attached to their backbone by only four sacral vertebrae, which was a weaker and less efficient arrangement than in later sauropods.

FAMILY CAMARASAURIDAE

(See pages 118 to 120)

Living in late Jurassic western North America and western Europe, the members of this family of sauropods were somewhat smaller than their relatives, the brachiosaurs and diplodocids: their necks and tails were shorter, their skulls were higher and they had much blunter snouts. The camarasaurids also had different teeth from other sauropods: these were long, forward-pointing and spoon-shaped. This suggests that these sauropods had a different diet to that of the other larger sauropods in the vicinity, so they were not competing for the same food. Less closely related sauropods in this family lived in Asia, in Mongolia, in China and in Thailand, South-east Asia.

FAMILY BRACHIOSAURIDAE

(See pages 116 to 117)

The members of this family were the giants of sauropods: until recent finds, this family could claim *Brachiosaurus* to be the most massive dinosaur ever to have lived, and as the largest animal ever to have walked on Earth. Although now overtaken in the size stakes, they remain a very impressive family. From the mid-Jurassic period to early Cretaceous times, these great herbivores roamed across North America, eastern Africa and Europe. They all shared a similar body structure: small heads perched on top of extra-long necks, deep bodies and shortish tails. These sauropods differed from others as their front legs were longer than their hind legs, so that their bodies sloped downwards from their shoulders, a little like a modern giraffe.

Brachiosaurus.

FAMILY DIPLODOCIDAE

(See pages 121 to 124)

This family of sauropod dinosaurs, the diplodocids, included the most spectacular of all dinosaurs. These had enormously long necks and even longer tails. They also had slender bodies and tiny heads. Despite their great lengths, the diplodocids were actually lightweights among the sauropods because their vertebrae had been reduced to a complex framework of bony struts that saved weight, but were also very strong. The diplodocids ranged across the world during the late Jurassic period and into the Cretaceous period, although the most famous members, *Diplodocus*, *Apatosaurus*, *Barosaurus* and the mighty, 'earth-shaking' *Seismosaurus* all hailed from the western region of the United States of America. The diplodocids take their name (which means 'double beams') from the twin extensions called chevrons in the caudal vertebrae (tail bones) in the middle of their tails.

FAMILY TITANOSAURIDAE
(See pages 125 to 126)

This family of sauropods was the largest, was spread worldwide, especially over the southern continents, and lived right to the end of the 'age of the dinosaurs' at the close of the Cretaceous period (65 MYA). Some 20 different kinds of titanosaurs are known from finds in Europe, Africa, Asia, India and North America, but the most significant finds have been in South America. Named after the mythical giants of Greek legend, not all of the members of this family were, in fact, titanic: most averaged only around 12.2–15.2m (40–50ft), quite small in comparison to the diplodocids and brachiosaurids. So far, only fragmentary remains of titanosaurs have been found, yet it appears that they had a similar structure to *Diplodocus* (see page 122), but had a shorter neck and a high, steeply sloping head. Unlike the diplodocids, however, titanosaurs had solid vertebrae that were not hollowed out to give them a weight-saving advantage. A striking feature, and unique among sauropods, is that on some titanosaurs there is evidence of bony armour on their backs.

FAMILY EUHELOPODIDAE
(See page 127)

This family hails from China, and has about a dozen genera, but because they share similar characteristics with the diplodocids, some palaeontologists attribute some of the dinosaurs in this family to the family Diplodocidae. The 'Chinese sauropods', which include *Euhelopus*, *Omeisaurus* and *Mamenchisaurus*, varied in length from 10m to 26m (33 to 85ft) and lived during the late Jurassic period until the early Cretaceous. The striking feature of this family is that its members appear to have had very, very long necks.

Mamenchisaurus.

FAMILY SEGNOSAURIDAE
(See page 128)

The *infra*-order Segnosauria was named as recently as 1980 for some very strange dinosaurs that were found in south-eastern Mongolia. This family is an unusual group of saurischian dinosaurs whose features include those that are reminiscent of theropods (see page 67), prosauropods (see page 104) and ornithischians (see page 129). Consequently, these dinosaurs are remarkable puzzles: lightly built bipeds, with curious skulls, they may well have been plant-eating theropods. The most unusual feature was the hips, which were untypical of saurischian 'lizard hips' because instead of one pointing backwards and the other forwards, the two bones ran parallel and sloped backwards. Palaeontologists believe that there were three segnosaurs, all discovered in China: *Segnosaurus* ('slow reptile'), an animal called *Erlikosaurus* ('king of the dead [Erlik] reptile') and a third, recently discovered form called *Enigmosaurus* ('enigma reptile'). These three segnosaurs may form part of a group of dinosaurs that lies between the saurischians and the ornithischians.

PLATEOSAURUS

Pronounced: 'PLAT-ee-oh-SORE-us'

This 'flat lizard' is one of the best-known of the larger prosauropods; dozens of skeletons have been found in the Triassic rocks of central Europe, and this also suggests that these dinosaurs may have lived in herds and possibly migrated to avoid droughts. *Plateosaurus* was a large animal – its flexible tail constituted about half of its overall length – and it had a stronger, deeper head than most other prosauropods, while its fairly short neck was also somewhat thinner than usual. Its many small, leaf-shaped teeth and low-slung jaw, which made for greater leverage, suggest that *Plateosaurus* was primarily, if not wholly, herbivorous. Small cheek pouches held the leaves in the mouth as the jaws worked up and down, chopping up the leaves. It would have roamed across the arid plains and semi-desert landscape of central Europe on all fours, sometimes, perhaps, rearing up on its hind legs to feast on various trees, such as the cycads and conifers that were growing at this time.

Plateosaurus had forelimbs with five digits of varying lengths: two short, outer fingers; two longer, middle fingers; and a huge, curving thumb. This large, clawed thumb was partially opposable: it could be moved around, a little like our own thumbs. This was useful since the thumb and its claw were so large that they would have interfered with walking when on all fours. It seems that *Plateosaurus* overcame this problem by being able to turn and lift its thumb clear of the ground. The thumb would also have made a pretty useful weapon for warding off predatory theropods, and along with the rest of the hand, it could also have been used for grasping and pulling down tree branches as *Plateosaurus* stretched and reared up to graze. An unusual feature of *Plateosaurus* – the reason for which is, as yet, unknown – was its very large nasal chamber; perhaps this functioned as a resonating chamber when calling to the rest of the herd or when frightening off predators.

NAME MEANS
'Flat lizard'

TIME
Late Triassic
(248–208 MYA)

LOCATION
Doubs, France;
Baden-Württemberg,
Germany; Aargau,
Switzerland

SIZE
8m (26ft)

WEIGHT
1,524kg (1½ tons)

DIET
Herbivore

RIOJASAURUS

Pronounced: 'ree-O-ah-SORE-us'

NAME MEANS
'La Rioja lizard'

TIME
Late Triassic
(248–108 MYA)

LOCATION
La Rioja, San Juan,
southern Argentina

SIZE
10m (33ft)

WEIGHT
1,016kg (1 ton)

DIET
Herbivore

Named after the Argentinian province of La Rioja, where it was found, *Riojasaurus* was one of the largest prosauropods, and one of the first truly large dinosaurs: it could grow as large as 10m (33ft) long, and some scientists have calculated its weight as high as 5,080kg (5 tons)! Its size alone would have offered it a good deal of protection from attack by carnivorous predators. As the prosauropods grew larger, the great weight of their intestines (plus that of the gastroliths, or stomach stones, that they swallowed to aid the digestion of plant material) in front of their forward-sloping hip bones made them front heavy, and consequently they were forced to live all of the time on all fours in order to support their weight. Accordingly, the skeleton was modified: the limbs were thick, solid and strong and held vertically under the body, while the hips were fused at the backbone by three vertebrae, making for a very solid attachment for the heavy hind legs. To keep weight to a minimum, however, *Riojasaurus'* vertebrae were made lighter by deep hollows. With its elongated and flexible neck, *Riojasaurus* was one of the first land animals to be capable of feeding on vegetation growing high above ground level. Like other prosauropods, *Riojasaurus'* skull was small for the size of its body, and it also shared the leaf-shaped teeth of its European cousin, *Plateosaurus* (see page 108).

ANCHISAURUS

Pronounced: 'AN-ki-SORE-us'

Anchisaurus was the first early dinosaur to be discovered in America, in 1818. At first, it was thought that the incomplete, fossilised remains belonged to a human, but it was identified as a dinosaur in 1885. It was only in 1925, however, that the remains were formally identified as *Anchisaurus*. This 'near lizard' was typical of the small prosauropods, in that it had a small head on a long, flexible neck and a long, slim body. Its head was long and narrow and its skull was relatively flat. Its forearms were shorter than its hind legs by about one-third, and each hand had five fingers, although the two outer fingers were quite short. On the first finger, or thumb, there was a large, curved claw that may have been used for both digging up roots and fighting. Despite its shorter arms, *Anchisaurus* was designed to walk on all fours, but it is possible that it may have been bipedal at least some of the time, or that it occasionally reared up on its hind legs – using its tail to complete a weight-bearing tripod – in order to feed on tree leaves. From track marks left in the Connecticut Valley in eastern North America, it appears that *Anchisaurus* lived in herds, and shared its habitat with harmless ornithischian ('bird–hipped') dinosaurs, as well as some dangerous theropods. It must have been well adapted to the landscape and capable of defending itself with its claws, or perhaps it simply ran away on its hind legs when it faced danger, because living in the Jurassic period, *Anchisaurus* survived long after it seems that most other prosauropods became extinct.

NAME MEANS
'Near lizard'

TIME
Mid-Jurassic
(208–144 MYA)

LOCATION
Connecticut,
Massachusetts, USA;
southern Africa

SIZE
2.4m (8ft)

WEIGHT
27kg (80lb)

DIET
Herbivore

MASSOSPONDYLUS

Pronounced: 'MAS-oh-SPON-die-lus'

NAME MEANS
'Massive vertebrae'

TIME
Late Triassic
(248–208 MYA)

LOCATION
North America: Arizona,
USA; Africa: Quthing,
Lesotho; Matabeleland,
Zimbabwe; Orange Free
State, Transvaal, and Cape
Province, South Africa

SIZE
5m (16ft 6in)

WEIGHT
150kg (330lb)

DIET
Herbivore

Massospondylus was the most common prosauropod in southern Africa. A few large, but broken, vertebrae were sent to England for examination by Sir Richard Owen, who named it 'massive vertebrae' in 1854. New fossils were found later, and now some 80 partial skeletons have allowed scientists to reconstruct *Massospondylus*. The discovery of fossilised remains in North America also point to the widespread distribution of the species – distribution made possible by the fact that the land masses during the time in which it lived were joined together. *Massospondylus* was a medium-sized prosauropod with a particularly tiny head perched on the end of a very long and very flexible neck. Its five-fingered hands were massive, and had a great spread, which they needed to support their weight when they walked, but they may also have been used for grasping food as each thumb had a large, curved claw. While *Massospondylus* probably spent most of its time on all fours, it could have reared up on its hind legs, using its tail as a support. While fossil remains show that in the stomach cavities of some specimens there were gastroliths (stomach stones swallowed to aid digestion by grinding up plant material to pulp), there have also been suggestions that *Massospondylus* was carnivorous. Scientists point to the unusually tall, strong, front teeth, which were ridged (a bit like a steak knife), as well as to the lack of wear, which together suggest that *Massospondylus'* teeth did not meet as they would in a herbivore, which needed them to grind up plants.

VULCANODON

Pronounced: 'vul-KAN-oh-don'

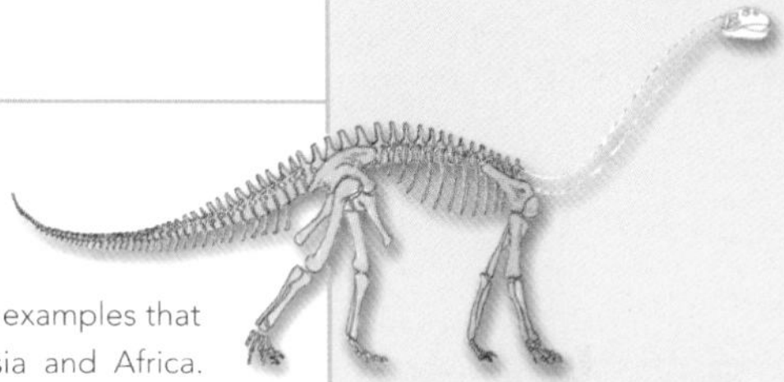

Vulcanodon belongs to the most primitive sauropod family, the Vulcanodontidae, which is composed of early Jurassic examples that measured up to 9m (29ft 6in) long from Europe, Asia and Africa. *Vulcanodon* was found in early Jurassic (208–144 million years ago) rocks in Zimbabwe, southern Africa, and is one of the earliest sauropod dinosaurs to be discovered to date.

Although the skeleton first described in 1972, and then later in 1984, is incomplete, it is apparent that *Vulcanodon* was a very large, quadrupedal, saurischian dinosaur. It had sauropod-like limbs, but whether it was a large prosauropod or a true sauropod is still hotly debated because *Vulcanodon* demonstrated some of the more primitive prosauropod features, especially in its hips, yet its vertebrae were beginning to develop along the lines expected of the sauropods.

NAME MEANS
'Volcano tooth'

TIME
Early Jurassic
(208–144 MYA)

LOCATION
Zimbabwe,
southern Africa

SIZE
6.5m (21ft)

WEIGHT
3,556–4,572kg
(3½–4½ tons)

DIET
Herbivore

NAME MEANS
'Whale lizard'

TIME
Mid-Jurassic
(208–144 MYA)

LOCATION
England; Beni Mellal,
Morocco, North Africa

SIZE
Up to 18.3m (60ft) long

WEIGHT
27,026kg (26.6 tons)

DIET
Herbivore

CETIOSAURUS

Pronounced: 'See-tee-oh-SORE-us'

During the 1830s, when the first sauropod bones were discovered in Oxfordshire, England, they were identified by Georges Cuvier as whale bones. However, by the early 1840s, Richard Owen recognised that the remains were less likely to be whales (which are mammals) and more possibly to be a whale-like lizard – a whale-sized crocodile, perhaps – and he coined the name *Cetiosaurus,* or 'whale lizard'. When more bones were discovered in 1848 and 1869 (a near-complete skeleton), scientist Thomas Henry Huxley recognised that *Cetiosaurus* was actually a land-living reptile.

Cetiosaurus was a massively built sauropod, but with a shorter neck and tail and much sturdier forelimbs than usual among sauropods The backbone was a solid mass, since the vertebrae were hardly hollowed out at all. A near-complete skeleton unearthed in Morocco in 1979 revealed the true size of the animal: the thigh bone was a massive 1.8m (6ft) long – as tall as a man – and one of the shoulder blades measured over 1.5m (5ft) in length. Its stiff neck stuck straight out, and its weight was counterbalanced by its raised tail. For a long time it was thought that *Cetiosaurus* was a tree-top browser, but, in fact, it could not raise its head much above shoulder height, although it could lower it to drink and swing it in an arc about 3m (10ft) across to crop ferns and small, bushy trees. Judging by its enormous bones, *Cetiosaurus* must have consumed an incredible amount of food each day to maintain its weight and to power its limbs.

SHUNOSAURUS

Pronounced: 'SHOON-oh-SORE-us'

Shunosaurus, or 'Shou lizard', was a mid-Jurassic sauropod from China, where there have been more than 20 discoveries of near-complete skeletons. This makes *Shunosaurus* one of the best-known sauropods, and only the second to be known in its entirety. These finds have revealed that this early sauropod already showed the basic characteristics of small head, long neck and tail, deep body and pillar-like legs, although these features were not yet fully developed. *Shunosaurus* had a relatively short neck and tail and had fewer vertebrae fused to its hip bones to support its body, while its spinal vertebrae were not yet hollowed out to reduce the weight.

Shunosaurus had only 12 neck vertebrae and 13 spinal vertebrae, four vertebrae fused to its hip bones and 44 tail bones. Later, larger sauropods would have nearly twice as many tail bones. The most surprising feature of *Shunosaurus*, however, is the fact that it had a small, bony club at the end of its tail, which was formed by enlarged vertebrae that had fused together. This means that *Shunosaurus* may have used its tail as a defensive weapon.

NAME MEANS
'Shou lizard'

TIME
Mid-Jurassic
(208–144 MYA)

LOCATION
China

SIZE
10m (33ft)

WEIGHT
10,160kg (10 tons)

DIET
Herbivore

BRACHIOSAURUS

Pronounced: 'brak-ee-oh-SORE-us'

The first *Brachiosaurus* bone to be discovered was found in 1900, by Elmer S Riggs, at the Grand River Valley, western Colorado, USA. One of largest, longest and heaviest of all dinosaurs, *Brachiosaurus* is also one of the best known as complete skeletons exist, except for the neural arches of the vertebrae at the base of its long neck. Its relatively slim, yet pillar-like, front legs were proportionally longer than the hind legs. The humerus (upper arm bone) averaged 2.1m (7ft) and gave the 'arm lizard' its name, and its shoulders were about 6.5m (21ft) from the ground. This gave *Brachiosaurus* a giraffe-like stance, and, when combined with its long neck, it is estimated that it could reach heights of up to 16m (50ft), enabling it to feed on leaves and branches high above the ground. Plant material was bitten off with 26 chisel-like teeth on each jaw, located towards the front of the mouth. It appears that plant matter was swallowed whole and digested with the aid of gastroliths (stomach stones) in its gizzard and gut.

The weight of the relatively small, oddly shaped and high-domed skull was reduced by replacing solid bone with a framework of light, bony struts that framed the orbits (eye sockets) and the nasal openings, which were placed above the eyes on the large bulge of the skull dome. This arrangement allowed *Brachiosaurus* to breathe while it ate, without getting leaves up its nose. Behind the eyes lay a tiny brain case: its brain was no more than 100,000th the weight of its whole body.

NAME MEANS
'Arm lizard'

TIME
Late Jurassic to mid-Cretaceous (153–113 MYA)

LOCATION
North America: Colorado, Utah, Wyoming; Europe: Estremadura, Portugal; Africa: Wargla (Algeria)

SIZE
25m (82ft)

WEIGHT
Up to 49,784kg (49 tons)

DIET
Herbivore

A scaffolding-like framework of bones supported the body: 13 neck bones (each elongated to 3 times the length of the dorsal vertebrae); 11 or 12 dorsal (back) vertebrae; and 5 vertebrae fused at the hips. To reduce weight, great hollows were scooped from the sides of each vertebra to leave a structures that was anchor-shaped in cross section and made of thin sheets and struts of bone. Each vertebra was angled and articulated to give optimum strength along the line of stress. By contrast, the thick-walled limb bones were immensely heavy, and the feet all had five toes, with fleshy pads behind. The first toe on each front foot bore a claw, while on the hind feet, the first three toes were also clawed.

CAMARASAURUS

Pronounced: 'kam-are-ah-SORE-us'

NAME MEANS
'Chambered lizard'

TIME
Late Jurassic
(203–135 MYA)

LOCATION
North America: Colorado,
Utah, Wyoming, USA;
Europe: Estremadura,
Portugal

SIZE
18m (59ft)

WEIGHT
19,812kg (19½ tons)

DIET
Herbivore

Camarasaurus, or 'chambered lizard', is possibly the best-known North American sauropod, with the most complete fossil skeletons. Furthermore, fossil remains have included juvenile specimens and the first fossilised embryo of a sauropod dinosaur ever found. *Camarasaurus* was named in 1877 by Edward Drinker Cope, and was called 'chambered lizard' on account of the roomy hollows in its backbone, which helped to limit the mighty weight of this sauropod. *Camarasaurus* had a high skull that was short from front to back, with bony struts surrounding window-like openings. The naris (nostril sockets) opened in front of very large eye sockets (orbits), and below each eye socket was a skull hole called the 'infra-temporal fenestra', from which the muscles that worked the jaw bulged. The large size of the fenestrae suggests that *Camarasaurus* had highly developed senses of sight and smell. The jaw bones themselves were very sturdy and housed deeply rooted, spoon-shaped teeth that would have been able to deal with fibrous plant material like horsetails and ferns.

Its vertebrae included 12 short neck bones, with long, straight, cervical (neck) ribs that overlapped those behind to stiffen the neck; 12 deeply hollowed dorsal (back) bones; five sacral bones fused to the hip bones; and 53 chevron-shaped, caudal (tail) bones. The chevrons guarded the blood vessel that ran under the cores of the vertebrae, and the long, lower prong on each chevron provided a site for the attachment of muscles. The front legs were relatively long and ended in stubby toes with sharp thumb claws, while the shorter hind legs had three clawed toes.

Because the remains of juveniles have been found with adult *Camarasaurus* in the same sequence of rock – the Morrison Formation in the western USA – it is likely that *Camarasaurus* travelled in herds, perhaps on migrations to new feeding grounds.

OPISTHOCOELICAUDIA

Pronounced: 'oh-PIS-thoh-SEEL-i-KOW-dee-a'

NAME MEANS
'Tail vertebrae
cupped behind'
(aka: 'posterior tail cavity')

TIME
Late Cretaceous
(135–165 MYA)

LOCATION
Mongolia, Asia

SIZE
12m (39ft)

WEIGHT
Unknown

DIET
Herbivore

The exact size and appearance of this tongue-twistingly named sauropod can only be guessed at since the one skeleton unearthed in the Gobi Desert of Mongolia, China, in 1965, is missing the neck and head. The rest of the body was fortunately well preserved, and scientists have been able to see that *Opisthocoelicaudia* was similar to the other non-brachiosaurid sauropods in its general shape and proportions and appeared to be a typical, though relatively small and more streamlined, camarasaur. The heavy, pillar-like legs supported a bulky body, the shoulders were quite high and the tail was held straight out. The curious feature of this creature – and what gives it its name – is that at the front end of each caudal (tail) vertebra, there is a large, hemispherical dome that fits into a deep cup or socket at the rear of the preceding vertebra. This arrangement makes the joints between each vertebra extremely strong. Furthermore, it was noted that the spines of the tail vertebrae were exceptionally roughened and enlarged in order that powerful muscles and ligaments could be attached. Why exactly *Opisthocoelicaudia* needed such a powerful, rigid tail is a mystery. Some palaeontologists have suggested that the tail may have been used as a body prop – a sort of third leg – to steady the creature as it raised itself up on its hind legs to feed off the upper leaves of trees.

APATOSAURUS (once known as *Brontosaurus*)

Pronounced: 'ah-PAT-oh-sore-us'

Many people know *Apatosaurus* ('deceptive lizard') by its old name of *Brontosaurus* ('thunder lizard', on account of the noise that its heavy footfalls would probably have made). The name was changed when it was discovered that *Brontosaurus* fossils were identical to the earlier named *Apatosaurus*. The body of this giant herbivore, which roamed across western America, was well known to scientists, for it had been discovered and described in 1877 by Edward Drinker Cope. But *Apatosaurus*' head was a mystery. Many assumed that it had a boxy skull like *Camarasaurus* (see page 118), but when a skull was finally discovered in 1975, it was realised that this creature was a giant sauropod, with the tiniest of long, low heads, only a mere 55cm (22in) long out of a total body length of over 20m (65ft)! While not as long overall as *Diplodocus* (see page 122), *Apatosaurus* was certainly weightier as its cervical (neck) vertebrae and limb bones were thicker and heavier. Both creatures shared the same body shape – the longer hind legs and shorter front legs – and had the same long, slender teeth at the front of their jaws. Both animals could rise up on their hind legs to reach into the tallest branches for leaves, but *Apatosaurus* had a longer tail than *Diplodocus*: no fewer than 82 interlocking vertebrae (as compared to *Diplodocus*' 70 or so caudal vertebrae) made up the tail, which ended in a

whiplash. Current thinking suggests that *Apatosaurus* did not drag its tail along the ground, but held it clear. This would have meant that other *Apatosaurs* wouldn't have stepped on it, and that predatory theropods would have been less able to grab it by its tail.

NAME MEANS
'Deceptive lizard'

TIME
Late Jurassic
(203–135 MYA)

LOCATION
Colorado, Oklahoma,
Utah, Wyoming, USA

SIZE
Up to 21.3m (70ft) long

WEIGHT
24,384kg (24 tons)

DIET
Herbivore

NAME MEANS
'Double beam'

TIME
Late Jurassic
(203–135 MYA)

LOCATION
Colorado, Utah,
Wyoming, USA

SIZE
27m (89ft)

WEIGHT
11,938kg (11¾ tons)

DIET
Herbivore

DIPLODOCUS

Pronounced: 'di-PLOH-de-kus'

Resembling a suspension bridge, the longest complete skeleton ever found belonged to *Diplodocus*, a massive sauropod whose length, on average, was greater than that of a tennis court. Most of this length was accounted for by the long neck (around 7.3m/24ft long) and the extra long tail (about 14m/46ft long) as the body was, on average, only around 4m (13ft) long, and the tiny head was a miniscule (proportionally, in dinosaur terms) 60cm (24in) long. In spite of these mighty measurements, *Diplodocus* weighed in, on average, at a mere 9,652–11,938kg (9½–11¾ tons), about one-eighth the weight of *Brachiosaurus* (see page 120). This was because *Diplodocus* had a particularly lightweight framework of vertebrae that were hollowed out to form huge cavities. The bony areas and struts that remained were, however, strong enough to bear the body weight of this large creature.

The name *Diplodocus* means 'double beam', which refers to the pair of anvil-shaped bones or skids that grew from the underside of each vertebra in the middle section of the tail. These extensions may have protected the delicate blood vessels and nerves that ran through the tail when it was pressed on the ground. The tail itself was made up of at least 70 (and perhaps as many as 80) vertebrae, the first 19 of which were lightened with cavities. Towards the tip of the tail, the vertebrae diminished into simple, rod-like bones that supported the whiplash tail tip. *Diplodocus'* pillar-like hind limbs rested on five-toed feet, which were supported by fibrous heels, and only the first three toes were clawed. The hind legs were longer than the front legs, as was usual for the sauropods (brachiosaurs excepting), and the body sloped downwards from the hips. The forelegs had only one clawed toe on each foot. For some time, it was thought that *Diplodocus* had three toes on the fore foot: this was because of the casts made from a well-preserved, but incomplete, skeleton found in Wyoming during a dig financed by American steel magnate Andrew Carnegie

in 1899. The bones of the feet of *Diplodocus* were missing, so the casts were constructed using feet modelled by the three clawed toes of *Camarasaurus* (see page 118), which was also living in Wyoming at the same time. A total of eight casts were made, and sent to museums worldwide, before the error was discovered. The casts presented by Carnegie also showed *Diplodocus* with its tail dragging along the ground. Modern interpretations, which are based on evidence provided by fossilised footprints and tracks that don't show the drag marks of a tail, show *Diplodocus* with its tail held well clear of the ground.

NAME MEANS
'Heavy lizard'

TIME
Late Jurassic
(203–135 MYA)

LOCATION
North America: South
Dakota, Utah, USA; Africa:
Mtwara, Tanzania

SIZE
23–27m (75–89ft)

WEIGHT
19,812kg (19½ tons)

DIET
Herbivore

BAROSAURUS

Pronounced: 'bar-oh-SORE-us'

The immensely long 'heavy lizard' had all the typical features of its family: a bulky body that stood highest at the hips, relatively short legs for its size, a long neck and tail and, it is assumed, a tiny head, although since Orthniel Marsh named *Barosaurus* in 1890, no skull has yet been discovered. Where *Diplodocus* (see page 122) had a very long tail, *Barosaurus* had a very long neck – it was one-third longer than *Diplodocus'* neck and constituted one-third of its overall length. Although both dinosaurs had the same number (15) of cervical vertebrae (neck bones), each of *Barosaurus'* neck bones were stretched, and up to 1m (3ft 3in) long. Each of these cervical vertebrae bore long, strut-like ribs to support them, but the vertebrae were also hollowed out to make them lighter in weight. Without this weight reduction, there was no way that *Barosaurus* would have been able to project its head and neck 9m (30ft) beyond its shoulders. This makes *Barosaurus* one of the tallest North American dinosaurs, whose head, if it reared up on its hind legs, would have towered a remarkable 15m (49ft) above the ground. Like its missing head, the structure of *Barosaurus'* tail tip is a palaeontological mystery. The known tail bones suggest that, like *Diplodocus*, *Barosaurus* had a whiplash tail that would have had to have been long enough to counterbalance its long neck.

SEISMOSAURUS

Pronounced: 'SIZE-moh-SORE-us'

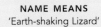

From the sole specimen found to date in New Mexico in 1986, and described in 1991 by David Gillete, *Seismosaurus*, the 'earth-shaking lizard', appears to have been the longest dinosaur and one of the largest animals ever to have walked on Earth. Measuring around 36m (120ft) long, and with weight estimates varying between a mere 33,528kg (33 tons) and an incredible 101,600kg (100 tons), a few palaeontologists consider *Seismosaurus* to be an 'aged *Diplodocus*'. While they share the same overall proportions and body structure, *Seismosaurus* seems to have had longer forelegs than *Diplodocus*. In spite of *Seismosaurus'* enormous size, it was very lightly built and had relatively short legs. As its extremely long neck would have required a very high blood pressure to maintain the flow of oxygen to the brain, it is possible that, in fact, *Seismosaurus* did not often raise its head up to its highest extent, but instead contented itself with browsing for food at relatively low levels.

The late Jurassic rocks in which this monster was found have yielded even larger creatures, including the aptly – though not officially – named *Supersaurus,* from western Colorado, whose remains were found in 1972.

NAME MEANS
'Earth-shaking Lizard'

TIME
Late Jurassic
(203–135 MYA)

LOCATION
New Mexico, USA

SIZE
36m (120ft) long

WEIGHT
101,600kg (100 tons)

DIET
Herbivore

SALTASAURUS

Pronounced: 'sal-ta-SORE-us'

The incomplete remains of this medium-sized sauropod were found in Argentina's north-western Salta Province in 1970, and these consisted of a group of partial skeletons surrounded by thousands of bony plates. For some time, it was believed that these bony lumps were the remains of armoured ornithischian dinosaurs (see page 129), but in 1980, analysis of fossilised skin proved that *Saltasaurus* did, indeed, have armour. Furthermore, it had two types! Close-packed, pea-sized lumps served to toughen the skin, while fist-sized, bony plates were arranged along its back and flanks. These larger plates may also have terminated in a bony spike. That this South American sauropod had body armour suggests that the continent could have been separate from the great land mass that included North America and Eurasia in the mid-Cretaceous period, with present-day Central America under water and forming a barrier between north and south. Sauropods in South America would then have developed in isolation and subject to different evolutionary forces. *Saltasaurus* had shortish, sturdy limbs and a flexible, whiplash tail. In its neck, a single, bony spine rose from each cervical vertebra (neck bone), while its hip girdle featured an extra vertebra. The tail vertebrae were articulated with ball-and-socket joints. These would have strengthened the tail, and perhaps allowed *Saltasaurus* to prop itself up when rearing on its hind legs to browse on higher branches; the bony neck tendons suggest that *Saltasaurus* was not particularly able to lift its small head much above shoulder height.

MAMENCHISAURUS

Pronounced: 'mah-men-chee-SORE-us'

With the longest neck of any dinosaur by far, *Mamenchisaurus* also had more cervical vertebrae (neck bones) than any other sauropod. There were 19 cervical vertebrae, each more than twice the length of the dorsal (back) vertebrae, so that *Mamenchisaurs'* neck constituted more than half of its overall length. These cervical vertebrae were, however, in parts very thin and lightweight, and to support this great neck, each had two rod-like ribs or bony struts that overlapped the vertebrae. While these struts would have offered support, they would also have stiffened the neck, restricting movement between the head and uppermost neck bones so that *Mamenchisaurus* would not have been able to hold its head much above shoulder height. The forelimbs were relatively long and, like the hind limbs, very sturdy. Like *Diplodocus*, *Mamenchisaurus'* tail chevron bones bore front and back extensions, and likewise, its tail may have ended in a whiplash. Because *Mamenchisaurus* is missing its skull, palaeontologists often reconstruct it wearing the head (and teeth) of *Diplodocus*. It is possible, however, that *Mamenchisaurus'* head was more like that of its Chinese relative, *Euhelopus* ('good marsh foot'), which was shorter- and deeper-snouted, with larger teeth that grew from the sides of the jaws, as well as at the front of the mouth.

NAME MEANS
'Mamenxi
[Mamen Brook] lizard'

TIME
Late Jurassic
(203–135 MYA)

LOCATION
China: Sichuan, Gansu
and Xinjiang

SIZE
22m (72ft)

WEIGHT
19,304kg (19 tons)

DIET
Herbivore

SEGNOSAURUS

Pronounced: 'SEG-noh-SORE-us'

NAME MEANS
'Slow lizard'

TIME
Late Cretaceous
(135–65 MYA)

LOCATION
Mongolia, China

SIZE
6m (19ft 6in)

WEIGHT
1,016kg (1 ton)

DIET
Probably herbivore

The first segnosaur remains came to light in 1979, following the Soviet–Monglian expedition. Segnosaurus was the first of the three forms to be identified, and was reconstructed from a partial skeleton that included a lower jaw (but no skull), parts of the legs and backbone and a complete pelvis. Several other fragments, including a forelimb, were later found in the area of late Cretaceous rocks known as the Bayn Shireh Horizon, in south-eastern Mongolia. The first thing that struck palaeontologists was the pelvis, which was unusual for a saurischian ('lizard-hipped') dinosaur: the arrangement of bones was more like those found in ornithischian ('bird-hipped') dinosaurs. The second striking thing about *Segnosaurus* was its jaw: unusually, for a supposed theropod, the front part of its jaw was toothless, and the teeth at the rear of the mouth were small and pointed, rather than being like serrated daggers. It appears that the front end of the jaw was probably covered in a horny beak. The forelimbs were short, and ended in three clawed fingers, while the hind limbs ended in a short, broad, four-toed foot. In theropods, the feet are usually quite slender and bunched together. At around 6–7m (20–23ft) long, the limbs – its thighs were longer than its shins – suggest that *Segnosaurus* was capable only of a brisk walk or slow run. This implies that *Segnosaurus* was unlikely to have been a predatory carnivore, but was able to use its strong forearms and claws to dig at the earth, perhaps clawing at termite nests and anthills. The limited amount of fossil evidence so far means that the exact appearance and lifestyle of *Segnosaurus* remain a mystery. If, and when, more remains are discovered, scientists will be able to build up a much fuller picture of this extraordinary creature.

CHAPTER 7
ORNITHISCHIAN DINOSAURS

Members of the ornithischian ('bird-hipped') order of dinosaurs were exclusively herbivores – the other great order, the saurischian ('lizard-hipped') dinosaurs, as we have seen, had members that were both herbivore and carnivore. The ornithischian dinosaurs can be recognised by several features: the bird-like pelvis (from which the group takes its name); a peculiar, horn-covered, predentary bone at the tip of the lower jaw; a trellis-like arrangement of long, bony tendons along the backbone; and, in most, but not all, ornithischians, a strange bone called the palpebral in the eye cavity.

The ornithischian dinosaurs can be divided further into distinct types, or suborders: suborder Ornithopoda; suborder Thyreophora (which includes the *infra*-orders Stegosauria and Ankylosauria); and suborder Marginocephalia (which includes the *infra*-orders Ceratopsia and Pachycephalosauria).

SUB-ORDER ORNITHOPODA

Ornithopods, or 'bird feet', walked on two feet and may well have been the ancestral group from which all of the other ornithischian ('bird-hipped') dinosaurs evolved. As a suborder, they were a diverse group of animals in terms of their size, lifestyle and distribution, but structurally, they were all similar. They were also a highly successful group: they survived for nearly 150 million years and spanned the whole of the Jurassic (203–135 MYA) and Cretaceous (135–65 MYA) periods.

Heterodontosaurus.

The *sub*-order of Ornithopoda comprised a number of families: Fabrosauridae (these earliest-known ornithopods looked superficially like the small, carnivorous theropod dinosaurs, the coelurosaurs, and one specimen, called *Fabrosaurus*, may, in fact, be the same as *Lesothosaurus*, see page 62); Heterodontosauridae; Hypsilophodontidae; Iguanodontidae; and Hadrosauridae (which is further divided into two groups, the hadrosaurines and lambeosaurines).

FAMILY HETERODONTOSAURIDAE
(See page 137)

Members of this family of ornithopods, the heterodontosaurs, were small and lizard-like in appearance, but ran upright on their long, slender, rear legs. What distinguishes this family is their dental arrangement, which is unique among dinosaurs – and, indeed, among most other reptiles. Heterodontosaurs were the first dinosaurs to have developed cheeks that kept their food inside their mouths. They also had three kinds of teeth – hence their name of 'varied-toothed lizards' – each performing a different function.

FAMILY HYPSILOPHODONTIDAE
(See page 138)

Among the most successful of the dinosaurs, the hypsilophodonts flourished as a group for about 100 million years, from the late Jurassic to the end of the Cretaceous period 65 million years ago, and were widespread across the world, except in Asia. They are an important family in the evolution of dinosaurs as palaeontologists believe that they gave rise to two other major groups of ornithopods: the iguanodonts (see page 131) and the 'duck-billed' hadrosaurs (see page 131).

Hypsilophodon.

Although they were structurally similar to the fabrosaurs, even the primitive hypsilophodonts had developed the retaining cheeks that stopped their food from falling out of their mouths. Furthermore, their upper and lower teeth occluded (met) in regular rows, rather than interlocking alternately. But it was their hips that were significant, and more advanced than those of fabrosaurs: part of the pubis bone projected forwards and provided an extra area to which the leg muscles could be attached, which gave extra running power to the hypsilophodonts.

FAMILY IGUANODONTIDAE
(See pages 139 to 141)
This family of large, herbivorous ornithopods is named after its most famous member, *Iguanodon*. The iguanodonts evolved in the mid-Jurassic period (203–135 MYA) and spread worldwide: fossilised remains have even been found in what is now the Arctic Circle, although these lands would have been ice-free when the iguanodonts roamed the Earth some 170 million years ago. Scientists suspect that the ancestors of the iguanodonts were the hypsilophodonts (see above), but unlike them, iguanodonts did not evolve as running animals: their bodies were bigger and bulkier, their femurs (thigh bones) were longer than their tibias (shin bones) and both their fore- and hind feet had heavy, hoof-like nails. These features suggest that iguanodonts were slow-moving, quadrupedal browsers of low-growing plants.

Ouranosaurus.

FAMILY HADROSAURIDAE
(See pages 142 to 147)
The largest ornithopod family was the Hadrosauridae, the 'duck-billed' dinosaurs, and although preyed upon by carnivorous theropods, they were also some of the biggest dinosaurs. Probably evolving in central Asia, by the late Cretaceous period, the Hadrosauridae dominated as herbivores in most parts of the northern hemisphere, migrating eastwards into Europe and across the land bridge that existed at the time into North America. The southern land mass of Gondwanaland had, by this time, broken up, and the continents were drifting apart. While no hadrosaurids have been found in Africa, India or Australia, some managed to reach South America, probably crossing from the north via the chain of volcanic islands that existed where Central America is now.

Hadrosaurus.

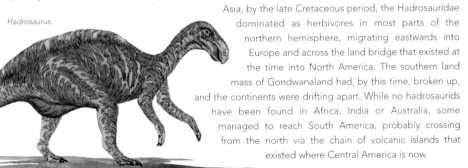

As their name suggests, the hadrosaurids had a wide, expanded mouth packed with hundreds of teeth arranged in batteries on both the upper and lower jaws, with new teeth continuously replacing old or broken ones. This was a unique development in dinosaurs, which, no doubt, contributed to their success.

HADROSAURINES AND LAMBEOSAURINES

Superficially, hadrosaurids looked quite different: there were many variations in the crests and bumps on their heads, and consequently hadrosaurids are divided into two distinct subfamilies. Some animals had flat heads crowned with solid, bony crests, others had no crest at all. These are the hadrosaurines (see pages 142–47). The second subfamily had high-domed heads topped by quite magnificent, hollow crests. This subfamily is the lambeosaurines (see pages 148–54) and appears to have evolved in, and been largely confined to, North America. Hadrosaurids – 'duck-billed' dinosaurs – with hollow head crests are known as lambeosaurs. Their head crests, which varied in size and shape between species and individuals, appear to be linked to gender and maturity, although some theories propose that they also functioned as snorkels and air tanks, allowing the lambeosaurines to feed under water, as sites for salt glands, as foliage detectors and as signalling devices. The crests were hollow structures, with a complex series of tubes inside, and were connected to the noses and throats of the lambeosaurines, so it is possible that the crests were used as resonating devices, with each shape creating a different sound. The lambeosaurines seem to have been particularly widespread in the Cretaceous period across North America.

SUB-ORDER THYREOPHORA

Corythosaurus.

Thyreophorans, whose name means 'shield-bearers', were a diverse group of heavy-limbed, mainly quadrupedal and armoured ornithischian dinosaurs. They were distinguished by their rows of protective, bony scutes (bony studs, with a horny outer covering embedded into the skin), plates or spikes running along their backs. These dinosaurs are considered to have been more primitive ornithischians than ornithopods or marginocephalians on account of their small cheek teeth and jaw formations. The most primitive thyreophorans were from the early Jurassic period, and these were relatively small – around 4m- (13ft-) long animals – such as *Scelidosaurus* (see page 159), with the more developed species being grouped into two *infra*-orders or families: Stegosauria and Ankylosauria.

INFRA-ORDER STEGOSAURIA

Stegosaurus.

(See pages 155 to 158)

All of the familiar stegosaurs, including the famous *Stegosaurus*, belong to this *infra*-order. They evolved in Asia during the mid-Jurassic period, some 170 million years ago, and reached their peak of diversity by the end of the Jurassic period. Stegosaurs were widespread throughout North America, western Europe, east Africa and eastern Asia. By the early Cretaceous period, the stegosaurs had started to decline, although some species appeared to have survived in isolated pockets, such as in India, until the end of the Cretaceous period, and the end of the 'age of the dinosaurs' around 65 million years ago. Like their ornithopod relatives, stegosaurs were herbivores and probably lived in herds. Unlike the more agile ornithopods, though, stegosaurs were exclusively quadrupedal, and were unable to rise up on their hind legs. The stegosaurs were medium- to large-sized creatures with toothless beaks, and most had long, thick, pillar-like hind limbs: this meant that their back was arched and was highest over the hips. The most distinctive features, however, were the two rows of tall, bony plates and/or spikes that stood up along the back and ran from head to tail, and at least two pairs of tail spikes. A large area in the hip region – once mistaken for a second brain, helped to control the tail and hind legs. In addition to this armour, some stegosaurs were equipped with shoulder spikes.

INFRA-ORDER ANKYLOSAURIA

Ankylosaurs ('fused' or 'joined-together lizards') were the tanks of the dinosaur era. They were low-slung dinosaurs, with broad heads, rather short necks and heavy, barrel-shaped bodies carried on four sturdy limbs, with fairly long and muscular tails. Instead of tall plates of spines, these ornithischians were armoured with bands of bony studs or plates, some of which were sheathed in horn. These covered the neck, flanks and backs and, in some specimens, the belly. They are known chiefly from fossil finds in North America and Asia, but discoveries in Australia show that they also spread to the southern continents, replacing the stegosaurs by the early Cretaceous period. The ankylosaurs are divided into two subfamilies: Nodosauridae and Anklosauridae. The nodosaurs were the more primitive ankylosaurs, lived from the middle Jurassic to late Cretaceous times and occurred in Asia, Australia, Europe and North America. The ankylosaurs flourished from early to late Cretaceous times in Asia and North America.

In a 'family' of its own, but placed here alongside the ankylosaurs, are the Scelidosauridae. Some maintain that these early thyreophorans were primitive members of the Ankylosauridae; others maintain that they were the ancestors of the stegosaurs.

Scelidosaurus.

FAMILY SCELIDOSAURIDAE
(See page 159)
The scelidosaur family of primitive, quadrupedal herbivores ranged from heavily armoured dinosaurs to more lightly built creatures equipped for running, varying in size from 1 to 4.5m (3¼ to 14¾ft) long. They lived in the late Triassic to early Jurassic periods, possibly inhabiting wet, marshy areas.

FAMILY NODOSAURIDAE
(See pages 160 to 165)
The nodosaurs ('node [or lumpy] lizards') were the earlier, and more primitive, of the two families of ankylosaurs. Their skulls had an unusual, hourglass-shaped palate, and the skull overall was longer than it was wide. Solid, bony plates covered the body from neck to tail, and while nodosaurs did not have a tail club, long spikes guarded the flanks. Nodosaur remains are generally poorly preserved, and consequently, their whole family tree and relationships are subject to debate.

FAMILY ANKYLOSAURIDAE
(See pages 166 to 167)
Like the nodosaurs, the ankylosaurs were heavily built, quadrupedal herbivores. They were also armoured, but additionally had a 'club' of solid bone at the end of their tails. The ankylosaurs also differed from the nodosaurs in the shape of their skulls: where the nodosaurs had narrow skulls, ankylosaurs had broad skulls, at least as broad as they were long, with pointed 'corners', or 'horns', at the back and an intricate pattern of breathing passages. Ankylosaurs flourished from the early to the late Cretaceous period (135–65 MYA) and roamed Asia and North America. They ranged in size from 3 to 10m (10 to 33ft) in length, with massive, boned hips that were fused to the backbone by at least eight sacral vertebrae to form an extremely strong anchor for the hindquarters.

Nodosaurus.

SUB-ORDER MARGINOCEPHALIA

The Marginocephalia ('margined heads') were a suborder of the ornithischian ('bird-hipped') dinosaurs: herbivorous and bipedal/quadrupedal, the Marginocephalia had a narrow shelf, or deep, bony frill, at the back of their skulls. They were also distinguished by the structure of their hip bones: they had no obturator process (a projection on the ischium) and no symphysis (the cartilaginous joining of the bones) between the pubic bones. The earliest marginocephalians were late Jurassic bipeds with a small skull ridge, but the later, late Cretaceous marginocephalians included the huge, horned quadrupeds, with large, bony, skull frills. The marginocephalians are divided into two *infra*-orders: Pachycephalosauria and Ceratopsia.

INFRA-ORDER PACHYCEPHALOSAURIA

(See pages 168 to 172)

The 'thick-headed lizards' ranged in size from very small to large, bipedal herbivores that evolved thickened skulls: the skull roof was up to 25cm (10in) thick. Some, like the homalocephalidae (the 'even-headed'), were flat-headed pachycephalosaurs from late Cretaceous east Asia, while others developed high, domed skulls. Some species also had bony frills, knobs and even spikes on the backs and sides of their heads, and sometimes on their snouts. Rows of bony tendons stiffened the middle sections of their tails, and primitive ornithischian features included teeth at the front of the jaw and small, leaf-shaped cheek teeth. In many other respects, pachycephalosaurs were like other ornithopods: bipedal herbivores, with five-fingered hands and three-toed feet (with a tiny hallux, or first toe).

Stegoceras.

INFRA-ORDER CERATOPSIA

The second *infra*-order of the marginocephalians is the *infra*-order Ceratopsia. These 'horned faces' were bipedal and quadrupedal, ornithischian dinosaurs, and the *infra*-order includes all of the horned dinosaurs. It was one of the shortest-lived groups of dinosaurs as most lived during the late Cretaceous period in the last part of the 'age of the dinosaurs', which ended around 65 million years ago. Yet they were numerous, with many species arising, although they were confined to the northern continents of North America and Asia.

The *infra*-order contains two primitive families – Protoceratopidae and Psittacosauridae – and a larger, more advanced, family, the Ceratopidae, which some palaeontologists divide further into 'short-frilled' ceratopids and 'long-frilled' ceratopids as the long-frilled forms appear to be more advanced and occurred right at the end of the 'age of the dinosaurs'.

FAMILY PROTOCERATOPIDAE
(See page 173)

The protoceratopids, or 'first horned faces', include some eight genera of bipedal and quadrupedal herbivores, which ranged in size from 1m (3ft 3in) to 3m (10ft) in length. They constitute the early, primitive, horned dinosaurs – although only some of them had horns – and all had a bony frill at the back of the skull; some had bumps above the brow and nose. Smaller than their later relatives, they had teeth in their upper beak, which is considered a primitive feature. They arose in late Cretaceous times and occurred in central and eastern Asia and spread to western North America.

FAMILY PSITTACOSAURIDAE
(See pages 174 to 175)

The forms of ceratopians in this family represent an early evolutionary state. This rare group of 'parrot lizards' were bipedal herbivores, with an old-fashioned, ornithischian body, similar to hypsilophodonts (see page 130), but with a highly evolved skull that suggests that they were the ancestors of the ceratopians. The snout was deeper than those of other ornithischians, and formed a narrow beak, with high nostril holes. The family Psittacosauridae comprised only one known genus, *Psittacosaurus*, of which there were four known species living in the early Cretaceous period (135–65 MYA) in central, eastern and South-east Asia.

Triceratops.

FAMILY CERATOPIDAE
(See pages 176 to 183)

The most numerous, large herbivores of the late Cretaceous period, confined solely to western North America, were the 18 named genera of great horned dinosaurs of this family. Rhinoceros-like herbivores up to 9m (29ft 6in) long, some (the Chasmosaurinae) bore deep, shelf-like, bony, skull frills and great horns on their brows, while others (the Centrosaurinae) had shorter neck frills, with horns on their snouts. Exclusively quadrupedal, pillar-like legs, with heavy, hoofed feet, supported stocky bodies covered in a thick, protective hide.

HETERODONTOSAURUS

Pronounced: 'HET-er-oh-DONT-oh-SORE-us'

In 1962, in Cape Province, in South Africa, the rabbit-sized skull of *Heterodontosaurus* was discovered. Typical plant-eating dinosaurs had a toothless beak and cheek teeth, which were all one type and designed for grinding up plants. *Heterodontosaurus* amazed palaeontologists because it had three distinct types of teeth – a dental pattern that was reminiscent of a mammal, even though this dinosaur had no connection with the mammalian line of evolution. At the front of the upper jaw were some small, pointed teeth (like a mammal's incisors). There were no opposing teeth at the front of the lower jaw, but instead the chin bone had a horny beak. This bone is called the predentary bone, and is unique to ornithischian dinosaurs. Behind the upper teeth and the lower beak there were two pairs of large, canine-type teeth, or 'tusks', with the lower pair fitting into a socket in the upper jaw. Behind these canines were tall, chisel-like back teeth, with cutting edges. The pointed front teeth were used to snip and nip off leaves and greenery from trees, while the back teeth were used to cut up the leaves with a scissors-like motion and grind them into small pieces. But what the two pairs of canine-type 'tusks' were used for is a mystery, except, perhaps, for fighting other males, since it seems from other skulls found that the female *Heterodontosaurus* may have lacked these particular teeth. Living in the early Jurassic semi-desert regions of southern Africa, fossil remains show that *Heterodontosaurus* was about the size of a large turkey and had sturdy arms bearing five clawed fingers. Each foot had one short toe and three longer, forward-facing, clawed toes. The rear legs were more than a third longer than the arms, and the tibia (shin bone) was a third longer than the femur (thigh bone), making it capable of running at some speed. As it ran, its tail would have waggled, as this was not stiffened with bony tendons, as was the case with later ornithopods.

NAME MEANS
'Varied-toothed lizard'

TIME
Early Jurassic
(203–135 MYA)

LOCATION
Africa: Cape Province,
South Africa; Quthing,
Lesotho

SIZE
1.2m (4ft)

WEIGHT
2.5kg (5½lb)

DIET
Herbivore

137

HYPSILOPHODON

Pronounced: 'hip-sih-LOH-foh-don'

NAME MEANS
'High-ridge tooth'

TIME
Mid-Cretaceous
(135–65 MYA)

LOCATION
Europe: East Sussex,
Isle of Wight, England;
Teruel, Spain;
North America:
South Dakota, USA

SIZE
2.3m (7ft 6in)

WEIGHT
68kg (150lb)

DIET
Herbivore

Hypsilophodon was an ornithischian ('bird-hipped') dinosaur whose name means 'high-ridged tooth'. It was first discovered in 1849 on the Isle of Wight, off England's south coast, but experts at the time believed that it was an *Iguanodon* (see page 140). Later finds examined by Thomas Huxley in 1870 revealed *Hypsilophodon's* distinctive teeth, and a new dinosaur genus was named – except that Huxley conceived it as a tree-dwelling, plant-eating ornithopod! It was not until 1974 that palaeontologists agreed that there was no evidence to suggest that it lived in a tree, but that it was, in fact, perfectly adapted to life on the ground. *Hypsilophodon's* small head had a horny beak and large eyes. In its mouth, its jaws were lined with 28 or 30 tall, grooved and self-sharpening cheek teeth, and there were incisor-like teeth on the front of the upper jaw. The upper and lower teeth met to form a flat surface for grinding up vegetable matter. *Hypsilophodon* has been described as a 'browsing sprinter'; it had very strong, mobile jaws and cheek pouches for storing food, and longer tibias (shin bones) than femurs (thigh bones). Unlike more advanced ornithopods (the four-fingered and three-toed hadrosaurs), the primitive *Hypsilophodon* had five fingered hands and four forward-facing toes. The fifth toe was tiny, and the fourth toe itself was too short to reach the ground. The legs appear to have swung backwards and forwards very quickly; in motion, the head and neck were counterbalanced by the long, tapering tail, which was stiffened by rows of bony tendons and was unlikely to have touched the ground unless *Hypsilophodon* was resting or sleeping. Since it was first discovered, the remains of more than 20 *Hypsilophodon* have been found in the Isle of Wight alone. Some of these remains lay close together, suggesting that *Hypsilophodon* lived in herds.

OURANOSAURUS

Pronounced: 'OO-ran-oh-SORE-us'

Ouranosaurus shared many characteristics with its famous relative, *Iguanodon*, including longer hind limbs that were stronger than the forelimbs, hoof-like claws on the toes and the fingers, thumbs armed with smaller – though equally vicious – spikes and leaf-shaped teeth, with high-ridged crowns. But *Ouranosaurus* also had some very distinctive features of its own: a flat-topped skull, with a low bump over its eyes, a hadrosaur- (duck-billed-) like beak and a bony skin 'sail' held aloft by blades jutting from its backbone. The very tall back spines were unique among ornithischians, and the sail's purpose is, as yet, unknown. If the males had taller sails than females, these may have been part of mating rituals, either to attract a mate or to scare off rivals for a female's affections. The sail may also have served as a temperature regulator as it was made of skin and blood vessels must have flowed through it. *Ouronosaurus* (like the carnivorous *Spinosaurus,* see page 73, which also had a back sail and came from the same, arid region) may have angled its spine towards, or away from, the sun, either to heat up or cool down its body. The structure of *Ouronosaurus'* hand suggests that it rested, and perhaps ambled, on all fours: the wrist bones were very strong, and although the three middle fingers were hoofed and could not grasp objects, they could be stretched out or bent back to form weight-bearing feet if it went down all all fours. To run – perhaps from dangerous predators like *Spinosaurus* – the adults would have reared up on their hind legs. It appears, however, from fossilised remains, that juveniles were bipedal until mature as their forelimbs were substantially shorter.

NAME MEANS
'Brave monitor lizard'

TIME
Mid-Cretaceous
(135–65 MYA)

LOCATION
Africa: Agadez,
north-eastern Niger

SIZE
7m (23ft)

WEIGHT
3,048kg (3 tons)

DIET
Herbivore

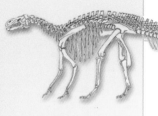

NAME MEANS
'Iguana tooth'

TIME
Early Cretaceous
(135–65 MYA)

LOCATION
North America:
South Dakota, USA;
Europe: south-east
England; Hainault,
Belgium;
Nordrhein–Westfalen,
Germany; Castellon,
Cuenca
and Teruel, Spain

SIZE
9m (29ft 6in)

WEIGHT
4,064kg (4 tons)

DIET
Herbivore

IGUANODON

Pronounced: 'ig-WHA-noh-don'

Iguanodon was the second dinosaur to be discovered, although then, in 1809, the word 'dinosaur' hadn't been invented! Part of its shin bone was found in southern England in 1809, and in 1819, some teeth and further bones were found. Scientists of the day thought that the creature was some great mammal, but Gideon Mantell recognised the teeth as being more reptilian, and as resembling the teeth of the modern iguana of Central and South America. In 1825, Mantell described and named *Iguanodon* and, using the rather sparse information that he had, he attempted a reconstruction. Mantell's *Iguanodon* was a four-legged beast, with a heavy tail and small, lizard-like head, with a short horn on it. This horn was, in fact, an *Iguanodon* thumb claw. It was only in 1877 that the true nature of *Iguanodon* became clear, when 31 skeletons were found in Bernissart, Belgium, by coalminers.

Originally believed to have been primarily quadrupedal, *Iguanodon* is now thought to have been capable of bipedal walking as its legs were thick and sturdy and its forelimbs were considerably thinner and shorter. Since *Iguanodon* was first discovered, scientists have found its fossilised footprints in the rocks of southern England: these show that when *Iguanodon* passed by, it was walking upright. Similar footprints, although no bones, have also been found as far away as South America and in Spitzbergen, to the north of the Arctic Circle, which demonstrate just how widespread the iguanodonts were.

The rear legs were pillar-like, with three stout toes ending in heavy, hoof-like nails. Each arm had a five-fingered hand: the middle three fingers on each hand had hoof-like nails and were joined by a pad of skin, while the fifth finger could be curled to grasp food. Meanwhile, the thumb was armed with a sharp spike, which stuck out sideways from the hand. The head of this great creature ended in a prominent snout and powerful, beak-like jaws. The cheek teeth needed to be especially strong because the bones in the upper jaw were hinged and could move apart when the lower jaw was raised up between them: the banks of cheek teeth then moved past each other, grinding up the plant matter.

NAME MEANS
'Big/sturdy lizard'

TIME
Late Cretaceous
(135–65 MYA)

LOCATION
North America:
New Jersey, Montana,
New Mexico, South
Dakota, USA

SIZE
Up to 10m (33ft)

WEIGHT
6,604kg (6½ tons)

DIET
Herbivore

HADROSAURUS

Pronounced: 'HAD-roh-SORE-us'

Hadrosaurus, meaning 'big' or 'sturdy lizard', has the distinction of being the first dinosaur ever to be discovered in North America. Its bones were found in New Jersey, and were reconstructed and named by Joseph Leidy in 1858. Leidy recognised that *Hadrosaurus* was structurally related to *Iguanodon* (see page 140), whose remains had been found earlier (in 1825) in England. But unlike the quadruped described by Mantell, Leidy also recognised that although *Hadrosaurus* would have spent much of its time browsing on all fours, it could rear up to be bipedal as its forelimbs were much shorter than its hind legs. It probably used its tail, held outstretched to balance it as it walked. *Hadrosaurus* was typical of the duck-billed dinosaurs: its tough, horny bill (used for snipping off vegetation) at the front of the jaw had no teeth, but at the back of the jaw, there were ranks of hundreds of teeth for chewing vegetation, each tooth replaced by a new one as it wore out. *Hadrosaurus* had no head crest; it did, however, have a large bump on its snout, which was made of bone and was probably covered with tough, thick skin.

EDMONTOSAURUS

Pronounced: 'ed-MONT-toh-SORE-us'

Many skulls of this large, flat-headed hadrosaur have been found that display many hundreds of teeth packing the jaws behind the beak to make an effective grinding machine. It is estimated that at any one time, *Edmontosaurus* had over 1,000 teeth, each with an outer edge coated with hard enamel that wore away more slowly than the rest of the tooth. The result: a tooth with a cutting edge of hard enamel, ideal for cutting through tough vegetation. The jaw structure of *Edmontosaurus* was like that of *Iguanodon*: the upper jaw could move over the lower jaw so that the teeth ground against each other when the jaw was closed. *Edmontosaurus* was a large dinosaur – one of the largest hadrosaurs – up to 13m (43ft) long, with long, strong, pillar-like hind legs and a long tail to balance the weight of the front of the body, flexible neck and short front limbs. The fleshy pads between the digits (fingers) gave *Edmontosaurus* the hadrosaurid's paddle-like hands, while claws on the first two fingers were large and hoof-like. A trellis of bony tendons attached to the vertebral spines of the back tied the bones together so that the body didn't sag on either side of the pelvic girdle. While it was crestless, many palaeontologists believe that *Edmontosaurus* was equipped with an inflatable sac on its nose that it could use to make a noise with, perhaps making distinctive, bellowing calls to members of its family or group, in the same manner that elephant seals do today.

NAME MEANS
'Edmonton lizard'

TIME
Late Cretaceous
(135–65 MYA)

LOCATION
North America:
Alberta, Canada;
Montana, USA

SIZE
10–13m (33–43ft)

WEIGHT
3,962–4,572kg
(3.9–4.5 tons)

DIET
Herbivore

ANATOSAURUS

Pronounced: 'AN-at-oh-SORE-us'

NAME MEANS
'Duck lizard'

TIME
Late Cretaceous
(135–65 MYA)

LOCATION
North America:
Alberta, Canada

SIZE
10m (33ft)

WEIGHT
3,962kg (3.9 tons)

DIET
Herbivore

Anatosaurus was a relatively common hadrosaur, and it is one of the best-known crestless forms. The popular name for the hadrosaurids, 'duck-billed dinosaurs', was coined after the discovery of the broad, flat skull of this creature in Alberta, Canada. The name *Anatosaurus* itself means 'duck lizard', and refers to the creature's horny beak or bill. Several, well-preserved skeletons of *Anatosaurus* have been found, and palaeontologists have been able to deduce that it was some 9–10m (30–33ft) long and stood around 4m (13ft) tall. It was also closely related to *Edmontosaurus* and to another North American hadrosaur, *Anatotitan* (so closely related that some scientists suggest that all three should be referred to as *Anatosaurus*), although *Anatosaurus* appears to have been distinguished by its skull shape and extremely long snout. A great deal of information was provided by the discovery of two mummified specimens, complete with dried-up tendons and intact stomach contents, including their last meals of pine needles, twigs, seeds and fruits. Also preserved were impressions of the skin, showing that it was covered in a thick, leathery hide and that it had webs of skin between the three main fingers on each hand. At first, these webs appeared to give substance to the notion that hadrosaurs were aquatic animals that used their hands and flattened tails as paddles for swimming. Closer examination showed that the skin could not stretch particularly wide, and that these webs were more likely to be the remains of shrivelled-up fleshy pads used for walking on, a little like the fleshy walking pads on camels' feet. The 'pad theory' also ties in with the fact that *Apatosaurus* had hoof-like nails on two of the main fingers of each hand. *Apatosaurus* was, then, a land-dweller that walked on all fours.

KRITOSAURUS

Pronounced: 'KRITE-oh-SORE-us'

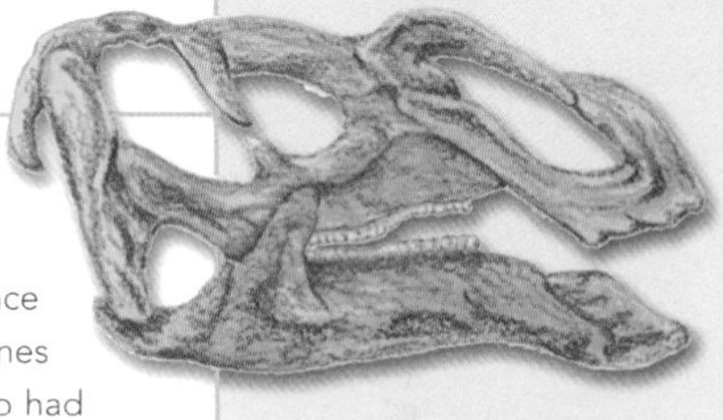

In addition to the main distinguishing feature marking the difference between hadrosaurines (non-crested hadrosaurs) and lambeosaurines (crested hadrosaurs), which was on their heads, the hadrosaurines also had broad, duck-like beaks and quite large nostrils. There was also a less obvious difference, though: the pelvis of crested hadrosaurs had a large, plate-like extension on the front pelvic bone (pubis), and the rear pelvic bone (ischium) was wide and shaped at the lower end like a hook. A medium-sized, crestless hadrosaurid, *Kritosaurus* was in many respects similar to *Hadrosaurus* (see page 142), but while it had no crest, there was the beginning of one in the form of a large, bony hump on the snout in front of the eyes. The function of the hump is unknown; it is possible that only the males had one, and that it was used in courtship and mating. Alternatively, the thickened, bony hump may have served the same purpose as the thickened skulls of the pachycephalosaurs (see page 135): to absorb the impact during head-butting contests between males at the start of the mating season. It is also possible that *Kritosaurus* and *Hadrosaurus* were, in fact, two species of the same animal.

NAME MEANS
'Chosen lizard'

TIME
Late Cretaceous
(135–65 MYA)

LOCATION
North America: Alberta,
Canada; Montana,
New Mexico, USA

SIZE
9m (30ft)

WEIGHT
4,572kg (4½ tons)

DIET
Herbivore

MAIASAURA

Pronounced: 'MY-ah-Sore-ah'

NAME MEANS
'Good earth-mother lizard'

TIME
Late Cretaceous
(135–65 MYA)

LOCATION
Montana, USA

SIZE
9m (30ft)

WEIGHT
4,572kg (4½ tons)

DIET
Herbivore

Maiasaura, whose name means 'good earth-mother lizard', is one of the most important recent dinosaur discoveries. In 1978, a skeleton of an adult was found in Montana by John Horner and Robert Makela, complete with her nest and young. It seems that scientists had found the remains of a dinosaur nursery some 75 million years old. The adult – the mother, presumably – was about 9m (30ft) long, and several youngsters were around 1m (3ft 3in) long. Their presence suggests that young *Maiasaura* remained with their parents for some time to be looked after. There was also a group of hatchlings each about 50cm (20in) long, together in their fossilised nest, while further nests revealed intact eggs and broken eggshells where the young had hatched.

The nests themselves had been made of scooped-up mud (now fossilised into solid rock), and were about 3m (10ft) in diameter and 1.5m (5ft) high, with a crater-like depression in the centre of the mound about 2m (6ft 6in) across and 75cm (2ft 6in) deep. The spacing between each nest was about 7m (23ft); given the size of the adults, the nests were placed quite close together. The fossilised, sausage-shaped eggs found in the nests had been laid and arranged with great care in circles in the crater depression, layer upon layer, possibly with each layer carefully covered with sand to keep it safe and warm, and then finally covered with earth.

With its broad, duck-billed beak and rows of self-sharpening teeth, *Maiasaura* was also a typical hadrosaurid. It had no hollow crest on its long, rather horse-like, head, but instead had a solid hump above its eyes and triangular projections on its cheekbones.

LAMBEOSAURUS

Pronounced: 'LAMB-ee-oh-SORE-us'

NAME MEANS
'Lambe's lizard'

TIME
Late Cretaceous
(135–65 MYA)

LOCATION
North America: Montana,
USA; Alberta, Canada;
Baja California, Mexico

SIZE
15m (49ft)

WEIGHT
3,810kg (3¾ tons)

DIET
Herbivore

Named in honour of Lawrence Lambe (1863–1918), the pioneering Canadian fossil hunter, *Lambeosaurus* was discovered in 1913 by Charles H Sternberg. It was a large, sturdy hadrosaurid (duck-billed dinosaur), with a head crest often compared to a hatchet. In fact, *Lambeosaurus'* head was quite unique, in that it had two head structures: the tall, hollow hatchet-shaped crest leaning over the snout, and a tall, solid and backwards-pointing spike of bone behind it. The nostrils ran up from the snout and through the crest, which may have supported a flap of skin that ran down the head, back and tail. Some of the specimens found had larger crests than others: in some, the crest was larger than the skull, and it was first assumed that these were different species. It now appears that they may, in fact, have been males, females and juveniles of the same species. *Lambeosaurus* was a large hadrosaurid, about 15m (49ft) long, with massive bones. The Baja California, Mexico, specimen, however, seems to have been a giant at around 16.5m (54ft) long, making it one of the largest hadrosaurs known. Like other members of its family, *Lambeosaurus* had a deep, narrow tail formed by tall, vertebral spines and chevrons that made the tail stiff and immobile. It also moved around on all fours, browsing for plant food, using its flexible neck to reach around a wide area without it having to shift its whole body into a new position.

SAUROLOPHUS

Pronounced: 'Sore-oh-LOAF-us'

Saurolophus was an advanced, crested, duck-billed dinosaur that is known from several skeletons, ranging in size from 9 to 12m (29ft 6in to 40ft) long. The Asian species had a larger crest than its North American relative, and a correspondingly larger body. The face of this large, duck-billed dinosaur swept up in a graceful curve from a broad, rather flattened, and much shorter snout than that of other hadrosaurids, to the tip of a solid, bony, horn-like crest that sloped backwards from the top of its head. The solid crest implies that *Saurolophus* was a hadrosaurine (a duck-billed dinosaur with a solid crest) rather than a lambeosaurine (a duck-billed dinosaur with a hollow crest). The crest was an extension of the nasal bones, and in *Saurolophus,* the nasal passages would have run through it. *Saurolophus,* then, would have been an intermediate between the two subfamilies. Some palaeontologists think that there may have been a mass of nasal tissue that could have been inflated to produce a honking noise through the nose, and so the bony crests would

NAME MEANS
'Ridged lizard'

TIME
Late Cretaceous
(135–65 MYA)

LOCATION
North America: Alberta, Canada; California, USA; Asia: Mongolia

SIZE
9–12m (29ft 6in–40ft)

WEIGHT
3,556–5,080kg
(3½–5 tons)

DIET
Herbivore

have acted as supports for the inflatable skin sac. Because hadrosaurids were herd-dwellers, communicating with each other, and signalling alarm, was vital to their survival.

149

CORYTHOSAURUS

Pronounced: 'koh-rith-oh-SORE-us'

NAME MEANS
'Helmet lizard'

TIME
Late Cretaceous
(135–65 MYA)

LOCATION
North America; Montana,
USA; Alberta, Canada

SIZE
10m (33ft)

WEIGHT
3,556kg (3½ tons)

DIET
Herbivore

One of North America's best-known hadrosaurids (duck-billed dinosaurs), thanks to a complete skeleton found in 1912, 'helmet lizard' was named for its huge, hollow, bony, head crest, which rose steeply from just in front of its eyes into a narrow fan shape, or, as some describe it, half a dinner plate, about 30cm (1ft) high, that curved down to the back of the head. However, not all *Corythosaurus* had such well-developed crests: according to extensive research by Dr Peter Dodson, of the University of Pennsylvania, the size and shape of the head crests are related to the sex and maturity of the *Corythosaurus*. Before this was established, there were seven species, where now only one is recognised. While the actual function of the crest is still a mystery, Dodson's work has given us a major insight into the growth and development of hadrosaurids and the sexual dimorphism of the species. The domed crest was made up of expanded nasal bones: the hollows inside the crest were the actual nasal passages, which ran up into the crest and then looped downwards, into the duck-billed snout. The most likely function of the crest, beyond distinguishing males and females, is that the tubular cavities inside the crest operated as a resonator, allowing *Corythosaurus* to produce distinctive sounds and calls.

Like other hadrosaurids, *Corythosaurus* was a land-dweller, browsing in low-growing vegetation and spending most of its time on all fours, although it could walk on its two hind legs alone. Living in the warm plains between the Rocky Mountains and the vast, inland sea that, in the late Cretaceous period, divided North America into western and eastern halves, *Corythosaurus* lived in herds, browsing through the pine forests, fern prairies and coastal marshes. If threatened by hungry, carnivorous theropods, *Corythosaurus* may even have sought to escape by wading into shallow water.

PARASAUROLOPHUS

Pronounced: 'par-a-SORE-oh-loaf-us'

NAME MEANS
'Beside *Saurolophus*'

TIME
Late Cretaceous
(135–65 MYA)

LOCATION
North America: Alberta,
Canada; New Mexico
and Utah, USA

SIZE
10m (33ft) long

WEIGHT
3,556kg (3½ tons)

DIET
Herbivore

Like *Saurolophus* (see page 149), this lambeosaurine had a shorter snout than other hadrosaurids, but is distinguished largely by the magnificent single, backward-pointing, horn-like crest on top of its head. The crest was a hollow tube (unlike the solid crest of *Saurolophus*), and could be as long as 1.8m (6ft). The shape and size of the crest seem to have been dependent on sex and maturity, with males apparently having the largest crests, and there may also have been a brightly coloured frill of skin joining the crest to the neck. Inside the crest was a pair of nasal passages that ran from the nostrils right up to the tip of the crest and then curved back down to the snout. In the backbone of *Parasaurolophus,* there was a unique notch, just behind the shoulders, where the tip of the crest would abut the back of the neck when the animal held its neck and head in an 'S'-shaped position. Some palaeontologists suggest that *Parasaurolophus* held its crest into its neck when it moved through dense forest growth, deflecting branches from its head and body. *Parasaurolophus* also had a very deep tail, which, some researchers suggest, was brightly patterned and was used, along with the neck frill, as a signalling device, for social recognition and perhaps during courtship to attract a female.

HYPACROSAURUS

Pronounced: 'HIGH-pak-roh-SORE-us'

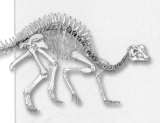

Hypacrosaurus was another hadrosaurid (duck-billed dinosaur) with a semi-circular head crest. The crest was similar to that of *Corythosaurus* (see page 150), but it was not as tall or narrow, and it did not rise as steeply from its face. Instead, *Hypacrosaurus'* crest sloped gently upwards. *Hypacrosaurus* remains were found in rock deposits that postdate those of *Corythosaurus,* and some palaeontologists have suggested that the 'high-spine lizard' in fact evolved from this species. Although they were both similar-sized duck-bills, *Hypocrasaurus* differs in that it had dorsal vertebrae (back bones) that were extended upwards, into tall spines, which formed a prominent, skin-covered ridge along its back, giving it its name. This 'skin sail' may have been a heat-exchange mechanism used to regulate body temperature. By angling the 'sail' towards, or away from, the sun, *Hypocrasaurus* could have warmed up or cooled down its body. A similar method appears to have been used by the carnivorous *Spinosaurus* (see page 73), in what is now northern Africa.

NAME MEANS
'High-spine lizard'

TIME
Late Cretaceous
(135–65 MYA)

LOCATION
North America: Alberta,
Canada; Montana, USA

SIZE
9m (29ft 6in) long

WEIGHT
4,064kg (4 tons)

DIET
Herbivore

TSINTAOSAURUS

Pronounced: 'ching-dow-sore-us'

NAME MEANS
'Tsintao lizard'

TIME
Late Cretaceous
(135–65 MYA)

LOCATION
Asia: China

SIZE
10m (33ft)

WEIGHT
4,572kg (4½ tons)

DIET
Herbivore

Tsintaosaurus was one of the most unusual crested hadrosaurs: its crest pointed forwards, rather like the horn of the mythical unicorn. The tall, hollow tube of bone pointed straight up from between its eyes; the tip was expanded and notched; and there was a connection between the base of the tube and the nostrils. These features have led some palaeontologists to suggest that *Tsintaosaurus* had a flap of skin attached to its horn, or perhaps stretched between the tip of the horn and its beak. The flap may have been inflatable, like a balloon, and may have been used as a signalling device to call to other members of the herd or to attract a female in the mating season. Other palaeontologists believe that the remains of *Tsintaosaurus* that were found in China (the skull and skeleton), suggest that it was related to *Saurolophus* (see page 149), and that the 'horn' has been reconstructed facing the wrong way. This is quite possible as both *Saurolophus* (as well as being found in North America) and *Tsintaosaurus* remains have been found in China. While the sea barrier that separated the southern continent of Gondwanaland (South America, Africa, India, Australia and Antarctica) from the northern continent of Laurasia in the mid-Cretaceous period may have impeded the hadrosaurids from spreading from their northern area of origin southwards (except, perhaps, via an island chain running through what is now Central America), they were able to spread across the northern continents because the Turgai Sea (which separated Europe and North America on one side from Asia on the other) was shallow, and although they were land-dwellers, the hadrosaurids could certainly swim, especially across shallow water.

KENTROSAURUS

Pronounced: 'KEN-troh-SORE-us'

Kentrosaurus is an east African contemporary of *Stegosaurus* (see page 156), whose remains were found in Tendaguru, Tanzania. Up to 5m (16ft) long, *Kentrosaurus* had a long, narrow head, which it held low when walking and browsing for food, and its jaws were equipped with small cheek teeth. It appears likely that *Kentrosaurus* fed on the low-growing ferns and shrubby vegetation that grew in the moist soil alongside the prehistoric riverbanks of eastern Africa. While it was smaller than its American relative, *Kentrosaurus* was equally well armoured, and its pattern of plates and spikes was quite distinctive. A double row of narrow, triangular, bony plates rose from either side of the backbone, and were grouped in pairs along the neck, shoulders and front part of the back. At the middle of the back, these flat plates were replaced by five pairs of sharp spikes, some as long as 60cm (2ft), and these continued down the back and tail. In addition, there was a pair of extra-long spikes that stuck out at hip level on each side and pointed diagonally backwards. The arrangement of these spikes suggests that *Kentrosaurus* may have been able to rush backwards at predators in the same way that modern porcupines do. The flexible tail could have been swung from side to side to lash out at predators. *Kentrosaurus'* tail structure was unusual in that in most stegosaurs, the caudal neural spines (the high, narrow tops of tail vertebrae) slope backwards (towards the tip of the tail); in *Kentrosaurus*, after caudal vertebrae number 18, the neural spines slope forwards, towards the base of the tail.

NAME MEANS
'Spiky lizard'

TIME
Late Jurassic
(203–135 MYA)

LOCATION
Tanzania, Africa

SIZE
5m (16ft)

WEIGHT
1,524kg (1½ tons)

DIET
Herbivore

STEGOSAURUS

Pronounced: 'STEG-oh-SORE-us'

NAME MEANS
'Roof lizard'

TIME
Late Jurassic
(203–135 MYA)

LOCATION
North America: Colorado,
Oklahoma, Utah,
Wyoming, USA

SIZE
Up to 9m (30ft)

WEIGHT
2,032–2,540kg
(2–2½ tons)

DIET
Herbivore

The largest, and most familiar, of the stegosaurs, *Stegosaurus* had massive hind legs and heavy hooves that were over twice the length of their forelimbs. This was unusual in a four-legged animal, since it meant that the body sloped forwards from the highest point at the hips. Tall spines projected from the vertebrae of the hips and tail and probably acted as anchor points for the immensely strong back muscles. *Stegosaurus* had a long, narrow head that was very small in relation to its size – about 40cm (16in) long – and housed a brain about the size of a walnut. To compensate for the small brain, a large cavity in the hip vertebrae above the hind legs, where the spinal cord would have passed, held a mass of nerve tissues controlling the rear legs and tail. All vertebrates (backboned animals) have this so-called 'second brain', but its size related to the size of the animal's hips: in big-hipped animals, such as dinosaurs, this 'brain' was often larger than the one in their skulls.

Stegosaurus had a toothless beak at the front of its jaws and small cheek teeth. Consequently, in order to digest tough plant matter, *Stegosaurus* probably made use of gastroliths, small stones that it swallowed to help to grind up the food in its gizzard and stomach. The most recognisable feature of *Stegosaurus* is undoubtedly its body armour: a double row of broad, bony plates, covered in tough horn and shaped like huge arrowheads, some over 60cm (2ft) high, were embedded in the skin on its back. Since none of these plates have been found attached to a skeleton, some palaeontologists maintain that the plates were arranged to lie flat in, or on, the skin – like a tiled roof – to form a protective layer. The commonly held belief, however, is that the plates were arranged vertically to form a 'fence' down either side of the backbone, from just behind the head to halfway along the tail. This arrangement has suggested to some palaeontologists that the plates may not have been for defence, but may have been covered in a blood-rich skin and may have been used as heat-exchange mechanisms, warming up or cooling down the stegosaur by angling the plates towards, or away from, the sun. The heavy tail itself was armoured with pairs of spikes, each about 1m (3ft 3in) long. The number of pairs of spikes, and the size, varied from species to species: *S. ungulatus* had four pairs, while *S. stenops* had only two pairs. The spikes were probably used for defence, with the heavy tail being swung from side to side to ward off attacks from hungry, carnivorous theropods.

TUOJIANGOSAURUS

Pronounced: 'too-hwang-oh-SORE-us'

NAME MEANS
'Tuo river lizard'

TIME
Late Jurassic
(203–135 MYA)

LOCATION
Sichuan, China

SIZE
7m (23ft)

WEIGHT
1,016kg (1 ton)

DIET
Herbivore

The Chinese 'Tou river lizard' is one of several armoured dinosaurs found in China, and the first to be discovered in Asia. Known from an almost complete skeleton, *Tuojiangosaurus* was smaller than *Stegosaurus* (see page 156), averaging 6–7m (18–23ft), although structurally similar, with a small, narrow head, low-ridged teeth and a heavy, humped-back body. Up to 15 pairs of bony plates surmounted its back, neck and tail, becoming taller and more spine like over the hips and down the tail. As in *Stegosaurus,* two pairs of long, slim spikes stuck up from the end of the tail, and a long spine jutted out from each shoulder. Unlike *Stegosaurus,* though, *Tuojiangosaurus* appears not to have been able to rear up on its hind legs: the tail spines that projected upwards from the back vertebrae of *Stegosaurus,* providing muscle attachment points, are absent in *Tuojiangosaurus* – and in *Kentrosaurus* (see page 155) as well – which suggests that these were exclusively quadrupedal animals. Holding its head low, *Tuojiangosaurus* browsed on ferns and cycads, which grew in the rich river valley soil of southern China, cropping the vegetation with its horny beak and chewing it with its small, ridged teeth.

SCELIDOSAURUS

Pronounced: 'skel-IDE-oh-SORE-us'

Until the discovery of *Heterodontosaurus* (see page 137) in 1962, *Scelidosaurus* was the earliest-known ornithischian dinosaur. Remains of *Scelidosaurus* discovered in Dorset, southern England, in 1859, were first described by Richard Owen, and again by him in 1863, following the discovery of an almost complete skeleton. A third discovery was made as recently as 1985, by a group of amateur fossil hunters in Charmouth, Dorset, which added greatly to the knowledge of this dinosaur. One of the most primitive ornithischian dinosaurs, *Scelidosaurus* was about the size of a small car and had a long, heavy body, with pillar-like hind legs longer than the forelegs – although *Scelidosaurus* was quadrupedal – and broad, four-toed feet designed for bearing its body weight. Its flanks were covered with parallel rows of bony studs, while along the neck, spine and top of the stiffened tail was a row of bony spikes (the underside of the tail was covered with bony studs). This arrangement of body armour has led some palaeontologists to suggest that *Scelidosaurus* was a primitive type of ankylosaur (see page 133). The head was small and pointed, and behind the neck was a pair of triple-spiked, bony plates. Inside the mouth were small and simple, leaf-shaped teeth, extending right down to the tip of the snout. At the front of the upper jaw were six small, conical teeth, so if there was a horny beak, it was very small. The less complex jaw and teeth arrangement meant that this dinosaur would have chewed its food using a simple, up-and-down jaw motion.

NAME MEANS
'Lower-hind-limb lizard'

TIME
Early Jurassic
(203–135 MYA)

LOCATION
Europe: Dorset,
England; North America:
Arizona, USA

SIZE
4m (13ft)

WEIGHT
250kg (550lb)

DIET
Herbivore

POLACANTHUS

Pronounced: 'pol-a-KAN-thus'

NAME MEANS
'Many spikes'

TIME
Early Cretaceous
(132–112 MYA)

LOCATION
Europe: Isle of Wight,
England; North America:
South Dakota, USA

SIZE
4m (13ft)

WEIGHT
2,032kg (2 tons)

DIET
Herbivore

Polacanthus was discovered in 1865 by the Reverend William Fox on the Isle of Wight, just off the south coast of England. The skeleton consisted of the hind parts of the animal, including various spines, back and tail vertebrae, hips and hind legs. It appears that the front part of the skeleton was lost after being washed out to sea following a cliff fall that exposed the rear end. Consequently, the 'reconstruction' of *Polacanthus* is a matter of conjecture and debate. This debate is heightened by the fact that living at the same time in England as *Polacanthus* was another nodosaur, *Hylaeosaurus* ('woodland lizard'), which had been discovered in 1833 in the Tilgate Forest area of Sussex, also on England's south coast. Of this nodosaur, we have remains of the front end. The front and back parts of these two animals do not overlap, so it is impossible to compare the two skeletons directly to prove conclusively that they belonged to the same, or to different, animals. Furthermore, because the spines of *Polacanthus* were founded scattered near the remains of the skeleton, even their position is a matter of guesswork. It is presumed that the long, dorsal (back) spines arranged in pairs may have formed a protective frill around the sides of the body to protect the flanks and legs. While a shield of fused bone covered the hips, two lines of smaller, vertical spines ran down to the tip of the deep, heavy tail.

SAUROPELTA

Pronounced: 'SORE-oh-PEL-ta'

Sauropelta was the earliest, and most primitive, member of the nodosaur family to live in what is now North America. It is also the largest-known member of the family, estimated to have weighed around 2,540kg (2½ tons). Its massive body was encased in bony armour consisting of bands of horn-covered plates, with raised keels or studs – which were elongated into spines – that ran transversely over the body from the neck to the end of the long, tapering tail that did not have a tail club. The plates were embedded in the skin to form a strong, but flexible, covering over the animal's back. As a slow-moving herbivore – its heavy, pillar-like legs and blunt claws would not have been capable of much more than a slow trot, and then only for a short distance – *Sauropelta* needed such protection against attack from predatory carnivores like *Deinonychus* and *Struthiomimus,* against whom its best defence was simply to stand its ground, or better still, 'lie' its ground: by lying down, *Sauropelta* would have guarded its most vulnerable parts (the lower flanks and underbelly). The structure of *Sauropelta*'s forelimb bones suggests that it had very strong shoulder muscles, which may have allowed it to bend its elbows more easily than other nodosaurs.

NAME MEANS
'Shielded lizard'

TIME
Early to mid-Cretaceous
(135–65 MYA)

LOCATION
North America: Montana,
Wyoming, USA

SIZE
7.6m (25ft)

WEIGHT
2,540kg (2½ tons)

DIET
Herbivore

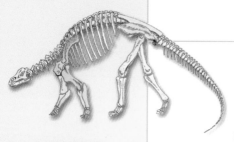

NODOSAURUS

Pronounced: 'No-doh-SORE-us'

The typical nodosaur, and the one that gave its name to the whole family, *Nodosaurus* was first mentioned by Marsh in 1889, but was only described in some detail in 1921, by Richard Lull, on the basis of partial remains. However, a later, and more unusual, find in Kansas consisted of several skeletons, all supine (lying on their backs), that were found in marine sediments dating from the late Cretaceous period. It is possible that this was a small herd of *Nodosaurus* whose members died at the same time, their bodies then being washed towards the prehistoric sea. As they were swept down river, the weight of their body armour would have made them top heavy, and they would have flipped over, on to their backs, before eventually sinking into the mud of the sea bed, belly side up.

Nodosaurus' body armour was arranged from neck to tail in bands consisting of narrow, rectangular plates that covered the ribs and alternated with broader plates that covered the spaces in between. Hundreds of bony nodes studded the broad plates, giving *Nodosaurus* its name. The shoulders and hips were powerful and strong, as were the stout legs and broad, hooved feet. The pelvis was a rather different shape to other ornithischians': the bones of the hips were modified as weight-bearing structures, so the ilium at the top of the hips was much more enlarged, while the lower hip bones (the pubis and ischium) were much reduced in size. Large, powerful leg muscles were attached to the underside of the ilium. The front legs were short and powerfully built. Unlike ankylosaurs, nodosaurs had a narrow skull, with a more pointed snout, and did not have the horn-like projections on the rear corners of the skull. Nodosaurs also had an opening on the side of the skull, behind the eye, again a feature that is absent in ankylosaurs.

NAME MEANS
'Node lizard'

TIME
Late Cretaceous
(135–65 MYA)

LOCATION
North America: Kansas,
Wyoming, USA

SIZE
5.5m (18ft)

WEIGHT
1,778kg (1¾ tons)

DIET
Herbivore

NAME MEANS
'Fully plated lizard'

TIME
Late Cretaceous
(135–65 MYA)

LOCATION
North America: Alberta,
Canada; Montana, South
Dakota, Texas, USA

SIZE
4.4m (15ft)

WEIGHT
3,048kg (3 tons)

DIET
Herbivore

PANOPLOSAURUS

Pronounced: 'pan-OP-loh-SORE-us'

Although a medium-sized animal, as its name, 'fully plated lizard', implies, *Panoplasaurus* was encased in heavy body armour consisting of broad, square plates, with keels arranged in wide bands across the neck and shoulders, while the rest of the body was covered in smaller, bony studs. Protecting the flanks, especially on the shoulders, were massive spikes that were angled to the front and side. Equally well armoured was its head: thick, bony plates were so solidly fused together that the underlying skull and toothless beak on the snout were hidden. Inside this solid, bony box was, however, a network of cavities and air passages, with a bony palate separating the nasal system from the mouth. This allowed *Panoplosaurus* to breathe and eat at the same time, chewing its vegetable food with simple, ridged teeth in the cheeks.

Unlike other nodosaurs, which may have lain down and relied on their body armour to protect them from attack, *Panoplosaurus* may have mounted a more active defence by directing its spiked shoulders at its attackers. Its forelegs were especially strong, and suggest that *Panoplosaurus* was quick on its feet and could manoeuvre its forequarters to react to an enemy's onslaught, rather like a modern, charging rhinoceros.

EDMONTONIA

Pronounced: 'ed-mon-TONE-ee-ah'

Among the largest of the nodosaurs, *Edmontonia* was also the latest, and is known from several skulls and skeletons, two of which are complete with their armour. *Edmontonia* was a heavily built nodosaur, with a bulky, barrel-shaped body, thick legs (the hind legs were longer than the forelegs) and wide, flat feet, a short tail supporting, without a club at the end, and a short neck, carrying a low-slung, long head. It was the armoured tank of the nodosaurs: too slow to sprint away from danger, it seems likely that *Edmontonia* lunged at its enemies with its long, forward-projecting shoulder spikes in order to inflict crippling injuries to the legs of theropods.

Meanwhile, flank and shoulder spines helped to protect it from attack from the sides, two collars of bony plates shielded the base of its neck and its wide hips formed a solid, broad base that would have made it difficult to overturn. This heavy-bodied animal browsed through western North America, feeding on low-growing plants, ripping at them with its narrow, toothless, but horny, beak and chewing them with rows of ridged, leaf-shaped cheek teeth arranged along the side of the jaw. Each tooth was about 4cm (1½ in) long (including the root), was flattened from side to side and was enamelled on both sides to resist wear and tear. The teeth were in-curved, so that room was left in the large cheek pouches to store food. *Edmontonia*'s teeth appear to have been small for a nodosaur, but even so, they were larger than the teeth of ankylosaurs.

NAME MEANS
'Lizard from Edmonton'

TIME
Cretaceous
(135–65 MYA)

LOCATION
North America: Alberta,
Canada; Montana,
Texas, USA

SIZE
7m (23ft)

WEIGHT
3,556kg (3½ tons)

DIET
Herbivore

ANKYLOSAURUS

Pronounced: 'an-KIE-loh-SORE-us'

NAME MEANS
'Fused lizard'

TIME
Late Cretaceous
(135–65 MYA)

LOCATION
North America: Alberta,
Canada; Montana, USA

SIZE
7–10m (23–33ft)

WEIGHT
4,572–6,858kg
(4½–6¾ tons)

DIET
Herbivore

Ankylosaurus was the largest-known ankylosaur, and one of the last of the group to survive, right up to the end of the Cretaceous period (65 million years ago). It was massively built – it is often described as a 'living tank' – and its stocky body, measuring about 5m (16ft) wide at its largest point, neck and head were protected by thick bands of armour-plating, while the tip of its tail culminated in a great, bony club. The armour consisted of a thick, leathery skin studded with hundreds of oval, bony plates and parallel rows of bony spikes. In addition, a pair of long spikes stuck out from the back of the head, while the cheekbones were drawn out into another pair of spikes, protecting the face. *Ankylosaurus* had a skull about 75cm (2ft 5in) long, with a broad face and blunt snout that ended in a toothless, horny beak. In contrast to the relatively simple, paired tubes running from the nostrils to the back of the throat of the nodosaurs, ankylosaurs' nasal tubes followed an 'S'-shaped course through the head, and on the side of these were additional passages (sinuses). These may have served to filter, warm and moisten the air that they breathed, also allowing for an improved sense of smell or for making distinctive calls or noises. The backs of ankylosaurs were at least partly stiffened by bony tendons running down the spine, but were most obvious towards the end of the tail, where the tail club was located. Along the back, these stiffening tendons provided firm anchorage for the tail-swinging muscles, while at the end of the tail, they stopped any whiplash from damaging the bones of the tail. The main part of the tail had no stiffening tendons, and could therefore be swung freely from side to side.

PINACOSAURUS

Pronounced: 'pin-AK-oh-SORE-us'

Pinacosaurus is one of several ankylosaurs to have been discovered in Asia. Smaller than most of its relatives at around 5m (16ft 6in), and of relatively slender build, *Pinacosaurus* was first described by Charles Gilmore in 1933 from material collected in the Gobi Desert during the American Museum of Natural History–Mongolian expeditions of the 1920s. Although lightly built, *Pinacosaurus* was still well armoured: its back and tail were covered with bony spines, and the end of the tail bore a heavy, bony club that could have been used as a defensive weapon, being swung with considerable force by strong tail muscles anchored to the hips. *Pinacosaurus* had a rounded beak and the top of its skull was covered with small, bony plates. A recent discovery of a juvenile skull shows that these plates were at first separate, only later fusing together into a solid, heavy sheet of bone as the animal matured. Its eyes were set quite far back in the skull, and it is also remarkable for having two small openings in the skull near the nostrils, the purpose of which is still unknown. In the nasal passages of *Pinacosaurus* (and found in a second Asian ankylosaur, *Saichania*), were thin, curved bones that resemble the turbinal, or scroll, bones found in the noses of mammals. These bones are covered in membranes that filter, moisten and warm the air that we breathe, and it could be that *Pinacosaurus* also had this facility. The front of the skull sloped downwards to form a parrot-like, horny beak. Inside its mouth were small, rather weak, teeth that suggest that *Pinacosaurus* must have fed on only very soft vegetation.

NAME MEANS
'Plank lizard'

TIME
Late Cretaceous
(135–65 MYA)

LOCATION
Asia: Mongolia
and China

SIZE
5m (16ft 6in)

WEIGHT
3,048kg (3 tons)

DIET
Herbivore

HOMALOCEPHALE

Pronounced: 'home-ah-loh-SEFF-ah-lee'

NAME MEANS
'Even head'

TIME
Late Cretaceous
(135–65 MYA)

LOCATION
Asia: Mongolia

SIZE
3m (10ft)

WEIGHT
80kg (180lb)

DIET
Herbivore

Homalocephale means 'even head', and makes reference to the fact that this pachycephalosaur did not have the high-domed top to its skull that is a feature of other members of the family. Instead, it had a flat, wedge-shaped head, although the bones of the skull were immensely thickened and there were numerous dents, or pits, and bony knobs scattered all over it. Because the skull was thickened, this part of the animal fossilised the most easily, and consequently many of the 'bone-head' dinosaurs are known only from these remains. *Homalocephale* is remarkable that in addition to its skull, other parts of its skeleton are known. It is thought that rival male pachycephalosaurs charged at each other in head-butting contests; this is something that sheep and goats do, but it can also be seen in the modern marine iguanas of the Galapagos Islands. The force of the impact was absorbed by the thick cranium that protected the brain, and nuchal ligaments that ran from the back of the head to the neck were also large and powerful and helped to absorb a great deal of the impact. The force of the impact would also have run down the backbone, so this was strengthened with bony tendons, while the joints between individual bones in the back had special, grooved surfaces to stop them from twisting around too much. The wide hips may also have been part of the shock-absorbing system, although other palaeontologists have suggested that this could indicate that *Homalocephale* gave birth to live young rather than laying eggs.

STEGOCERAS

Pronounced: 'ste-GOs-er-as'

A medium-sized herbivore, *Stegoceras* was first described by Lawrence Lambe in 1902, on the basis of two skull fragments found in the Belly River Formation of Alberta, Canada, to which he gave the name 'horny roof'. The skull fragments were unusually thick, and were at first thought to belong to a certopian dinosaur (see page 135). In 1924, Charles Gilmore described a skull and partial skeleton found on the Red Deer River in 1920 by George Sternberg, and although incomplete, the material gave a much better picture of *Stegoceras*. Although quick on its feet, *Stegoceras* was not a particularly fast runner as its femurs (thigh bones) were longer than its tibias (shin bones). But it had a body designed to withstand impact from head-butting – either from rival males or, perhaps, in defence from predators. The skull was thickened into a dome of solid bone (protecting its small brain), and the grain of the bone was angled to the surface, enabling it to withstand the force of impact even more efficiently. During head-butting contests, the head was held face down, so that the ramming surface of the head and the neck joint were in a straight line with the horizontally held spinal column. The battering force would then be transmitted through the skull and would be absorbed by the backbone.

NAME MEANS
'Horny roof'

TIME
Late Cretaceous
(135–65 MYA)

LOCATION
North America: Alberta,
Canada; Montana,
Wyoming, USA

SIZE
2m (6ft 6in)

WEIGHT
55kg (120lb)

DIET
Herbivore

PRENOCEPHALE

Pronounced: 'pren-oh-SEF-a-lee'

NAME MEANS
'Sloping head'

TIME
Late Cretaceous
(135–65 MYA)

LOCATION
Asia: Mongolia

SIZE
2.4m (8ft)

WEIGHT
75kg (150lb)

DIET
Herbivore

All pachycephalosaurs had a bony shelf jutting out from the back of their skulls, but in the case of *Prenocephale*, while this was evident, it was less distinct. It did, however, have a most bulbous dome – rather like a bowling ball – surmounting the top of its skull and a row of bony bumps and spikes surrounding the back and sides of the solid skull.

This thickening of the skull in pachycephalosaurs gives them something of a passing resemblance to the ankylosaurids (see page 133). In ankylosaurids, however, the thickened skulls were created by plastering new bones on the skulls, while in pachycephalosaurs, it was the actual bones of the skull that became thicker. Because this bone-thickening process is unique, it has made it difficult for palaeontologists to decide how the pachycephalosaurs related to other dinosaur genera. Because of their bipedal stance, some place them in the suborder of ornithopods, while others attribute them to marginocephalia. However, *Prenocephale*, like other pachycephalosaurs, is undoubtedly an ornithischian because of the existence of the tell-tale, horn-covered, predatory beak in the lower jaw. What these creatures ate as herbivores is uncertain, though. Their small, ridged teeth were not capable of chewing tough vegetation, so it is likely that they survived on a mixed diet of fruit, leaves and maybe insects.

PACHYCEPHALOSAURUS

Pronounced: 'PAK-ee-SEF-a-loh-SORE-us'

The largest member of the family found so far, *Pachycephalosaurus* was also the last to exist before the extinction of the dinosaurs at the end of the Cretaceous period, around 65 million years ago. A giant among the 'boneheads', *Pachycephalosaurus* is known, in fact, only from one well-preserved, 60cm- (2ft-) long skull found by William Winckley in Montana, USA, in 1940, and a few immensely thick skull roofs. The domed head case, rather like a huge crash helmet, was up to 25cm (10in) thick. Bony knobs projected from the rear rim of the skull dome, and short spikes projected upwards from the snout. As well as the horny beak, *Pachycephalosaurus* had curved, fang-like teeth at the front of its jaws, and tiny cheek teeth lining the sides of the jaws. Because remains other than the skull are unknown, scientist have reconstructed *Pachycephalosaurus* using known skeletons of other pachycephalosaurs, especially *Stegoceras* (see page 169), with the body proportions and sizes estimated. The overall picture is of a bipedal animal, about the length of a large car, standing about 1.8m (6ft) high, with a fairly short, thick neck, short arms, with five fingered hands, long rear legs, three-toed feet and a sturdy body counterbalanced by a heavy tail stiffened by hard, bony tendons.

NAME MEANS
'Thick-headed lizard'

TIME
Late Cretaceous
(135–65 MYA)

LOCATION
North America:
Montana, South Dakota,
Wyoming, USA

SIZE
5m (16ft)

WEIGHT
1,778kg (1¾ tons)

DIET
Herbivore

STYGIMOLOCH

Pronounced: 'STIJ-ee-MOH-loc'

NAME MEANS
'River of Hades
[Hell Creek] devil'

TIME
Late Cretaceous
(135–65 MYA)

LOCATION
North America: Montana,
Wyoming, USA

SIZE
Estimated 2–3m
(6ft 6in–10ft)

WEIGHT
Unknown

DIET
Herbivore

Because the pachycephalosaurs are a relatively rare group, they are also quite puzzling. The first remains – a tooth from the Judith River Beds in Montana – found by Ferdinand Hayden in the 19th century, were described and named by Joseph Leidy as *Troodon formosus,* who suggested that it belonged to a large monitor lizard or to some extinct, carnivorous reptile. It was not until the turn of the century, and later in the 1930s and 1940s, that more remains were found, especially in Montana, South Dakota and Wyoming, which shed more light on the pachycephalosaurs. More recent finds in many parts of the world have turned up a number of pachycephalosaurs, including the marvellously named *Stygimoloch*, or 'River of Hades [Hell Creek] devil', which was found in the Hell Creek Formation of Montana, USA. At the moment, *Stygimoloch* is known only from parts of its skull, but what a skull it is! Not only did *Stygimoloch* have the high, domed and thickened skull characteristic of the pachycephalosaurs, but this was embellished with a large, elaborate horn core that formed clusters of horns on either side of its domed head. These horns would have made it difficult for *Stygimoloch* to indulge in the ritualistic head-butting contests between males that scientist believe their thick heads developed for. Instead, *Stygimolochs'* crown of horns may have been sufficient to establish and maintain a position in the social hierarchy.

PROTOCERATOPS

Pronounced: 'PROh-toh-SERRA-tops'

The first protoceratopid to be discovered, *Protoceratops* was found in Mongolia in the 1920s, with later finds revealing complete skulls and skeletons of individuals that ranged from newly emerged hatchlings to adults, as well as nests and eggs that gave a clear indication that *Protoceratops* probably lived in herds. The numerous remains belonged to quadrupedal herbivores with large heads, bony neck frills, sharp, shearing teeth and parrot-like beaks. Although *Protoceratops* had no horns, it did have a prominent bump halfway along its snout, which seems to have been larger in more mature males, suggesting that it was used in ritual mating battles. Spending most of its time on all fours, *Protoceratops'* hind legs were slightly longer in comparison to the forelegs; this is usual in most land animals, as the rear legs are the source of locomotion, while the forelegs act like shock-absorbers as the body is propelled forwards. Although the front legs were supporting the front of the body, there were still trellis-like bones spanning the vertebrae that helped to stop the body from sagging. Each hind limb ended in a long foot, with four toes bearing tapered, though blunt, claws. The forelimbs had three long, spreading digits, with the fourth and fifth digits very much reduced. Like later ceratopids, *Protoceratops* had an arched sacrum (fused sacral vertebrae) that made its tail curve downwards.

NAME MEANS
'First horned face'

TIME
Late Cretaceous
(135–65 MYA)

LOCATION
Asia: Gansu (Inner
Mongolia), Omnogov
(Outer Mongolia)

SIZE
1.8m–2.7m (6–9ft)

WEIGHT
180kg (400lb)

DIET
Herbivore

PSITTACOSAURUS

Pronounced: 'si-TAK-oh-SORE-us'

NAME MEANS
'Parrot lizard'

TIME
Early Cretaceous
(135–65 MYA)

LOCATION
Asia: Gorno-Altayskaya,
(Siberia); Dundgov,
Ovorhangay (Outer
Mongolia); Liaoning,
Shandong, Xinjiang Uygur
Zizhiqu (Inner Mongolia);
Chaiyaphum, Thailand

SIZE
2m (6ft 6in)

WEIGHT
80kg (175lb)

DIET
Herbivore

While the ancestors of the ceratopians (which are often incorrectly called ceratopsians) are believed to be among the 'parrot dinosaurs', it is unlikely that *Psittacosaurus* ('parrot lizard') was itself an ancestor since this dinosaur had only four fingers on each hand, while the ceratopians had five. Furthermore, *Psittacosaurus* had no teeth in its beak, while the later protoceratopids (see page 136) had teeth in their upper beaks.

Psittacosaurus was a two-legged herbivore about 2m (6ft 6in) long and resembled the gazelle-like ornithopod *Hypsilophondon* (see page 138) in that it could rear up on its long, thin hind legs to run from predators. However, *Psittacosaurus* had a deeper and longer body, a shorter tail and longer arms, which ended in a four-fingered, grasping hand. Its most peculiar feature was, however, its skull and toothless, parrot-like beak. A thick ridge of bone on the top of the skull squared off the head at the back and served as an anchor point for very powerful muscles that worked the lower jaw.

Over the course of millions of years, this bony ridge would develop into the huge, bony, neck frills of the later ceratopians. The cheekbones were drawn out into a pair of horn-like projections on the side of the head – again, the forerunners of the horny spikes on either side of the head shields of later ceratopians – and were thought to be used for fighting or for sexual display. Beneath the horn-covered part of the upper beak, *Psittacosaurus* had the characteristic rostral bone that is found in all ceratopians. The cutting beak and self-sharpening cheek teeth that lined the jaw suggest that *Psitticosaurus* had, perhaps, evolved to eat either new forms of vegetation that needed this beak to crop them or that it had evolved the 'parrot beak' to feed on existing vegetation that had previously been inedible for dinosaurs.

Whatever its diet, *Psitticosaurus* made use of gastroliths (stomach stones) to help to grind up the plant matter in its food. Bipedal when it walked or ran, *Psittacosaurus* would have used its hands, with their stubby, short claws, to pull down branches to its mouth.

STYRACOSAURUS

Pronounced: 'sty-RAK-oh-SORE-us'

NAME MEANS
'Spiked lizard'

TIME
Late Cretaceous

LOCATION
North America: Alberta, Canada; Montana, USA

SIZE
5.5m (18ft)

WEIGHT
2,286kg (2¼ tons)

DIET
Herbivore

Perhaps not the most famous ceratopid, *Styracosaurus* was certainly one of the most spectacular of all of the 'horned lizards'. While it had the neck frill of all ceratopids, *Styracosaurus* was unique in having six long spikes that had grown out from the epoccipital bones at the edge of the frill. These epoccipital bones were usually small knobs of bone that gave a scalloped edge to the rim of the frill. Each of the four longest spikes on the neck frill was probably about the length of a man's arm. *Styracosaurus* also seems to have had unusually large nostrils, but the reasons for this are unknown. To lessen the overall weight carried by the neck, the bony frill had parietal openings, or 'windows', covered by tough skin. *Styracosaurus* would certainly have been a formidable animal: charging head down like a rhinoceros, its long nasal horn would have ripped into the soft underbelly of a predatory carnivore, while the array of spikes protected its own vulnerable neck from onslaught by sharp teeth and claws. Standing head-on to its enemy, the frill and spikes would have made *Styracosaurus* appear much larger than its 5.5m (18ft), and this alone may have helped to deter some attackers; modern African elephants adopt a similar technique by holding their ears out at the sides of their heads to warn off other elephants.

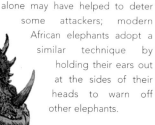

CHASMOSAURUS

Pronounced: 'KAZ-moh-SORE-us'

Known from a number of well-preserved skulls and skeletons that were discovered along the Red Deer River in Alberta, Canada, by Lawrence Lambe and the Sternberg family, *Chasmosaurus* was one of the earliest of the long-frilled ceratopids, and was smaller than many of its relatives. Its skull was quite long and narrow, with a pair of long, upwardly curving horns on its brow and a single, shorter horn on its snout. The bony frill, however, was quite enormous: it stretched from the back of the skull over the neck and shoulders. It was made lighter by two very large, parietal openings that were covered with skin. These reduced the bony structure of the frill to a mere scaffold that allowed the head and frill to be moved around with ease. The frill edge was embellished with epoccipital bones – triangular, bony knobs and spikes. The spectacular frill was undoubtedly for display; it may have been brightly coloured – perhaps with 'eyes', as on peacock feathers – which, when seen head on, would have warned off attackers. A brightly coloured frill may also have been the male *Chasmosaurus'* method of attracting females. Skeletally, *Chasmosaurus* was typical of a slow-moving, heavy dinosaur. Both the hip and shoulder girdles, as well as their respective legs, were very solidly constructed and designed not for speed, but for bearing weight. In the neck and back regions, the vertebrae were also very strong, and had extended spines to which the head-supporting muscles would have been attached. The stout ribs would have supported the bulky gut as a substantial space was needed in order to process large quantities of vegetable matter.

NAME MEANS
'Cleft lizard'

TIME
Late Cretaceous
(135–65 MYA)

LOCATION
North America: Alberta,
Canada; Texas, USA

SIZE
4.2m (16ft)

WEIGHT
1,778kg (1¾ tons)

DIET
Herbivore

CENTROSAURUS

Pronounced: 'SEN-troh-SORE-us'

NAME MEANS
'Horned/sharp-point lizard'

TIME
Late Cretaceous
(135–65 MYA)

LOCATION
North America: Alberta,
Canada; Montana, USA

SIZE
6m (20ft)

WEIGHT
2,794kg (2¾ tons)

DIET
Herbivore

A medium-sized ceratopid, *Centrosaurus* had a single horn on its snout and small spines around the back of its short neck frill. There were also two horns on the posterior (back) edge of the frill that pointed forwards and downwards. While these two tongues of horn were unique to *Centrosaurus*, this horned dinosaur was typical of the short-frilled ceratopids (the Centrosaurines), but was once known by another name: *Monoclonius* ('single stem'). Its remains were first found in 1855, by Ferdinand Hayden, during a geological expedition of the upper Missouri, around the mouth of the Judith River in Montana. These remains, which included fragments of the crest and fragments of skeleton, were described and named (as *Monoclonius*) by Cope in 1876.

In 1904, however, Lawrence Lambe, using another frill, this time from the Red Deer River, and having the curious tongues of bones that point downwards, towards the frill, described and named it *Centrosaurus*. The frill itself had two window-like holes in the bone in order to reduce the weight, and their edges also served as anchor points for the powerful jaw muscles. These 'windows' would have been covered over with tough skin, as was the rest of the frill. A strong ball-and-socket joint connected the head to the neck. This joint was positioned forwards in the skull – under the region of the eyes – so that the weight of the frill at the back of the head was balanced by the huge horn on the snout. This mobile joint allowed *Centrosaurus* to turn its head quickly, which was vital since its only weapons of defence were on its head. To strengthen the neck, some of the neck vertebrae behind the ball-and-socket joint were fused together. *Centrosaurus* also had a parrot-like, toothless beak at the tip of its jaws, and teeth that were set in at the sides of the jaws to give room for cheek pouches.

NAME MEANS
'Three-horned face'

TIME
Late Cretaceous
(135–65 MYA)

LOCATION
North America: Alberta,
Saskatchewan, Canada;
Colorado, Montana, South
Dakota, Wyoming, USA

SIZE
9m (30ft)

WEIGHT
4,572–9,652kg
(4½–9½ tons)

DIET
Herbivore

TRICERATOPS

Pronounced: 'try-SERRA-tops'

The most famous of all of the horned dinosaurs, *Triceratops* was also the largest, the heaviest and the most abundant of the group. *Triceratops* belongs to the group of 'long-frilled' chasmosaurines, whose brow horns were longer than their nasal horns. Scientists estimate that *Triceratops* could reach weights of 9,652kg (9½ tons) – heavier than a modern African bull elephant – and *Triceratops'* skull alone was over 2m (6ft 6in) long. Great herds of these horned dinosaurs roamed western North America during the late Cretaceous period, some 70–65 million years ago, and hundreds of well-preserved specimens have been found over the years since Orthniel C Marsh first named the creature in 1889.

The massive structure of the skull and frill meant that these were more likely to be fossilised than less robust dinosaur skulls, and so far 50 *Triceratops'* skulls have been found. Unlike other members of its group, *Triceratops* was unique in that its neck frill was a solid piece of bone: there were no parietal openings, or 'windows, in it to lighten the weight. This suggests that the main function of the frill was as a defensive shield rather than as an anchorage point for jaw muscles. It is possible that the skin over the frill was filled with blood vessels; this means that the frill could also have been used as a heat-exchange mechanism, cooling up or warming down the body as it was angled towards, or away from, the sun. The nasal horn was relatively short and thick, while two long brow horns, each over 1m (3ft 3in) long, curved forwards and slightly outwards over the long, low face and the long snout. Using their sharp, horny beaks to snip at twigs and leaves, food was then sliced up in the mouth by rows of shearing cheek teeth. These teeth were self-sharpening: one side of the crown was hardened by enamel, the other side wasn't; as *Triceratops* chewed, the softer side of the tooth wore down quickly, leaving the hard side with a sharp cutting edge.

PENTACERATOPS

Pronounced: 'PEN-ta-SERRA-tops'

NAME MEANS
'Five-horned face'

TIME
Late Cretaceous
(135–65 MYA)

LOCATION
North America:
New Mexico, USA

SIZE
5–8m (16–26ft)

WEIGHT
2,032–7,620kg
(2–7½ tons)

DIET
Herbivore

Pentaceratops may well have been a descendent of *Chasmosaurus* (see page 177), which lived earlier in late Cretaceous times. It, too, had a huge neck frill, its edges embellished by triangular, bony knobs and spikes. The remains of *Pentaceratops* were found in the San Juan Basin of New Mexico, and were first described in 1923 by Henry Fairfield Osborn. The name *Pentaceratops* was suggested to him by William Diller Matthew to recognise the fact that in addition to the usual three horns of the head – a straight horn on the snout and two curved brow horns – this new species appeared to have had five horns. The two smaller horns were, in fact, outgrowths of the cheeks beneath and behind the eye. These cheekbones are not particularly horn like, especially when compared to the nasal or brow horns, and some specimens and other ceratopids (but not long-frilled ones) had equally large cheekbones. Nevertheless, the rather fanciful name, 'five-horned face', stuck.

Pentaceratops did have a remarkably enormous head: reconstructed in 1998, the skull alone measured over 3m (10ft) long. To reduce the weight of the large, bony, neck frill, four parietal openings, or 'windows', punctured it. These may have been filled with muscles, the edges of the 'windows' providing anchor points, and would have been covered with tough skin, possibly brightly coloured for sexual display.

ANCHICERATOPS

Pronounced: 'AN-ki-SERRA-tops'

Discovered in the Red Deer River formation of Alberta, Canada, and living very near to the end of the late Cretaceous period (and the end of the 'age of the dinosaurs'), *Anchiceratops* was similar in some respects to *Chasmosaurus* (see page 177), from which it may have descended: it had quite a long face, but was larger, had longer horns above its eyes and the frill was rather different. *Anchiceratops* seems to have had a much more streamlined form: its body was longer, narrower, and with a shorter tail, and the tall neck frill was also quite narrow. The 'windows' in the frill were smaller than in *Chasmosaurus*, and there were three pairs of enlarged epoccipital bones (bony projections) on the posterior margins, but none around the sides. A further pair of triangular, horny epoccipital projections pointed forwards on the top rear edge of the frill. These were much smaller than, but still reminiscent of, the curious tongues of bone that projected into the frill openings of *Centrosaurus* (see page 178). *Anchiceratops* had two horns that curved forwards from the brows, and a shorter nasal horn that pointed straight out in front. As most of the ceratopians had similar skeletal structures, and the main distinguishing features were confined to their heads, it may be that the horn arrangements and frill sizes and shapes (and maybe colours) acted as species-recognition signals for the various ceratopids living in North America in the late Cretaceous period.

NAME MEANS
'Close-horned face'

TIME
Late Cretaceous
(135–65 MYA)

LOCATION
North America:
Alberta, Canada

SIZE
6m (20ft)

WEIGHT
4,572–5,588kg
(4½–5½ tons)

DIET
Herbivore

CHAPTER 8

REPTILES OF THE SEA

Dinosaurs lived only on land, but sharing the Mesozoic world with them were the reptiles of the sea and air. Scientists believe that all life came from the sea and appeared about 3,500 million years ago. Only relatively recently did life come on to land: about 400 million years ago for plants, and 300 million years ago for animals. Some of the first land creatures to evolve were reptiles and dinosaurs, but almost as soon as they had appeared, some reptiles returned to the seas to exploit the marine environment for food and for living. As early as 250 million years ago, there were aquatic animals that had evolved from land-living ancestors, even before the dinosaurs walked the Earth. In late Triassic times (250–203 MYA), other reptiles became adapted for life in the air, flying on wings of skin and diversified into many forms, among them the largest flying creatures of all time.

MARINE REPTILES

During the Mesozoic era, several groups of reptiles returned to the sea and became adapted to marine life. These include an ancient group of reptiles called chelonians, which differed from all other reptiles in having bodies – except for their heads, tail and legs – enclosed within a shell. Modern turtles, tortoises and terrapins are the only surviving members of this ancient group, and have changed very little in over 200 million years. Modern crocodiles have changed very little from their prehistoric relatives, which appeared in mid-Triassic times, some 230 million years ago. In addition to the chelonians and Crocodylia, there are four distinct types of marine reptiles, each of which demonstrates a different degree of adaptation to marine life. The least specialised were the placodonts of the Triassic period (250–103 MYA); there were also the nothosaurs (also of the Triassic period); the plesiosaurs, which swam in the open seas of the Jurassic (203–135 MYA) and Cretaceous periods (135–65 MYA); and the most specialised of marine reptiles, the ichthyosaurs, which also swam in Jurassic seas. Also included in this selection of marine reptiles are mosasaurs: these were a successful, but short-lived, offshoot of the family Varanidae, the monitor lizards.

ORDER CHELONIA

Even the earliest chelonians, dating from the late Triassic period, had a shell. They also had a solidly roofed skull, with no openings in it except for the eyes and nostrils. There are two distinct chelonian suborders that include the 230 species of living turtles, tortoises and terrapins. The two are distinguished by the way in which the animal retracts its head into its shell: pleurodires bend their necks sideways (a few members of this group survive today) and cryptodires bend their necks back vertically.

SUB-ORDER CRYPTODIRA

Most modern turtles and tortoises belong to this group, many of which can retract their heads into their shells by lowering their heads and pulling them back vertically. The cryptodires, the most successful group of chelodians, evolved during the Jurassic period. By the end of the period, they had become extremely diverse throughout the rivers, seas and lakes of the world, with new forms also developing on land.

FAMILY PROTOSTEGIDAE
(See page 190)

This family of sea turtles includes some of the most spectacular that ever lived. The protostegids developed two main features that distinguished all sea turtles from their land- or river-dwelling relatives. Firstly, since there were fewer predators in the sea, they did not need such heavy armour on their backs, so their shell was reduced to a lighter structure that also made them much more manoeuvrable. Secondly, the toes of the front and back limbs were more elongated and were modified into broad flippers for faster swimming.

ORDER CROCODYLIA

The most successful of the archosaurs, or 'ruling reptiles', crocodiles have changed very little since their relatives first appeared some 230 million years ago during the mid-Triassic period (25–203 MYA). Although modern crocodiles are more at home in water than on land, they evolved first as small, terrestrial carnivores that could run upright on their two hind legs. All crocodiles, including the earliest ones, have the characteristic long, low and massive skull that is designed to resist the powerful snap of their jaws shutting. The muscles are attached at the back of the skull, which allows the jaws to open wide to deal with large prey. An especially useful feature for water-dwellers is the secondary plate of bone that separates the mouth from the nasal passage, allowing the crocodile to eat and breathe at the same time. The order is divided into four *sub*-orders: *sub*-order Sphenosuchia, the earliest-known crocodiles from the mid-Triassic period; *sub*-order Protosucha, from the early Jurassic period; *sub*-order Mesosucha, which also evolved in the early Jurassic; and *sub*-order Eusuchia, which comprises the true crocodiles, including the 21 living species of modern crocodiles (and the 7 species of alligator and caiman and the single species of gavial or gharial).

SUB-ORDER MESOSUCHA

(See page 191)

There are some 70 genera of mesosuchians known, and these are arranged into 16 families, most of whose members were fully adapted land-dwellers or semi-aquatic species. However, four families were permanently aquatic. Most of the fossil crocodiles are from this *sub*-order Mesosucha, and of the permanently aquatic species, *Metriorhynchus* is the most famous, sharing the seas with the ichthyosaurs and plesiosaurs throughout the Jurassic period and into the Cretaceous period.

ORDER PLACODONTIA

Of all of the marine reptiles, the placodonts were the least specialised of the swimmers. They appeared (and disappeared) during the Triassic period (250–203 MYA), and while, during this time, many types evolved, none became fully adapted to life in the open seas. They were largely confined to the shallow, coastal waters of the Tethys Sea, which existed at the time between the two land masses of Laurasia, in the north, and Gondwanaland, in the south. Many types had turtle-like shells protecting their backs and underbellies. The order Placodontia includes the families Placodontidae, Cyamodontidae and Henodontidae.

Metriorhynchus.

FAMILY PLACONDATIDAE

(See page 192)

This family of semi-aquatic reptiles was equally at home on land, walking on the seashore, as when swimming in the shallow waters of the Tethys Sea. Both areas were rich feeding grounds for the shellfish on which they lived, which were crushed between their broad teeth. The warm, shallow waters had encouraged the formation of coral reefs during the Triassic period, and many new molluscs evolved.

Henodus.

FAMILY CYAMODONTIDAE

(See page 193)

Evolving during the mid-Triassic period, and living until the end of the period, this family of placodonts had developed turtle-like shells on their backs and were more adapted to an aquatic lifestyle. Although they began to look, and behave, like modern turtles (see order Chelonia, page 185), they were, in fact, unrelated. This phenomenon is known as convergent evolution.

FAMILY HENODONTIDAE

(See page 194)

Evolving during the late Triassic period, these armoured placodonts developed a great, bony shell that covered their backs and underbellies. They also lost most of their teeth, and instead had a horny beak, like a modern turtle. In spite of their turtle-like appearance, henodonts were not related to the turtles, which are members of the Chelonia order of reptiles.

ORDER NOTHOSAURIA

The Triassic seas contained many swimming, fish-eating reptiles. One very successful group was the nothosaurs, which ranged from lizard-sized to giant, 4m- (13ft-) long creatures. They were amphibious predators, with numerous sharp teeth. As their fossils have been found in marine sediments, this suggests that they were sea-going creatures, but probably rested and bred on land. Their fossils show that nothosaurs were long-necked, with a low skull and sharp teeth for piercing slippery fish. They also had a narrow tail and broad, paddle-like limbs with webbed feet, which were used for swimming.

FAMILY NOTHOSAURIDAE

(See page 195)

There are several families of nothosaurs, but this is the best known. Fossil remains have been found in the marine sediments of Europe and Asia, dating from the early to the late Triassic period (250–203 MYA).

ORDER ICHTHYOSAURIA

The ichthyosaurs were the most specialised of the marine reptiles – their name reflects this, and means 'fish lizards'. While they ate fish and were fish shaped (their overall body shape resembled a modern tuna), they were reptiles and breathed air. Unlike their contemporaries, the plesiosaurs, they did not rely on paddle-like flippers for swimming, but instead had a fish-like tail whose lateral (side-to-side) movements provided the propulsive force. Well adapted to marine life, the ichthyosaurs could no longer come ashore to lay eggs, but gave birth to live young – born tail first, and fully able to swim – at sea.

FAMILY ICHTHYOSAURIDAE

(See page 196)

Flourishing throughout the Jurassic period and into the Cretaceous, these typical 'fish lizards' are known from some spectacular fossils, including coprolites (droppings), stomach contents and even adult females with the bodies of young offspring inside them, making them among the best-known of all marine reptiles. They developed a streamlined body, with a stabilising, triangular dorsal (back) fin, short, paired paddles for steering and a large tail fin, with two equal lobes for propulsion. Ball-and-socket joints in the caudal (tail) vertebrae allowed for powerful strokes from side to side. While some ichthyosaurs measured only about 1m (3ft) long, others grew to more than 20m (65ft) long.

Ichthyosaurus.

ORDER PLESIOSAURIA

The great, sea-going reptiles of the Mesozoic era were the plesiosaurs. Some of these were giants, up to 14m (46ft) long, and had adapted to marine life by evolving their limbs into long, narrow flippers. Instead of there being only five, or fewer, bones in each finger or toe, plesiosaurs had up to ten in each. The hydrofoil-shaped flippers required modification to the hip and shoulder girdles: the structure of the massive collarbones and two of the three hip bones formed broad plates on the underside of the body, and was unique to these marine reptiles. A dense series of ribs connected the bones to the shoulders and the hip girdle on the underside, making the body more rigid and offering a strong, solid body against which the swimming flippers could move. The gastralia (belly ribs) also protected the body when the animal left the water and, using its flippers, dragged itself ashore on its belly to lay its eggs. There are two major groups, or *super*-families of Plesiosauria that differed in the lengths of their necks: plesiosaurs had long necks and small heads, while pliosaurs had short necks and larger heads. The head size is indicative of the size of the prey that each sought, and means that the two related families did not compete for the same prey, although they did have ichthyosaurs to contend with.

SUPER-FAMILY PLESIOSAUROIDAE
(See pages 197 to 200)

The early members of this *super*-family were long-necked marine reptiles that first appeared in the early Jurassic period (203–135 MYA), flourishing throughout that period. One member of the family, *Elasmosaurus* (see page 200), was the last member to survive, living right to the end of the 'age of the dinosaurs' in the Cretaceous period, which ended around 65 million years ago. Feeding on small fish and squid, plesiosaurs used their long necks to raise their heads high above the surface of the water to scan the waves in search of schools of fish on which to prey. The *super*-family Plesiosauroidae contains many genera and species, forming two families: Plesidosauridae and Elasmosauridae.

SUPER-FAMILY PLIOSAURIDAE
(See page 201)

The short-necked, large-headed pliosaurs appeared in early Jurassic (203–135 MYA) times alongside, their long–necked relatives. Some, like *Kronosaurus*, survived into the late Cretaceous period (135–65 MYA). Pliosaurs grew to a length of around 8–10m (25–33ft), although some were even bigger, but their skulls could constitute as much as one-third of their entire body length. Their strong jaws were powered by huge muscles, allowing pliosaurs to tackle larger prey, such as ichthyosaurs and their own relatives, plesiosaurs. Having no flexible neck, pliosaurs jumped their prey, grabbing it with sharp, sometimes three-sided, ridged teeth. Streamlined for speed, their necks became progressively shorter; some had only 13 cervical (neck) vertebrae, compared to 28 in even the shortest necks of the long-necked plesiosaurs.

FAMILY MOSASAURIDAE
(See page 202)

This family of highly successful, although short-lived, marine reptiles was an offshoot of the family Varanidae, the monitor lizards, which are today the largest of all land lizards. (The family Varanidae is part of the order Squamata, the most successful group of reptiles, which today comprises the lizards and snakes.) The mosasaurs ('lizards from the [River] Meuse') were fish-eating reptiles – some of which were giants – which diversified in the late Cretaceous period. This was a time when the ichthyosaurs had died out and the plesiosaurs were in decline. With large, conical teeth and strong jaws, they preyed on large fish, turtles and plesiosaurs, as well as other mosasaurs.

Tylosaurus.

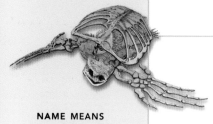

ARCHELON

Pronounced: 'Ar-KAY-lon'

NAME MEANS
'Ancient/ruling turtle'

TIME
Late Cretaceous
(135–65 MYA)

LOCATION
North America:
Kansas, South Dakota,
Wyoming, USA

SIZE
4m (13ft)

WEIGHT
2,032kg (2 tons)

DIET
Jellyfish, squid

This giant turtle – the biggest ever known, and more than twice the size of its largest, modern relatives – swam in the inland sea that covered much of North America, from Alberta, Canada, in the north, to Texas, USA, in the south, during the late Cretaceous period (135–65 MYA). Known from many fossilised skeletons in the limestone deposits of this once shallow seaway, *Archelon* was named, in 1896, 'ruling' or 'ancient turtle'. Instead of the heavy, plated shell characteristic of fresh-water and land-living turtles, which need armour to protect them from predators, *Archelon's* shell was reduced to a wide, flattened shell of bony struts covered with skin (rather like the contemporary, leatherneck turtle). The bony framework was made from the belly ribs (gastralia) that grew out from the body wall. This bony framework may well have been visible under the skin in live animals. The limbs of this massive sea creature were huge paddles, which would have cut through the water in vertical strokes; the same vertical method can be seen when penguins swim, flapping their wings to propel them through the water. With a rather weak and toothless jaw, but having a hooked beak, *Archelon* probably fed on a diet of soft jellyfish and squid.

METRIORHYNCHUS

Pronounced: 'Met-ree-or-RINE-cus'

A sea-going crocodilian, *Metriorhynchus* (and other members of its family, such as *Geosaurus*) was one of the most specialised of the aquatic crocodiles. It had dispensed with the heavy back armour of its relatives, since such protection was not needed in the sea. The reduction in armour also allowed its body to become more manoeuvrable, especially as it is believed that females would have had to haul themselves on to land to lay their eggs.

Metriorhynchus had a streamlined shape, with a long, slim head, long body and thin tail. Its skin was smooth, which reduced the amount of drag, or resistance through the water, and it had a vertical, fish-like tail, which it lashed from side to side to move it through the water. The tail was supported by a sharply down-turned tip of the backbone. Increasing its speed and mobility were flipper-shaped hind limbs and smaller, paddle-shaped forelimbs. The long snout, with nostrils set forwards, suggests that *Metriorhynchus* would lie submerged in water, with its nostrils above the waterline, ready to launch an attack. The long jaws had long, strong muscles attached to the rear of the skull, allowing *Metriorhynchus* to open its jaws wide and snap them shut on its prey. Inside, the jaws were lined with small, but razor-sharp, conical-shaped teeth with which to seize slippery fish and squid.

NAME MEANS
'Medium nose'

TIME
Mid-Jurassic
(203–135 MYA)

LOCATION
Europe: England, France;
South America: Chile

SIZE
3m (9½ ft)

WEIGHT
120kg (265lb)

DIET
Fish

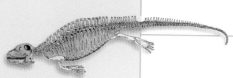

PLACODUS

Pronounced: 'PLAK-oh-dus'

NAME MEANS
'Flat tooth'

TIME
Early/mid-Triassic
(250–203 MYA)

LOCATION
Europe: the Alps

SIZE
2m (6½ ft)

WEIGHT
Unknown

DIET
Shellfish, crustaceans

With a stocky body, short neck and sprawling limbs, like those of the early, land-living reptiles, *Placodus* was not particularly well adapted to pachystosis (aquatic life). Its only swimming aids were useful webs of skin between the five toes on each foot and the long, slender tail that was flattened from side to side. The tail may also have had a fin along its length. The skeleton was quite massive, with three distinctive features, the chief of which was the structure of the vertebrae of the trunk. These all had special processes, which fitted exactly into corresponding grooves on the adjacent vertebrae so that they were all fixed tightly together, making the trunk rigid and immobile. The structure of the cervical (neck) and caudal (tail) vertebrae was quite different, and they were very flexible. A second feature was the curiously formed abdominal ribs, which turned upwards at right angles; like all of the placodonts, the underside of its body was protected by gastralia (belly ribs), which formed a strong armour, covering the whole of the abdomen. The third feature occurred above the backbone, where there was a row of raised, bony knobs to provide at least some protection for this otherwise defenceless animal. First described in 1830 by George Munster, *Placodus* got its name from its flat, blunt teeth, which protruded at the front of its jaw. These front teeth were designed to pluck shellfish off rocks, while a battery of flat teeth arranged on the upper and lower jaws was designed for crushing the shells. The jaws were powered by strong muscles, which could extend through openings in either side of the skull to give a truly strong bite.

PLACOCHELYS

Pronounced: 'PLAK-oh-KEE-lis'

Well suited to pachystosis (an under-water way of life), although it still needed to come to the surface to breathe, the rather newt-like body of *Placodus* (see page 192) had given way to a much broader and flatter, 'turtle-like' body in *Placochelys*, a point that is emphasised by its name, as the Greek word *chelys* means 'turtle'.

As slow-moving animals, many placodonts were vulnerable to carnivorous predators, and so developed a shell as protection. Covering the back of *Placochelys* was a mosaic of knobbly plates. Its tail was short, and its limbs, elongated and flattened to act as paddles, while the claws at the ends of its digits may have been used to scratch at shellfish on rocks. While *Placochelys* no longer had the protruding front teeth of *Placodus,* which were designed to pick off clinging shellfish from rocks, it was still a specialised shellfish-eater, using its very horny, but toothless, beak to pluck them off. Strong muscles worked the powerful jaws, which were lined along the sides and across the palate (the roof of the mouth) with a battery of broad, flat, shell-crushing teeth.

NAME MEANS
'Flat turtle'

TIME
Mid–late Triassic
(250–203 MYA)

LOCATION
Europe: Germany

SIZE
3m (9ft)

WEIGHT
Unknown

DIET
Shellfish

HENODUS

Pronounced: 'HEN-oh-dus'

NAME MEANS
'Single tooth'

TIME
Late Triassic
(250–203 MYA)

LOCATION
Europe: Tübingen,
Germany

SIZE
1m (3ft 3in)

WEIGHT
Unknown

DIET
Shellfish

Henodus was unusual among placodonts in that it was able to live in the fresher, less salty waters of lagoon-like seas. Usually, changes in the level of salt in water can be stressful – even fatal – to marine animals, but shelled animals, such as turtles and *Henodus,* are better equipped to cope with such changes. The body of *Henodus* was as broad as it was long, the same shape as a modern turtle. Its back and underbelly were covered in a tough casing of polygonal (many sided and irregularly shaped), bony plates, which formed a defensive shell to protect it from attack from other marine species, such as ichthyosaurs (see page 188), which also swam in the waters at this time. Unlike a turtle, *Henodus* had many more such plates in its shell, but like a turtle, the shell was covered in plates of horn. *Henodus* also had a strangely square-shaped snout, and there were no teeth in its mouth. Instead, it is believed that there was a strong, horny beak at the front of the mouth that could be used to prise shellfish off rocks. A modern sea animal that also subsists on shellfish is the walrus, whose two great tusks are used for prising shellfish from rocks, and it is possible that *Henodus'* beak worked in the same way. Scientists also think that *Henodus'* clawed feet may have been webbed.

NOTHOSAURUS

Pronounced: 'noh-thoh-SORE-us'

The best-known nothosaur, and the one that gives the family its name, is *Nothosaurus*, whose name means 'false lizard'. This nothosaur was typical of the family: its long neck, body and tail were quite streamlined and very flexible, and it probably lived – as modern seals do today – fishing at sea and resting (and nesting) on land. Some fossils have impressions of webbed skin between the five toes and fingers of the feet and hands, which was one of the adaptations to marine life, along with knee and ankle joints that were highly flexible. Because the limb bones were not joined strongly together, and the hips and shoulders were quite weak, *Nothosaurus* would not have found it particularly easy to walk on land for long periods.

Its forearms were sturdier than its legs, so it appears that these provided *Nothosaurus* with most of its propulsion under water, although the length of the spines on the caudal (tail) vertebrae suggests that the tail carried a fin, which would have helped movement and direction. Its long snout, lined with long, sharp, pointed teeth all the way to the back of the cheek region of its head, was ideally suited to catching slippery fish.

NAME MEANS
'False lizard'

TIME
Triassic
(250–203 MYA)

LOCATION
Asia: China, Mongolia;
Middle East: Israel;
Europe: Germany, the
Netherlands, Switzerland;
North Africa: Tunisia

SIZE
3m (10ft)

WEIGHT
80kg (175lb)

DIET
Fish, shrimps

ICHTHYOSAURUS

Pronounced: 'ik-THEE-oh-SORE-us'

NAME MEANS
'Fish lizard'

TIME
Early Jurassic
(203–135 MYA)

LOCATION
Europe: England,
Germany, Greenland;
North America:
Alberta, Canada

SIZE
2m (6ft 6in)

WEIGHT
90kg (200lb)

DIET
Fish

One of the best-known ichthyosaurs, which gave its name to the family, *Ichthyosaurus* was a medium-sized marine reptile that had a streamlined body, a long, pointed snout lined with small, sharp, conical-shaped teeth and foreflippers larger than its hind flippers. The foreflippers enclosed six greatly elongated digits – some later ichthyosaurs, such as *Platypterygius,* from the Cretaceous period, had eight digits. The nostrils were set far back on the snout, near to the eyes, so it had to break the surface of the water to breathe. While the bones of the ears were huge, suggesting that *Ichthyosaurus* had extremely acute hearing – that is, it transmitted vibrations from the water to the inner ear – making it able to judge the location of potential prey, its main sense for hunting was its sight. The eye sockets were filled with a ring of bones (the sclerotic ring), which helped to support the massive eyeball. Because *Ichthyosaurus'* eyes were large and highly sensitive, it may have been able to hunt at night or in poor visibility, such as in murky or very deep waters. Several hundred complete skeletons of *Ichthyosaurus* have been found since it was first described in 1818 by Charles Keonig, and many show their bones still articulating with each other. Tiny bones of young were also found inside the bodies of adults: at first, palaeontologists suspected that *Ichthyosaurus* was a cannibal, but other remains show the young emerging tail first (like modern whales) from the bodies of their parents. In addition to offspring, coprolites (droppings) and fossilised stomach contents showing the fish diet of ichthyosaurs have been found. One of the most exciting fossilised remains, however, is of pigment cells from the smooth, thick skin, which reveal that *Ichthyosaurus* was a dark-reddish-brown colour in life.

PLESIOSAURUS

Pronounced: 'PLEEZ-ee-oh-SORE-US'

Some of the first fossilised reptiles to be seen by scientists may have been plesiosaurs: fossil specimens of *Plesiosaurus* were found over 200 years ago, on the coasts of Dorset and Yorkshire, in England, before the term 'dinosaur' had been invented. Many fine examples had been found by Mary Anning between 1800 and 1820 in Lyme Regis, Dorset, an area rich in fossils. The earliest member of the family, *Plesiosaurus* had already developed the main structural features that characterise these marine reptiles: it had the typical short and wide body that tapered towards the tail, with a flexible neck that was much longer than the body. Its head was relatively small, but its jaws were long and contained numerous sharp, conical-shaped teeth. Its nostrils – two holes on the palate – were located further forward than the nostrils on the outside of the snout. This arrangement suggests that *Plesiosaurus* sniffed the water for prey: water flowed through the snout and into the internal nostrils, where scent particles were detected, and then the water left through the external nostrils. The four wide, paddle-shaped flippers are thought to have been used in a combination of sculling (back-and-forth) movements and flying (up-and-down) movements, making *Plesiosaurus* built for manoeuvrability rather than speed: forward strokes by the flippers on one side of the body, combined with backward strokes of the flippers on the other side, would have turned *Plesiosaurus*' body on the spot. Its long neck would have then darted out to seize prey. On land, however, the long neck would have made *Plesiosaurus* a clumsy beast, and one that was very vulnerable to attack by hungry carnivores.

NAME MEANS
'Ribbon reptile'

TIME
Early Jurassic
(203–135 MYA)

LOCATION
Europe: England,
Germany

SIZE
2.3m (7ft 6in)

WEIGHT
90kg (200lb)

DIET
Fish, squid

CRYPTOCLIDUS

Pronounced: 'KRIP-toh-CLY-dus'

NAME MEANS
'Hidden-closed tooth'

TIME
Late Jurassic
(203–135 MYA)

LOCATION
Europe: England

SIZE
4m (13ft)

WEIGHT
7,620kg (7½ tons)

DIET
Fish, small
marine animals

This plesiosaur is well known from fossils from England. *Cryptoclidus* had the familiar, long neck made up of around 30 vertebrae – compared to the more usual 7 or 8 in a reptile. The small skull had a long snout, with the nostrils set far back on the head. The jaws contained numerous sharp teeth, as well as a number of longer, pointed and curved teeth that interlocked when the jaw was closed to make a trap for small fish or shrimps; it was this feature that gave *Cryptoclidus* its name, 'hidden-closed tooth'. Although it was a good swimmer, *Cryptoclidus* would not have been very fast or capable of pursuing its prey for long distances. It seems more likely that it caught its prey at close quarters, by shooting out its long neck: the vertebrae in the cranial end of the neck appear to have been particularly flexible. *Cryptoclidus* had a relatively short tail and had transformed its limbs into flippers by greatly increasing the number of bones in each of the five digits to produce the long, flexible, hydrofoil-shaped front paddles and long rear flippers that it used to propel and steer itself through the water. The gastralia (belly ribs) were moulded into bony plates that provided some protection for the underbelly when *Cryptoclidus* came ashore, either to escape attack at sea from an ichthyosaur (see page 188) or to lay its eggs.

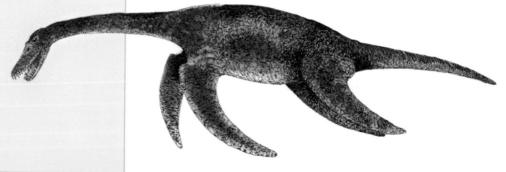

MURAENOSAURUS

Pronounced: 'MURE-rain-oh-SORE-us'

The most successful family of plesiosaurs was the Elasmosauridae, of which *Muraenosaurus* was an early member. Evolving during the late Jurassic period (203–135 MYA), and surviving well into the Cretaceous (135–65 MYA), the elasmosaurs had the longest necks of all of the plesiosaurs. *Muraenosaurus* had a neck that was as long as its body and tail combined and was supported by 44 vertebrae. It is uncertain just how flexible such long necks were, but the vertebrae at the head end of the neck indicate that this part, at least, was highly flexible. There appears to have been a good deal of lateral (side-to-side) movement possible, but in the vertical plane (up and down), movement of the neck appears to have been restricted. While it could hold its head downwards, lifting its head up, on to the surface like a swan, would have been impossible for *Muraenosaurus*.

Perched at the end of this long neck was a tiny head, measuring only about one-sixteenth of the total body length. The short, stiff plesiosaur body had now also become quite stout and rigid; the inflexibility of the body would have meant that the flippers were more effective as propellers.

NAME MEANS
'Sea-eel lizard'

TIME
Late Jurassic
(203–135 MYA)

LOCATION
Europe: England,
France

SIZE
6m (20ft)

WEIGHT
9,144kg (9 tons)

DIET
Fish, small
marine animals

ELASMOSAURUS

Pronounced: 'eh-LAZ-moh-SORE-us'

NAME MEANS
'Plate lizard'

TIME
Late Cretaceous
(135–65 MYA)

LOCATION
North America: Kansas,
USA; Asia: Japan

SIZE
14m (46ft)

WEIGHT
2,540kg (2½ tons)

DIET
Fish, squid, shellfish

'Snakes threaded through the bodies of turtles' is the description of these long-necked plesiosaurs given by Dean Conybeare, a 19th-century British palaeontologist who undertook much of the early scientific investigation into these marine reptiles. *Elasmosaurus* means 'plate lizard', and is derived from the massive, plate-like shoulder bones that covered its chest and formed its arm sockets. The huge muscles that powered the foreflippers were anchored to this plate. *Elasmosaurus* was the longest-known plesiosaur; more than half of its entire body length was made up of its neck. Where earlier plesiosaurs had only 28 cervical (neck) vertebrae, *Elasmosaurus* had 72 – more than any other plesiosaur, or, indeed, any other animal. This incredibly long neck would have allowed *Elasmosaurus* to bend it around sideways and make almost two complete circles on either side of its body. In the vertical plane (upwards and downwards), it was only half as flexible. Moving the neck around while submerged would have been difficult, though, as it would have met with considerable water resistance, and this led some scientists to suggest that as *Elasmosaurus* paddled along, propelled by its four long, paddle-shaped flippers, it held its head just out of the water in order to spot prey. In its small head, *Elasmosaurus* had bony, sclerotic rings around the eyes, suggesting that it had flattened eyeballs, which would have been better suited to seeing under water, and some skulls have been found with ear bones. These are fused to the surrounding skull and suggest that *Elasmosaurus* was not particularly well suited to hearing sound waves transmitted through the air.

KRONOSAURUS

Pronounced: 'CRO-noh-SORE-us'

The Australian *Kronosaurus* was the giant of the pliosaurs. During the Triassic (250–203 MYA) and Jurassic (203–135 MYA) periods, the modern continent of Australia had been dry land. But during the Cretaceous period (135–65 MYA), the seas flooded in and submerged vast areas of land. The environment was warm, and the waters shallow, conditions that would have supported large numbers of fish and other marine life. Fossilised remains, including the stomach contents of *Kronosaurus,* show that it lived rather like a modern shark, devouring anything that came its way.

Its flat-topped skull alone measured 2.7m (9ft), making it substantially larger, and even more powerful, than that of the greatest land-dwelling carnivorous dinosaurs like *Tyrannosaurus rex*. The snout was long and triangular, and inside the mouth were sharp, pointed teeth around 25cm (10in) long and 5cm (2¼in) in diameter (although much of the tooth was deeply embedded in the jaw). Large eyes faced slightly forwards, which suggests that *Kronosaurus* had an overlapping field of vision. Highly manoeuvrable, *Kronosaurus* had a body that was held stiff by tightly linked gastralia (belly ribs). It had two pairs of flippers, the rear ones longer than the front ones, and there may have been a fin at the top of the tail to help to steer it through the water.

NAME MEANS
'Kronos [Time] lizard'

TIME
Late Cretaceous
(135–65 MYA)

LOCATION
Australia: Queensland

SIZE
15m (49ft)

WEIGHT
6,604kg (6½ tons)

DIET
Marine reptiles, fish, molluscs

TYLOSAURUS

Pronounced: 'TIE-loh-SORE-us'

This giant, long-skulled, marine lizard was one of the later members of the mosasaur family, and a fearsome predator. One of the most distinctive features of *Tylosaurus* – and that which gave it its name, 'knob lizard' – was the hard, bony tip of its snout, which it may have used as a ramming weapon for stunning prey, or perhaps to see off rival males. The snout tip was not made of solid bone, though, and some fossil remains show specimens with broken noses, which suggests either that they were quite fragile or that *Tylosaurus* was apt to ram with great force. It is also thought that *Tylosaurus*, like other mosasaurs, had a forked tongue as its skull shows that it had the Jacobson's organ: this is a structure in the roof of the mouth, found in snakes and lizards, that is used to detect scent particles in the air, or, in *Tylosaurus*' case, in water. In addition to having large eyes and acute eyesight, it appears that *Tylosaurus* could sniff out its prey. Inside the long, slim snout were teeth on the jaws and palate bones. The skull bones could also move quite freely at the joints, which allowed *Tylosaurus* to expand its jaws to swallow very large prey.

NAME MEANS
'Knob lizard'

TIME
Late Cretaceous
(135–65 MYA)

LOCATION
North America, Japan

SIZE
11m (36ft)

WEIGHT
6,096kg (6 tons)

DIET
Turtles, fish, other
mosasaurs

The arms and legs of its land-living ancestors had evolved into streamlined flippers, with extra-long toe and finger bones making the flippers longer. These were probably not used for swimming, but for steering, the main propulsive force being delivered by the high, but narrow, flexible tail that was waved from side to side.

CHAPTER 9

REPTILES OF THE AIR

The Mesozoic era, around 250–65 million years ago, is often called the 'age of the dinosaurs'. But the dinosaurs lived only on land. In the sea, and in the air, other reptiles also existed. The Mesozoic reptiles were among the first vertebrates (back-boned animals) to take to the air: flapping their wings, or gliding on wings of skin, they cruised through the air across the world. None of these extraordinary flying reptiles would survive beyond the end of the Cretaceous period, their only legacy being their fossilised remains.

The pterosaurs were the most important of the flying reptiles, and they have been known about for some time, with some of the most magnificent finds coming from the Solnhofen quarries in southern Germany. In late Jurassic times, Solnhofen was covered by a lagoon filled with stagnant water, flanked by mountains to the north and the deeper waters of the Tethys Sea (what is now the Mediterranean Sea) to the south. When flying reptiles (and marine reptiles) became trapped in the poisonous water and died in the lagoon, their dead bodies floated on the surface of the water and the soft tissues decayed. The heavier parts of their bodies – their bones – sank to the bottom, where they were buried, along with the fine sediment that settled beneath the water at the bottom of the lagoon. Because the waters of the lagoon were oxygen-starved, no further decay of the bones was possible.

The technical name for such geological occurrences (which are quite rare, with only a dozen sites known worldwide) is lagerstratten. The Romans first excavated the quarries at Solnhofen to make paving stones; during the 18th century, the fine-grained, limestone rock was found to be ideal for lithography (literally, 'stone-printing'), which led to the rapid expansion of the quarry. This in turn led to the discoveries, in the 19th century, of fossil remains – not only of pterosaurs, whose name, appropriately, means 'stone lizards', but of early birds (which appeared halfway through the Mesozoic era), small dinosaurs and marine reptiles.

Peteinosaurus.

ORDER PTEROSAURIA

The pterosaurs were the first group of vertebrates to take to the skies, flying on 'wings' of skin that were attached along the length of their greatly elongated fourth fingers on each hand and that rejoined the body at thigh level. These flying reptiles evolved during the late Triassic period (250–203 MYA), and about 70 million years before the first-known bird, *Archaeopteryx*, appeared. The pterosaurs thrived during the Jurassic (203–135 MYA) period, survived into the early Cretaceous period (135–65 MYA) and diversified into numerous forms. Among these were the largest flying creatures of all time. Like many of their land- and marine-dwelling reptile relatives, the pterosaurs began their decline during the Cretaceous period, and were extinct by the end of the Mesozoic age, around 65 million years ago. There are two *sub*-orders of pterosaurs: the earliest, and most primitive, types were the rhamphorhynchs, while the later types include the more familiar – and more famous – pterodactyls.

SUB-ORDER RHAMPHORHYNCHOIDEA

(See pages 206 to 218)

The Triassic period of the Mesozoic age was a highly significant period of reptile evolution, with many diverse groups, such as dinosaurs, turtles and crocodiles, appearing. While the fossil finds of the earliest pterosaurs have been found in late Triassic rocks (250–203 MYA), even the earliest-known pterosaurs were advanced flyers. The rhamphorhynchoids were generally small animals, with a long tail stiffened by bony ligaments.

SUB-ORDER PTERODACTYLOIDEA

(See pages 219 to 233)

The pterodactyls (whose name means 'wing finger') are undoubtedly the most familiar of all of the flying reptiles, so famous that many erroneously call all pterosaurs 'pterodactyls'. The pterodactyls were, in fact, short-tailed pterosaurs, which were already established as a group in the late Jurassic period (203–135 MYA), when their relatives, the rhamphorhynchoids – the long-tailed pterosaurs – became extinct. The pterodactyls survived through the Cretaceous period (135–65 MYA), although only a few types lasted to the end of that period. These pterosaurs had the same general structure as the rhamphorhynchoids, but their tails were shorter, their necks longer and their skulls and beaks more elongated. They ranged in size from some of the smallest-known pterosaurs to some of the largest flying vertebrates that ever lived.

NAME MEANS
'True two-form tooth'

TIME
Late Triassic
(250–203 MYA)

LOCATION
Cene, near Bergamo,
northern Italy

SIZE
11m (36ft)

WEIGHT
Unknown

DIET
Piscivorous

EUDIMORPHODON

Pronounced: 'YOO-die-MORF-oh-don'

About the same size as a large seagull, *Eudimorphodon* is the oldest pterosaur to have been found to date. Its remains were discovered on the western slopes of Monte Bo, in the Alpine foothills near Bergamo, Italy, by Mario Pandolfi in 1973. The fossilised skeleton – which is missing its winged fingers and most of its hind legs – was discovered in a thin shale layer from the rubble of the village of Cene's former quarry. *Eudimorphodon* was typical of a fully developed, rhamphorhynchoid pterosaur: it had a short neck, large head and long, bony tail stiffened by a network of bony ligaments, and with a diamond-shaped flap at the tip that probably acted as a rudder. The structure of its breastbone indicates that it was able to flap its wings, which would have measured about 1m (3ft 3in) from tip to tip. What is unique, however, are the unusual teeth found in no other pterosaur. These are not the usual row of teeth with a single cusp, but are divided into a few large front fangs and, behind them, a series of smaller teeth, with three to five cusps. In the upper jaw were two more large teeth, with additional cusps between the series of three- and five-cusped, smaller teeth. In the upper jaw were 58 teeth in all, and in the lower, 56 teeth. This makes a total of 114 teeth, all in a jaw measuring only 8cm (3⅛in) long! This type of dentition suggests that *Eudimorphodon* was piscivorous (a fish-eater), although juveniles, which had slightly immature dentition, probably ate insects, such as dragonflies.

PETEINOSAURUS

Pronounced: 'pet-INE-oh-SORE-us'

This pterosaur, whose remains were found in 1978, in Cene, near Bergamo, northern Italy, is one of the earliest vertebrates whose skeleton shows evidence of its ability to flap its skin-covered 'wings'. The long-tailed *Peteinosaurus,* which lived on the shore of the late Triassic Tethys Sea, was smaller than its contemporary, *Eudimorphodon* (see page 206), and, unlike it, *Peteinosaurus* had only single-cusped teeth, which were flattened, with sharp, cutting edges at the front and back. At the front of the lower jaw were two large 'fangs'.

Although the upper skull remains unknown, scientists believe that *Peteinosaurus* was an insectivore and, in more ways, more primitive than *Eudimorphodon.* It had a light-boned skeleton, a long tail stiffened by bony ligaments and its wings were relatively short, only twice as long at its hind legs. (In all other pterosaurs, the wings were at least three times as long, if not longer.) With a wingspan of only 60cm (24in), *Peteinosaurus* is considered by many scientists to be the direct ancestor of the oldest Jurassic-period (203–135 MYA) pterosaur, *Dimorphodon* (see page 210).

NAME MEANS
'Winged lizard'

TIME
Late Triassic
(250–135 MYA)

LOCATION
Cene, near Bergamo,
northern Italy

WINGSPAN
60cm (24in)

DIET
Flying insects

PREONDACTYLUS

Pronounced: 'PRAY-on-dak-TIE-lus'

NAME MEANS
'Preone finger'

TIME
Late Triassic
(253–203 MYA)

LOCATION
Preone Valley,
northern Italy

WINGSPAN
45cm (18in)

DIET
Insectivorous, possibly
piscivorous

Preondactylus is the third genus of pterosaur known to date. Its remains were discovered first in 1978, and consisted of three connected, digital (finger) phalanges. In 1982, another skeleton was discovered in the Preone Valley, in the Veneto, northern Italy, by Nando Buffarini, but unfortunately the slab of rock that contained it shattered as it was being extracted. The tiny fragments of bones embedded in the rocks were, after Buffarini had pieced the rock back together, washed away when he cleaned the rock. All that remained was the negative print of the skeleton on the surface of the rock, but a cast of silicon rubber was made to recreate the pterosaur in three dimensions. Once examined, it was found that this was a new species of pterosaur in the Rhamphorhynchidea family, and it was named 'Preone finger', after the three flight digits found earlier, which scientists believe also came from this species. This small, long-tailed genus, about the size of a pigeon, is among the earliest of the pterosaurs in the fossil records found so far. The wings were relatively short, and the legs long, proportions that palaeontologists consider 'primitive' characteristics in pterosaurs. Its jaws were lined with sharp, single-cusped teeth of different lengths. In 1984, one more fossil was discovered, but this time the bones were packed tightly into a ball. It appears that this *Preondactylus* had fallen prey to a predatory fish, which later spewed out the indigestible bones as a gastric pellet, which then sank to the bottom of the sea and was later fossilised.

CAMPYLOGNATHIODES

Pronounced: 'CAMP-ee-lon-ATH-ee-oh-dees'

This pterosaur takes its name from the Greek words *kampylos*, meaning 'curved', and *gnathos*, meaning 'jaws', which describe the crooked ends to its jaws. So far, there are two species known: *C. liasicus*, with a wingspan of about 1m (3ft 3in), and the larger *C. zitelli*, with a span of around 1.75m (5ft 7in). *Campylognathiodes* was a long-tailed, rhamphorhynchoid pterosaur, with a short head, small teeth and a skull dominated by large, circular, eye sockets, suggesting that it had extremely acute eyesight, and that it could possibly have been able to see in poor light, or even, perhaps, at night. The end of the snout was pointed and toothed with sharp, short, conical teeth set upright in the jaw. Its sternum consisted of a broad, rectangular plate of bone that had a short crest (known as a cristopina) projecting forwards.

In 1986, a fossil pterosaur pelvis was found in Lower Saxony, Germany; this find was of great significance as the hip sockets had survived in good condition, and scientists examining the lateral and upward orientation deduced that this pterosaur, at least, was not capable of bipedal walking as the upper leg bones (femora) could not be oriented vertically. (A vertical orientation is vital in order for the legs to 'swing' to and fro when walking or running.)

NAME MEANS
'Curved jaw'

TIME
Early Jurassic
(203–135 MYA)

LOCATION
Europe: Germany

WINGSPAN
1–1.75m
(3ft 3in–5ft 7in)

DIET
Piscivorous

DIMORPHODON

Pronounced: 'DIE-morf-oh-don'

NAME MEANS
'Two-form tooth'

TIME
Early Jurassic
(203–135 MYA)

LOCATION
Europe: England

WINGSPAN
1.4m (4ft 6in)

DIET
Piscivorous

Dimorphodon is the earliest Jurassic pterosaur, and was about 1m (3ft 3in) long, with a wingspan of about 1.4m (4ft 6in), with a large head, typical of the rhamphorhynchoids, measuring about 20cm (8in) long. The skull was relatively high, was shaped like that of a modern puffin and had large side 'windows', consisting of eye sockets, upper and lower temporal openings, pre-orbital openings and nostrils, all separated by thin bars of bone. So despite the size of the skull, it was quite lightweight. It had four large front teeth on each side of the upper jaw, behind which was a row of smaller teeth. In the lower jaw, there were also four or five large teeth, which were followed by 30 to 40 tiny, pointed teeth. This specialised dentition suggests that *Dimorphodon* was piscivorous (a fish-eater). A typical, long-tailed pterosaur, *Dimorphodon* had a long, vertebral tail made up of over 30 caudal (tail) vertebrae: the first 5 or 6 of these were short, and could move against each other, but subsequent caudal vertebrae were elongated and stiffed with bony tendons. This structure stabilised the pterosaur in flight, and it was probably further assisted by a small, diamond- or triangular-shaped, terminal tail 'vane', which acted as a drag rudder. Its short wings were also typical of early pterosaurs: the first of the four flight-digit phalanges was only a little longer than the lower arm, and was shorter than the second and third phalanges of the flight digits. The hind legs were relatively long and powerfully developed; the first four digits had claws, while the fifth digit was fairly long and splayed sideways.

It has been suggested that *Dimorphodon* was well suited to bipedal, bird-like walking, its long tail balancing its head as it moved around: fossilised tracks show the marks of hind feet walking in a narrow track, with marks apparently made by the forelimbs in a wider track at each side. It would have been a rather clumsy walk – using its 'arms' rather like crutches or walking sticks – and it probably spent much of its time perched on cliffs or branches, from which it launched itself into flight.

DORYGNATHUS

Pronounced: 'DOOR-ee-NAY-thus'

NAME MEANS
'Spear jaw'

TIME
Early Jurassic
(203–135 MYA)

LOCATION
Europe: Germany

WINGSPAN
1m (3ft 3in)

DIET
Piscivorous

Discovered in 1830, but named and described later, in 1860, *Dorygnathus* was a long, stiff-tailed pterosaur, with a relatively small wingspan of only around 1m (3ft 3in). Its skull was elongated (which gave it its name, 'spear jaw') and larger than that of its contemporary, *Campylognathiodes* (see page 209), with huge eye sockets and long, curved front teeth in the upper and lower jaws that pointed forwards and meshed alternately when the jaws were closed. At the rear of the jaws were only very small teeth. Together, the arrangement and shape of the teeth were ideal for seizing and holding on to slippery fish. A small, triangular-shaped sternum (breastbone) served as the area of attachment for the flight muscles, and the flight digits (and therefore the wings) were quite short. However, the fifth digit of the foot was very long and set at an angle. The reason, and thus the function, for this is unknown; it may have been used to spread a small web of skin, giving the animal more lift at take-off if it landed on the surface of the sea. *Dorygnathus* appears to have been abundant during the early Jurassic period, around what was once the Liassic Sea, an extensive, but shallow, sea that flooded broad areas of central Europe some 200 million years ago. Numerous outstanding fossilised records are from the slate quarries around Holzmaden and Ohmden, in the northern foothills of the Schwäbische Alb.

ANUROGNATHUS

Pronounced: 'AN-yoor-oh-NAT-us'

This very small pterosaur – its trunk was only 5cm (2in) long – was unlike any other rhamphorhynchoid, in that it had a very short tail – its name, in fact, means 'without tail and jaw'. The greatly reduced tail formed a kind of bird-like pygostyl, better known as the 'parson's nose'. This odd pterosaur is known from a single fossil specimen from the Solnhofen limestone quarry in Germany, which was described in 1923 by Ludwig von Ammon. It is classed with the rhamphorhynchoids, however, because it shares their general body proportions, as well as certain skeletal characteristics, including a short, high skull, short neck and peg-shaped teeth. Its narrow head had short, strong, broad jaws, with teeth designed for crushing and grinding, suggesting that *Anurognathus* was an insectivore. It must therefore also have been a proficient flyer if it was to catch in-flight dragonflies and other insects, such as wood-wasps (*Pseudosirex*), which were also preserved in the limestone deposits at Solnhofen. *Anurognathus* had wings that reached a maximum span of about 50cm (20in) and were composed of a thin membrane of skin that stretched from the elongated fourth finger to the ankle. A second wing was supported by a pteroid bone and stretched from each wrist to the neck.

NAME MEANS
'Without tail and jaw'

TIME
Late Jurassic
(203–235 MYA)

LOCATION
Europe: Germany

WINGSPAN
50cm (20in)

DIET
Insectivore

SCAPHOGNATHUS

Pronounced: 'SCA-fo-NAY-thus'

NAME MEANS
'Tub jaw'

TIME
Late Jurassic
(203–135 MYA)

LOCATION
Europe: Germany

WINGSPAN
90cm–1m
(36in–3ft 3in)

DIET
Piscivorous, possibly
insectivorous

Known from only two specimens preserved in the limestone of the Solnhofen quarry in Germany, *Scaphognathus* was one of the earliest pterosaur finds of all, and was described as early as 1831 by the German palaeontologist August Goldfuss, but as the tail section was missing, he believed that he was examining a pterodactyl, which he named *Pterodactylus crassirostris* ('thick-beaked flight finger'). When a second specimen was discovered – of an immature specimen whose bones were not fully ossified, but with its long, flexible tail intact – the genus was renamed *Scaphognathus* and was classified with the rhamphorhynchoids. In its general body proportions and long tail, *Scaphognathus* resembles *Rhamphorhynchus* (see page 218), but had some interesting characteristics of its own. *Scaphognathus* had a shorter, more compact head, but with a larger pre-orbital fenestra (opening in the skull in front of the eye socket). Its slender and widely spaced teeth – 18 in the upper jaw and 10 in the lower jaw – did not point forwards, but were set upright in the jaw. The ends of the jaw didn't meet in a point at the end, but were instead fairly blunt, like the bow of a boat, hence its name, 'tub jaw'.

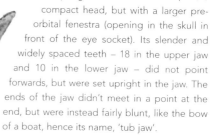

It is not clear, however, whether *Scaphognathus* was a fish-eater or an insectivore, but its long, slender wings suggest that it could fly for long distances in the hunt for food.

BATRACHOGNATHUS

Pronounced: 'ba-TRAK-oh-NATH-us'

The limestone deposits of the north-western foothills of the Karatau mountains, in Kazakhstan, are approximately the same age as those in Solnhofen, Germany, and both show a great similarity in the insect fauna (animal life) demonstrated by their fossil remains. In 1948, the remains of an incomplete and disarticulated (the bones were separated and jumbled up) skeleton of a pterosaur was found. Fragments of the skull and jaws, vertebrae and ribs, and bones from the wings and hind legs could be distinguished. The shape of the jaws suggested that this pterosaur had a high, short skull about 48mm (2in) long, with a broad mouth, rather like a frog. In its mouth were small, peg-like teeth, designed for crushing and grinding insects. It was named *Batrachognathus volans*, or 'flying frog jaw', and was likely to have been an insectivorous pterosaur that caught its prey in flight. *Batrachognathos* was a small, rhamphorhynchoid pterosaur, with a wingspan of around 50cm (20in), and appears to have been related to the *Anurognathos* (see page 213) found in Solnhofen, Germany. As the skeleton was incomplete, it may be that *Batrachognathos* also had a pygostyl ('parson's nose') rather than the more usual long tail of rhamphorhynchoid pterosaurs.

NAME MEANS
'Frog jaw'

TIME
Late Jurassic
(203–135 MYA)

LOCATION
Asia: Kazakhstan

WINGSPAN
50cm (20in)

DIET
Insectivore

RHAMPHORHYNCHUS

Pronounced: 'ram-FOR-ink-us'

NAME MEANS
'Beak snout'

TIME
Late Jurassic
(203–135 MYA)

LOCATION
Europe: England,
Germany, Portugal;
Africa: Tanzania

WINGSPAN
1m (3ft 3in)

DIET
Piscivorous

Rhamphorhynchus is probably the best-known pterosaur, and gives its name to the entire *sub*-order of Rhamphorhynchoidea. Evolving during the late Triassic (250–203 MYA) and surviving into the late Jurassic (203–135 MYA) period, the rhamphorhynchoid pterosaurs kept their long, vertebrate tails as a legacy of their land-dwelling, reptilian ancestors. Because of the fine grain of the limestone of the German Solnhofen quarry in which many specimens of *Rhamphorhynchus* have been magnificently preserved, we know that there was a rhomboid-shaped (an off-centre, diamond-shaped) membrane on the end of this long tail, which was used as a rudder during flight.

Long-tailed pterosaurs have not been found in any later rocks, so it appears that they became extinct shortly after they had populated the shoreline and islands of the Solnhofen lagoon. Also preserved in the German limestone were *Rhamphorhynchus'* fine wing structures and membranous wings, microscopic examination of which revealed that there were very fine fibres running from the front to the back of the wings, which strengthened them.

Rhamphorhynchus was evidently a very skilful flier: it had a broad sternum (breastbone), with a forward-pointing cristopina (crest), to which strong muscles were attached. The neck was short, with short, compact vertebrae, and the skull was large, elongated and pointed, with large orbital openings (eye sockets) and smaller openings in the skull in front of eyes (the nostrils and pre-orbital fenestrae). A pointed, horny beak formed the tip of its jaw, which was lined with long, slightly curved and pointed teeth, directed forwards and outwards. These teeth were designed for catching slippery prey, such as fish: the fossilised remains of a small fish were discovered inside the stomach of a *Rhamphorhynchus* found at Solnhofen. When the jaws were closed, the 20 upper-jaw teeth and 14 lower-jaw teeth meshed alternately. Several different species of *Rhamphorhynchus* have been found in Solnhofen; the most

common species is *R. muensteri. R. longicaudus* is the smallest of the species, with a wingspan of 40cm (16in), while *R. longiceps* is the largest, with a wingspan of 1.75m (5ft 8in). In addition to the finds in Germany, *Rhamphorhynchus* species have also been found elsewhere in Europe (England and Portugal), and in Tanzania, east Africa.

NAME MEANS
'Hairy devil'

TIME
Late Jurassic
(203–135 MYA)

LOCATION
Asia: Kazakhstan

WINGSPAN
63cm (25in)

DIET
Piscivorous, possibly
insectivorous

SORDES

Pronounced: 'sor-DAYS'

The Jurassic deposits in Kazakhstan, Asia, have been noted for their rich fossil finds for many years, but during the 1960s, a spectacular pterosaur find was made by Russian zoologist A G Sharov while he was collecting fossil insects in the Karatau mountains. The find consisted of an almost complete skeleton, with imprints of the soft body parts and flight membranes. Because of the fineness of the sediment in which the fossil was contained, the rock revealed the most remarkable feature: this pterosaur, named *Sordes*, was covered in thick fur. While traces of hair had been found in Solnhofen fossils, never had hairs themselves been found. Here was proof at last that pterosaurs were not 'naked-skin' creatures or covered in reptilian scales, but were hairy. The significance of this body covering means that pterosaurs were likely to have been warm-blooded. A typical rhamphorhynchoid pterosaur, *Sordes* was a close relative of the Solnhofen *Scaphognathus* (see page 214), sharing a similar skull, dentition, short, metacarpal bone and long, vertebrate tail that fanned out slightly at the end to act as a rudder, but without the terminal vane, as in the Solnhofen *Rhamphorhynchus* (see page 216).

Long, dense and fairly thick hair covered the body – the longest body hairs were 6mm (¼in) – and there was also hair on the short, broad, flight membranes (which also extended between the hind legs), digits (fingers) and skin between the foot digits (toes). The root of the tail was also covered in hair, but the rest was 'naked'. A total of three specimens of skeletons of *Sordes* has been found to date; the skull averaged 8cm (3¼in) long, and its wingspan averaged 60cm (24in). It was probably piscivorous (fish-eating), but could also have fed on insects.

PTERODACTYLUS

Pronounced: 'TER-oh-DAK-til-us'

Pterodactylus shows us the typical features of the pterodactyl: a short tail (with no steering or flying function), a long neck, with the head meeting the neck at right angles (rather than in a straight line, as in rhamphorhynchoids), and greatly elongated metacarpals (hand bones), which, along with the fourth finger, supported the wings. The earliest evidence of *Pterodactylus* comes once again from the fine, Jurassic, limestone deposits at Solnhofen, in Germany, where six species have been distinguished, each adapted for a particular lifestyle and for eating a particular food – fish or insects. This is evident from the shape and length of their skulls, which range from 4.2cm (1½in) long to 10.8cm (4¼in) long. The smallest of the species is *Pterodactylus elegans*, with its long, thin teeth (found only in the front part of its jaw) and a wingspan of a mere 25cm (10in). The most common species is *P. kochi*, with its long, narrow jaw lined with sharp, fish-eating teeth. Adults had a wingspan of about 50cm (20in), but the smallest specimen ever found at Solnhofen was of a baby, whose body measured only 2cm (⅜in) long, and its wingspan only 18cm (7in). Although very young when it died, this *P. kochi* was already able to fly. Larger species at Solnhofen were *P. longicollum*, whose name means 'long-necked flight finger', whose wingspan reached some 1.45m (4ft 9in), about the same size as that of a modern herring gull. Of the largest species, *P. grandis*, only individual wing and leg bones are known, but suggest a wingspan of 2.5m (8ft 2in), about the same size as that of a modern vulture.

NAME MEANS
'Wing finger'

TIME
Late Jurassic
(230–135 MYA)

LOCATION
Europe: England,
France and Germany;
Africa: Tanzania

WINGSPAN
25cm–2.5m
(10in–8ft 2in)

DIET
Piscivorous,
insectivorous

GALLODACTYLUS

Pronounced: 'GAL-oh-DAC-til-us'

Gallodactylus is known from finds in France and Germany. The name 'Gallic finger' was introduced in 1974 by the French (hence the appellation 'Gallic') palaeontologist J Fabre, for a pterosaur that he examined from Var, in southern France. There were many features found to be shared with some specimens discovered in Germany during the 1850s, named *Pterodactylus suevicus*, and these early remains were assigned to *Gallodactylus*, as were later discoveries at Solnhofen.

Gallodactylus was one of the larger short-tailed pterosaurs, with a wingspan of around 1.35m (4ft 4in). In general appearance, it resembled *Pterodactylus*, but had a number of distinct features. Its elongated beak had a small number of forward-pointing, narrow teeth confined to the front end of the long, slender jaws, which made it ideal for catching and holding fish. Its skull was about 15cm (6in) long, with a large, naso-pre-orbital opening that reduced the weight of the skull. Most significant, however, was the short, horny, medial (mid-line) crest at the rear of its head that ended in a point. This may have been used for signalling or as a 'cut water' to stop the head from moving as the creature dived into water to hunt fish.

NAME MEANS
'Gallic finger'

TIME
Late Jurassic
(203–135 MYA)

LOCATION
Europe: Germany,
southern France

SIZE
1.35m (4ft 4in)

DIET
Piscivorous

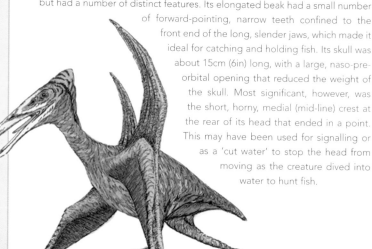

GERMANODACTYLUS

Pronounced: 'jer-MAN-oh-DAK-til-us'

Germanodactylus ('German finger') was a short-tailed pterosaur found first in Solnhofen, Germany, in 1925, but named in 1964 by the German-trained Chinese palaeontologist Dr Yang Zhong-jian (who is known familiarly as Dr C C Young). There have been very few finds of this genus, which is represented by two species: *Germanodactylus cristatus,* from Solnhofen, and the smaller of the two species, with a wingspan of around 98cm (3ft 2in); and *G. rhamphastinus,* found in Daiting, Bavaria, southern Germany, with a wingspan of around 1.08m (3ft 5in), making it the larger of the two.

Both, however, were characterised by having long, thin, bony crests on the mid-line of their skulls, starting at the nostrils and extending above the openings of the eye sockets. These were probably covered with a horny carina, or 'keel', and may have been used for signalling, or as a 'cut water'. Inside their jaws were a long row of powerful, short teeth. It has been suggested that *Germanodactylus,* which lived on the shores of the Solnhofen lagoon, may have used its strong finger claws to climb trees, and may also have hung, bat-like, from branches by turning its feet backwards to provide a strong grip.

NAME MEANS
'German finger'

TIME
Late Jurassic
(203–135 MYA)

LOCATION
Europe: Germany,
France

WINGSPAN
1.08m (3ft 5in)

DIET
Piscivorous

CTENOCHASMA

Pronounced: 'STEN-oh-KAS-mah'

NAME MEANS
'Comb jaw'

TIME
Late Jurassic
(203–135 MYA)

LOCATION
Europe: Germany

WINGSPAN
1.2m (3ft 9in)

DIET
Piscivorous

Although the late Jurassic skies over Germany appear to have teemed with pterodactyloid pterosaurs, *Ctenochasma* ('comb jaw') is a rare specimen. It was first described in 1851 by Hermann von Meyer (1801–69), although his specimen, from the Hanover area of Lower Saxony, consisted only of the front section of the lower jaw, with numerous tightly packed and strong teeth. Meyer named his find *Ctenochasma roemeri*, in honour of the palaeontologist F A Roemer. The first specimen to be found in the limestone at Solnhofen – a fragment of upper jaw – was also during the 1850s. Later, more complete skeletons were found, and were named *C. gracile* by Albert Oppel. *Ctenochasma*'s name was chosen on account of its long jaws, which were bent slightly upwards and were equipped with a total of 260 long, inwardly curved, slender teeth, which made it a perfect filter feeder. Rather than feed in flight, *Ctensochasma* would have waded into the shallow water and swept its jaw from side to side to strain small marine animals from the water. It was not until 1981 that another specimen came to light, this time with a porous, bony crest on its skull. This species was named *C. procristata*. The largest of the six specimens known so far had a skull around 20cm (8in) long and a wingspan of at least 1.2m (3ft 9in).

Because of its strange dentition, which is significantly different from that of other pterodactyloid pterosaurs, palaeontologists place *Ctenochasma* – along with another pterosaur, *Gnathosaurus* (see page 223) – in a family of its own known as the Ctenochasmatidae.

GNATHOSAURUS

Pronounced: 'NATH-Oh-sor-us'

Gnathosaurus is an extremely rare specimen of a pterodactyloid pterosaur from Solnhofen, in Germany: only fragments of two specimens are known. The first find consisted of a remnant of lower jaw discovered in 1832, but mistaken for a piece of crocodile jaw. Later, however, Hermann von Meyer assigned it the name of *Gnathosaurus subulatus*. *subulatus* is the Latin for 'awl-like', and describes the shape of the teeth that von Meyer found in this 'jaw reptile'. It was not until a second find in 1951 – a skull about 28cm (11in) long – that it was proved that *Gnathosaurus* was not a land-dwelling dinosaur, but, in fact, a pterosaur, a flying reptile, even though the rest of its skeleton has not been found.

Gnathosaurus was a large pterosaur, with a wingspan of around 1.7m (5ft 6in). While its teeth were fewer than *Ctenochasma*'s (see page 222), and they were much more powerful and less densely arranged in its jaw (*Gnathosaurus* had only 130 teeth), palaeontologists assume that *Gnathosaurus* was also a filter feeder. *Gnathosaurus* had teeth extending well towards the rear of its jaw, with the longest teeth at the front of the jaw, which was shaped like a spoon. Like *Ctenochasma*, *Gnathosaurus* also had a low crest of bone on its skull. Because of its strange dentition, *Gnathosaurus* is placed in the family known as Ctenochasmatidae.

NAME MEANS
'Jaw reptile'

TIME
Late Jurassic
(203–135 MYA)

LOCATION
Europe: Germany

WINGSPAN
1.7m (5ft 6in)

DIET
Piscivorous

ORNITHOCHEIRUS

Pronounced: 'OR-in-THOH-kiy-rus'

NAME MEANS
'Bird hand'

TIME
Cretaceous
(135–65 MYA)

LOCATION
Worldwide

WINGSPAN
2.5m (8ft 2in)

DIET
Piscivorous

Described by Henry Govier Seeley in 1869, from fossil material found in the Cambridge area of the east of England, *Ornithocheirus* was one of the most numerous pterosaurs of the Cretaceous period (135–65 MYA): a total of 36 species were distinguished. In 1914, R W Hooley re-ordered the material and reduced the number of different species to five different groups, which he named on the basis of their jaw bones.

Because of the fragmentary nature of the largely incomplete skeletal remains, there is still much controversy about what belongs to this genus of pterosaurs, with many other fragmentary remains from Europe, Africa, South America, Australia and New Zealand all ascribed to it. As a result, the generic name *Ornithocheirus* has become something of a catch-all, and palaeontologists are working on clearer definitions. So far, they have suggested that *Ornithocheirus* was a medium-sized, short-tailed pterosaur, with a wingspan of around 2.5m (8ft 2in), that lived worldwide. It had a long, slender skull, and the jaws were lined with numerous sharp, pointed teeth that extended to the very front of the jaw, indicating that it was likely to have been piscivorous. It is also highly probable that *Ornithocheirus* had a bony crest on its snout.

DSUNGARIPTERUS

Pronounced: 'D'SUNG-ah-RIP-ter-us'

The first pterosaur *Dsungaripterus* to be discovered in China was found by Dr Yang Zhong-jian (C C Young) during the 1960s. The fossil material consisted of front sections of the skull and lower jaw, and a large part of the rest of the skeleton. In 1973, a second find of compete skulls, a sternum (breastbone) and pelvic bones was made in the Junggar basin near Wuerho, Xingjian Province, China. *Dsungaripterus* was a fairly large pterosaur, with a wingspan of some 3–3.5m (9ft 8in–11ft 5in), and a skull up to 50cm (1ft 6in) long, but its most striking feature was the toothless tip of its jaws, which were bent slightly upwards and acted like a pair of giant forceps. Further back along both the upper and lower jaws were blunt knobs, which appear to have been used as crushing tools. Palaeontologists believe that *Dsungaripterus* used the upturned tip of the jaws to pluck bivalves, snails and crustacea from rocks, or out of crannies along the seashore, and their shells were then crushed by the bony knobs. A second feature of *Dsungaripterus* was the cranial crest on its skull. This was an elongated crest on the snout, along the mid-line, which extended over the eyes, with a short crest over the back of the head. The eye sockets were quite small, with the largest hole in the skull being the naso-pre-orbital opening. Like a bird, *Dsungaripterus* had a series of fused front dorsal (back) vertebrae (called a notarium) and fused sacral vertebrae (called a synsacrum).

NAME MEANS
'Junggar wing'

TIME
Cretaceous
(135–65 MYA)

LOCATION
Asia: China

WINGSPAN
3m (9ft 8in)

DIET
Piscivorous

NAME MEANS
'The frightening one'

TIME
Early Cretaceous
(132–112 MYA)

LOCATION
Asia: Mongolia

WINGSPAN
1.5m (4ft 9in)

DIET
Piscivorous

PHOBETOR

Pronounced: 'fo-BE-tor'

At the beginning of the Cretaceous period, shallow seas began to divide the southern continents (although South America and Africa were still attached to each other) and the Atlantic Ocean began to form. The northern and southern continents were now separated, and the sea dividing Asia from Europe was growing. By late Cretaceous times, the continents were in pretty much their now familiar positions, with South America and Africa drifting apart, and India moving eastwards, across the Indian Ocean. Australia and Antarctica had also detached themselves from what had been Gondwanaland. These changes affected the climate and the further development of plant and animal life: this period saw the first deciduous trees and flowering plants. While dinosaurs still dominated the land, and birds were becoming more numerous, the short-tailed pterosaurs dominated the air and were to be found on all of the continents, except for Antarctica.

Discovered in 1982, in Zagan Zabsk, western Mongolia, *Phobetor* was a close relative of the Chinese pterosaur *Dsungaripterus* (see page 225), but only about half its size. The first remains consisted of bones from the wing and hind legs; thought at first to belong to a species of small *Dsungaripterus*, they were named *D. parvus*. But later, skulls were also discovered, and it was clear that there were many differences between this pterosaur and the Chinese one, so it was renamed *Phobetor* ('the frightening one'). It had a similar, bony crest structure along its head, along with a toothless point to its jaw, but *Phobetor's* jaws were much straighter, and contained real, conical-shaped teeth rather than the bony, crushing knobs of *Dsungaripterus*.

NYCTOSAURUS

Pronounced: 'NIK-toh-SORE-us'

In his book *The Lost World* (1912), Sir Arthur Conan Doyle, the creator of Sherlock Holmes, told of pterosaurs still alive in South America. Living throughout the world (except Antarctica), in reality, the last of the pterosaurs survived until the end of the Mesozoic age, around 65 million years ago, and it would be as late as 1953 that the first exciting pterosaur remains would be discovered on the continent by L I Price, in Brazil. The first fossil was part of a humerus (arm bone); the complete bone would have been about 16.5cm (6½in) long, which would have made this a large pterosaur, with a wingspan of around 3.5m (11ft 5in). The humerus found in Brazil was seen to correspond with bones already discovered in Kansas, USA, and named *Nyctosaurus gracilis* by O C Marsh in 1876, but they were much larger. *Nyctosaurus* was a toothless, pterodactyloid pterosaur – a short-tailed pterosaur – which differed from its giant contemporary, *Pteranodon* (see page 232), by being smaller and having no bony crest on the back of its head.

The Brazilian find was named *Nyctosaurus lamegoi* in honour of A R Lamego, who was the divisional director of geology and mineralogy of the Department of Mineral Production in Rio de Janeiro. If future finds of this species are found, it could turn out that the Brazilian pterosaur is completely different from its North American cousin, and could be a completely new genus.

NAME MEANS
'Naked reptile'

TIME
Cretaceous
(135–65 MYA)

LOCATION
North America:
Kansas, USA; South
America: Brazil

WINGSPAN
3.5m (11ft 5in)

DIET
Piscivorous

ANHANGUERA

Pronounced: 'an-hang-GERR-ah'

NAME MEANS
'Old devil'

TIME
Cretaceous
(135–65 MYA)

LOCATION
South America: Brazil

WINGSPAN
4.15m (13ft 6in)

DIET
Possibly piscivorous

In north-eastern Brazil, on the slopes of the Araripe Plateau (Chapado do Araripe), and bordering the states of Piaui, Ceará and Pernambuco, is the Santana Formation, a layer of rock about 200m (656ft) thick, which was formed about 115 million years ago. From Santana come unique fossil preservations and strange, new pterosaurs. *Anhanguera* – 'old devil' – is one of the best-known pterosaurs from the Santana Formation, and takes its name from the local indigenous Tupi culture. This new pterosaur genus was described first in 1985, by D A Campos and A W A Kellner. It had a slender skull about 50cm (1ft 6in) long, with a medial crest along its snout, which was an outgrowth of the upper jawbone. A similar, though smaller, crest may have appeared on the lower side of the lower jaw. Its jaw was toothed, and it was probably a fish-eater, so its crest may well have acted as a 'cut water', stabilising the head as it dived into the water in the hunt for fish. The proportions of this pterosaur are quite unusual: it had a wingspan of more than 4 m (13ft), and the skull was twice as long as its body. The pectoral girdle was large and strong, while the pelvis was quite small. This means that the hind legs of *Anhanguera* could not have been brought into a vertical position under the body. Instead, they would have been slightly splayed at the sides, making bird-like, bipedal walking near impossible. It seems more likely that *Anhanguera* instead walked on all fours.

CEARADACTYLUS

Pronounced: 'SEE-ar-a-DAK-til-us'

Another new genus of pterosaurs was established in 1985, based on finds from the Santana Formation of north-eastern Brazil: *Cearadactylus* ('Ceará [one of the Brazilian states that borders the formation] finger'). The finds consist – so far – of an incomplete skull, the overall length of which (when reconstructed) would be around 57cm (1ft 9in). Using this skull length, palaeontologists estimate that *Cearadactylus* would have had an enormous wingspan of some 5.5m (18ft). An outstanding feature of the skull is the very powerful teeth: the front teeth are much longer and stronger than the back teeth. When the snout was closed, there was a gap in the front area. The long front teeth, set into jaws that broaden out into a spoon shape at the end – rather like the jaws of the modern gavial crocodile – suggest a pterosaur with a very strong 'fish grip'.

Until further fossil remains are found, palaeontologists can only assume certain features about a number of the varied pterosaurs that lived in this region. It is possible that when further finds are made, we may discover that some of them may have been related to North American and European forms.

NAME MEANS
'Ceará finger'

TIME
Cretaceous
(135–65 MYA)

LOCATION
South America: Brazil

WINGSPAN
5.5m (18ft)

DIET
Piscivorous

PTERODAUSTRO

Pronounced: 'TER-oh-DOW-stroh'

Nicknamed the 'flamingo pterosaur', *Pterodaustro* is one of the most unusual pterosaurs to be found to date. Discovered in 1969, and named by dinosaur-hunter *extraordinaire* Dr Jose Bonaparte, *Pterodaustro* was found in early Cretaceous rocks in the province of San Luis, in Argentina. A short-tailed pterosaur, *Pterodaustro* had the most remarkable, 'elastic' teeth: the skull was very elongated, and the front parts of the jaws were bent upwards. In the lower jaw was a groove into which were set a vast number of long, tightly packed teeth, which were more like bristles. Around 24 of these 'bristles' were embedded into 1cm (¼in) of jaw; in a jaw 20cm (8in) long, that works out at some 500 teeth in each half of the jaw! This made *Pterodaustro*'s lower jaw an effective sieve for filtering small marine organisms from the water, a feeding method similar to that used by blue whales. However, the collected food was then chopped up into smaller bits by blunt, short teeth in the upper jaw.

NAME MEANS
'South wing'

TIME
Cretaceous
(135–65 MYA)

LOCATION
South America:
Argentina

WINGSPAN
1.33m (4ft 4in)

DIET
Piscivorous

This filter device suggests that *Pterodaustro* did not feed on the wing, but instead had to wade into the water to feed. Its skull was only 23.5cm (9¼in) long, but its wingspan was 1.33m (4ft 4in). Although *Ctenochasma* (see page 222), found in Solnhofen, in Germany, was also a filter feeder, it had considerably fewer teeth, and for this reason, palaeontologists have placed the remarkable *Pterodaustro* in a family of its own, the Pterodaustridae.

QUETZALCOATLUS

Pronounced: 'KWETZ-al-CO-AT-lus'

Pteranodon sternbergi (see page 232) held the record for being the largest flying animal ever until 1971, when an even larger pterosaur fossil was found in late Cretaceous rocks in Big Bend National Park, Texas, USA. It was given the name *Quetzalcoatlus*, after the Aztec god Quetzalcoatl, who was worshipped in the form of a giant, winged snake. *Quetzalcoatlus* is the last-known pterosaur to have survived to the very end of the Cretaceous period, but unlike other pterosaurs, its remains were not found in marine sediment, but in river bedrock, which suggests that while it may have plucked fish from rivers, it may also have fed on carrion (the carcasses of dead animals). Only fragments of this immense pterosaur have been found to date, but the finds suggest a creature with enormously long and narrow wings. Some palaeontologists estimate the wingspan as being between 11 and 12m (36 and 39ft); among living birds, the royal albatross has the biggest wingspan, reaching a relatively small 3m (10ft). *Quezalcoatlus* had an estimated total body weight of 65kg (142lb). It also had an extremely long, though rather inflexible, neck, a slender, pointed and toothless jaw and a head topped by a long, bony crest.

It was probably more of an accomplished glider than a flyer, soaring high above the ground on rising thermals. Like a vulture, its keen eyesight would have spotted carrion from great distances. When it landed, it would have probed a dead beast's body cavity with its long neck and toothless jaws.

NAME MEANS
'Quetzalcoatl'
[an Aztec deity]

TIME
Late Cretaceous
(135–65 MYA)

LOCATION
North America:
Texas, USA

WINGSPAN
11–12m (36–39ft)

DIET
Piscivorous, possibly also
fed on carrion

PTERANODON

Pronounced: 'ter-AN-oh-don'

NAME MEANS
'Toothless flier'

TIME
Cretaceous
(135–65 MYA)

LOCATION
North America:
Kansas, USA

WINGSPAN
7m (23ft)

DIET
Piscivorous

The first fossil remains of North American pterosaurs were described by O C Marsh in 1871. In subsequent years, explorations of the Smoky Hill River, in west Kansas – which, in those days, was still Cheyenne territory – yielded great success, and the remains of Cretaceous reptiles were collected in large quantities. The first remains of a pterosaur consisted of half a metacarpal bone, from which Marsh estimated that this giant pterosaur had a wingspan of around 6m (20ft). Further finds yielded skulls, which Marsh discovered were toothless and had a long crest at the rear of the head. None of Marsh's finds of skulls were attached to any other bones of the skeleton, save for the neck vertebrae, which made it difficult to match up skeletons with heads. Nevertheless, he did distinguish various species of *Pteranodon* based on the different head crests.

Pteranodon ingens had a skull 1.70m (5ft 9in) long, of which almost half was the crest, which extended back to reach as far as the base of the tail. *P. sternbergi* had jaw that was longer than that of *P. ingens,* and an estimated wingspan of over 9m (30ft). It also had a high, upright crest that rose steeply and was broader at the top. *P. sternbergi* was the largest of the species, and was only exceeded in size by the azhdarchids, such as *Quetzalcoatlus* (see page 231). But unlike *Quetzalcoatlus*, *Pteranodons* had a rather short neck, with very strong cervical (neck) vertebrae. These creatures always had crests on the back of their heads, but never on their snouts or lower jaws. All of their bones were thin walled and hollow, with small air vents that possibly allowed the penetration of air sacs, which were connected to the lungs. The vertebrae also had lateral openings in order to lighten their construction.

In order to remain airborne for long periods, *Pteranodon* needed to keep its body structure as light as possible to sustain flying and soaring as it ranged far out over the seas to hunt. The strata of west Kansas, where the finds of *Pteranodon* have been made, are the deposits of the mid-continental seaway,

an extended sea that ran through the North American continent during the Cretaceous period, separating it into eastern and western halves. The fossil finds of *Pteranodon* were found some 160km (100 miles) from what was then the coast, suggesting that they flew great distances from their nesting sites on the coast.

GLOSSARY

Age of reptiles
Alternative name for the Mesozoic era.

Ammonites
Distant relatives of the octopus and squid; evolved during the Palaeozoic era, with a flat, spiral shell. Flourished during the Mesozoic era.

Amphibian
Moist-skinned animals that live in both water and the air.

Ankylosaurs
'Rounded reptiles': a group of low, heavy, armoured dinosaurs.

Apatosaurus
Giant sauropod dinosaur once known as *Brontosaurus* ('thunder lizard').

Archaeopteryx
The earliest-recorded bird from the Jurassic period.

Archosaurs
The group of reptiles from which dinosaurs evolved. Today, the crocodile is the only living archosaur, but the descendants of the early archosaurs are birds.

Arthropod
An invertebrate animal, with a jointed body and limbs. Insects, spiders and lobsters are all arthropods.

Biped/bipedal
Walking on the two hind legs only.

Brachiopods
Marine invertebrates, with a bivalve shell and a pair of tentacles inside the shell that they use to direct microscopic food to their mouths.

Brontosaurus
A dinosaur now known as *Apatosaurus*.

Carnivore
A meat- or flesh-eating animal.

Carnosaurs
Lizard-hipped, carnivorous dinosaurs, the largest of which was *Tyrannosaurus*.

Ceratopsians
Horned dinosaurs, the last group of dinosaurs to develop.

Club moss
A plant related to the fern; first appeared during the Devonian period and grew to great sizes during the Carboniferous period.

Coelyoposis
One of the earliest-known dinosaurs of the Triassic period.

Coprolite
Fossilised dung.

Cotylosaurs
A group of early reptiles of the late Palaeozoic era and Triassic period; often known as 'stem reptiles' as they gave rise to all other reptiles.

Cretaceous period
The third and final period of the Mesozoic age, during which time the dinosaurs became extinct.

Diapsids
A reptile group with two skull openings behind each eye socket.

Dicynodonts
'Two dog teeth': the first herbivorous, mammal-like reptiles of the Permian period, with a single pair of tusk-like teeth in the upper jaw.

Dinosaur
'Terrible lizard': used to refer to any now-extinct reptile that lived on Earth from 225 to 65 million years ago. Dinosaurs are divided into two main groups: lizard-hipped (saurischians) and bird-hipped (ornithiscians), according to the structure of their pelvic bones.

Gastroliths
'Stomach stones': stones swallowed to help to grind up food in the stomach.

Ginkgo
The South-east Asian 'maidenhair' tree.

Gondwana/Gondwanaland
The major land mass that made up the southern part of the super-continent Pangaea during the Triassic period. It included present-day Africa, Australia, India, Antarctica and South America.

Hadrosaurines
A hadrosaur ('duck-billed') ornithopod, with little or no bony head crest.

Hadrosaurs
'Duck-billed' dinosaurs. Bipedal dinosaurs of the Cretaceous period that lived on the northern continents. Had wide, toothless beaks and are grouped according to their various head crests (see hadrosaurines and lambeosaurines).

Herbivore
A plant-eating animal.

Ichnology
The study of footprints preserved in rocks.

Ichthyosaurs
A group of marine reptiles of the late Triassic period that resembled modern dolphins in appearance.

Iguanodonts
'Iguana-toothed', herbivorous dinosaurs.

Insectivores
Insect-eating animals.

Invertebrates
Animals without a backbone.

Ischium
One of the two lower hip bones of the dinosaur (the other was the pubis). Pointing downwards and backwards from the hip socket, the ischium anchored and powered the hind legs.

Jurassic period
The second period of the Mesozoic era.

Lambeosaurines
Hadrosaurs ('duck-billed' dinosaurs) with large, tubular crests on their heads.

Laurasia
The 'northern continent' in the Triassic period, comprising North America, Europe and Asia, which was separated from Gondwana by a sea, Tethys.

Lobe-finned fish
Lobe fins take their name from the fact that their fins were carried on short, scale-covered legs. They were the first land-living vertebrates; they had lungs and could breathe air. See rhipidistians.

Mammal
Any class of higher vertebrates – which includes humankind – which give birth to live offspring, which they feed on milk secreted from mammary glands.

Mesozoic era
The 'age of middle life', made up of three periods: the Triassic, Jurassic and Cretaceous. The dinosaurs evolved, and became extinct, in this era, from about 248–65 million years ago.

Mosasaurs
Giant, seagoing reptiles of the late Cretaceous period.

MYA
Million years ago.

Nothosaurs
A group of marine reptiles that flourished in the Triassic period and had back fins and webbed feet.

Ornithiscians
'Bird-hipped' dinosaurs: one of the two main groups of dinosaurs that are distinguished by the structure of their pelvic girdles.

Ornithopods
Herbivorous, 'bird-hipped' dinosaurs.

Palaeontology
The scientific study of flora (plants) and fauna (animals).

Pangaea
The single land mass or super-continent that stretched from pole to pole in the Triassic period.

Placodonts
'Plated teeth': Triassic-period aquatic reptiles. Some had 'paddle-like' limbs to propel them, while others had webbed digits and waggled their tails to create a forward motion through the water.

Plesiosaurs
Long-necked marine reptiles that swam with flipper-shaped limbs.

Pliosaurs
Short-necked plesiosaurs (see above).

Prosauropods
Early, herbivorous, saurischian dinosaurs.

Pterosaurs
'Winged lizards': Mesozoic 'skin-winged', flying reptiles.

Quadruped/quadrupedal
Walking on all fours.

Reptiles
Lizards, snakes, turtles, crocodiles and dinosaurs, as well as their living and extinct relatives.

Rhipidistians
A group of Devonian-period, carnivorous, lobe-finned fish that gave rise to the amphibians.

Saurischian
'Lizard hipped': one major grouping of dinosaurs based on hip structure, in which the pubis is long and points forwards and downwards from the hip.

Sauropodomorphs
Large, herbivorous, quadrupedal, saurischian dinosaurs. This group included the largest land animals ever to live.

Stegosaurs
'Plated/roof lizards': quadrupedal, herbivorous, ornithischian dinosaurs, with two rows of bony plates and/or spines along the neck, back and tail.

Synapsids
A reptile group characterised by a single opening low down on the skull, behind the eyes.

Thecodonts
'Socket teeth': a mixed group of archosaurs that were the ancestors of dinosaurs and pterosaurs.

Theropods
'Beast feet': predatory, carnivorous, saurischian (lizard-hipped) dinosaurs, armed with sharp teeth and claws.

Triassic period
The first period of the Mesozoic era.

Vertebrates
Animals with an internal backbone.

RESOURCES MUSEUMS, GALLERIES AND SITES

United Kingdom
Natural History Museum,
Cromwell Road, London SW7
www.nhm.ac.uk

Oxford University Museum of
Natural History, Parks Rd, Oxford
www.oum.ox.ac.uk

Sedgwick Museum, Downing
Street, Cambridge
www.sedgwick.esc.cam.ac.uk

Hunterian Museum, University of
Glasgow, University Avenue,
Glasgow
www.hunterian.gla.ac.uk

The Dinosaur Museum, Icen Way,
Dorchester, Dorset DT1 1EW

Crystal Palace Park, London SE20

Continental Europe
Institut Royal des Sciences
Naturelles de Belgique
Rue Vautier 29, B-1040 Brussels,
Belgium
www.kbinirsnb.be/general/eng/ma
in_e.htm

National Museum of Natural
History, Institute of Palaeontology,
Rue de Buffon 8, F-75005 Paris

Musee Parc des Dinosaures,
Beziers, France
www.musee-parc-
dinosaures.com/anglais/index.htm

USA
Academy of Natural Sciences,
19th & The Parkway, Logan
Square, Philadelphia, Pennsylvania
19103

American Museum of Natural
History, Central Park West/79th St,
New York, NY 10024
www.amnh.org

Carnegie Museum of Natural
History, 4400 Forbes Avenue,
Pittsburgh, Pennsylvania 15213
www.clpgh.org/cmnh

Smithsonian Museum of Natural
History, 10th Street & Constitution
Avenue, Washington, DC
www.mnh.si.edu

Field Museum of Natural History,
1400 Lake Shore Drive, Chicago,
Illinois
www.fmnh.org

Peabody Museum of Natural
History, Yale University, 17 Whitney
Avenue, New Haven, CT

Los Angeles County Museum of
Natural History, 900 Exposition
Blvd, Los Angeles, California
www.lam.mus.ca.us

Dinosaur National Monument
Quarry, PO Box 128, Jensen,
Utah 84035
www.nps.gov/dino/dinos.htm

Utah Museum of Natural History,
University of Utah, Salt Lake City,
Utah 84112

Canada
The Royal Tyrrell Museum of
Palaeontology, PO Box 7500,
Drumheller, Alberta
www.tyrrellmuseum.com

Royal Ontario Museum, Toronto,
Ontario, M5S 2C6

National Museum of Natural
Sciences, Ottawa, Ontario KA1
0M8
www.nature.ca/nature_e.cfm

Dinosaur Provincial Park, Patricia,
Alberta (excavation in progress)

Mexico
Natural History Museum, Mexico
City, Mexico

South America
Museo Argentinos de Ciencias
Naturales, Av. Angel Gallardo 470,
1404 Buenos Aires, Argentina

Museum of La Plata University, La
Plata, Argentina

Australia
Australian Museum, College Street,
Sydney, New South Wales 2000

Museum of Victoria, 328 Swanston
Street, Melbourne, Victoria 3000